BOEING B-29 SUPERFORTRESS

1942–60 (all marks)

COVER CUTAWAY Boeing B-29 Superfortress.
(Mike Badrocke)

First published in December 2015

Chris Howlett has asserted his moral right to be
identified as the author of this work.

A catalogue record for this book is available
from the British Library.

ISBN 978 0 85733 790 0

Library of Congress control no. 2014956839

Published by Haynes Publishing,
Sparkford, Yeovil,
Somerset BA22 7JJ, UK.
Tel: 01963 440635
Int. tel: +44 1963 440635
Website: www.haynes.com

Haynes North America Inc.,
859 Lawrence Drive, Newbury Park,
California 91320, USA.

Printed in Malaysia.

BOEING B-29 SUPERFORTRESS

1942–60 (all marks)

Owners' Workshop Manual

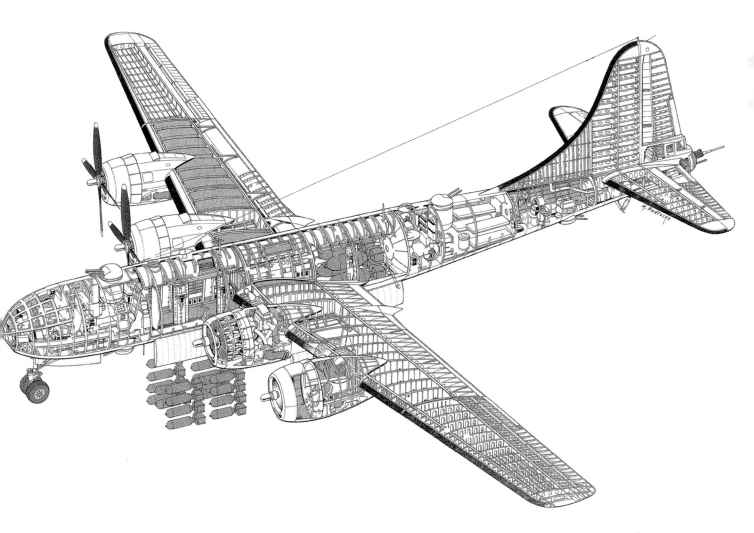

An insight into the design, operation, maintenance and restoration of the USA's giant long-range heavy bomber

Chris Howlett

Contents

OPPOSITE Possibly the most famous plane in the world. The fully glazed nose of *Enola Gay* illustrates well the streamlined shape of Boeing's super-bomber. *(Author)*

Acknowledgements

RIGHT Auxiliary fuel tanks fitted in the bomb bay of a B-29. The B-29 was able to carry four such tanks, two in the front and two in the rear bomb bay. Each tank had a capacity for 640 gallons. This image shows a B-29 equipped with a full set of tanks to ferry petrol across 'the Hump'. On operations B-29s seldom carried more than one of these tanks, normally in the rear bomb bay, allowing room for bombs at the other locations on the bomb racks. *(USAF)*

As with any book, the list of those who help with information or images is long and I am greatly appreciative of all the assistance I have been given by people with far greater knowledge of the B-29 than mine. Some have provided images while others have been patient in answering my many trivial questions. The total list is too long to include everyone but I would like in particular to thank the following whose support has made this book possible:

Dale Thompson and Donald England of the T Square 54 restoration team, who have been very helpful in providing many photos and explanations. Indeed, almost all the photos within the Anatomy section are of T Square 54 and show off the fantastic quality of the restoration work on this venerable plane.

Michael Hanz, whose encyclopaedic expertise of US radios and electronic countermeasures more than made up for my almost complete absence of knowledge.

Taigh Ramey, who has gathered much information on the B-29 central fire control system and has been unstinting in sharing this.

Bob Mann, a giant among B-29 experts, who has been a magnificent help with the fine points relating to serials, chronologies of the plane and maintenance details.

Bud Farrell, former B-29 air gunner and KB-29M hose operator, who allowed me to use the excerpts of his excellent book *No Sweat* that so well illustrates the use of the B-29 in Korea and as a tanker.

Scott Willey, who provided much needed information on the Silverplate B-29s backed up by several photos of *Enola Gay*.

Pete McLaughlin, formerly the chief engineering officer at Pyote AAF, who contributed information on the storage of B-29s.

Eric Nelson, who supplied me with many photos of *Miss America 62* that allowed me to fill in some of the gaps related to the anatomy, with images of equipment that has yet to be sourced or fitted on T Square 54.

John Szalay and Paul Stancliffe, who proofread the text and identified essential corrections and useful additions.

I thank all the contributors and hope that this book does justice to the plane and their assistance.

Introduction

Boeing's B-29 Superfortress more than lived up to its name. Able to carry twice the bomb load over twice the distance of its famous Second World War stablemate the Boeing B-17 Flying Fortress, it operated exclusively against Japan where its immense range made it ideal for crossing the vast expanse of the Asian continent or Pacific Ocean. This performance also made it the perfect choice to deliver the USA's first nuclear weapons, the dropping of which brought the Second World War to a rapid end and immortalised the B-29's fame (or maybe infamy).

Not considered obsolete at the end of the war the B-29s were stored rather than scrapped, then resurrected as the initial front-line nuclear bombers within Strategic Air Command. Finally, as newer and more capable bombers overtook it, the B-29 was thrown into a second war, this time against North Korea. Here, too, when allowed to operate as a strategic bomber it performed well.

However, the Korean War imposed restrictions on how the B-29 could be used, relegating it to little more than a tactical bomber, a role for which the aircraft was ill-suited. Also, modern jet fighters and improved radars made the Second World War vintage plane vulnerable and once the Korean War ended the B-29 was rapidly withdrawn from front-line service. It did continue serving, though, in support duties such as aerial tanker, offering the USAF's early jet fighters and reconnaissance planes much needed extended duration.

Today, of the 3,960 B-29s produced, a mere handful remain and only one of these still flies, although a second may soon take to the air. The others reside in museums where often dedicated teams of volunteer restorers continue to bring the ageing airframes back to the condition of their prime so that future generations can investigate the cutting-edge technology of a bygone era and still admire, even by current standards, a magnificent aeroplane.

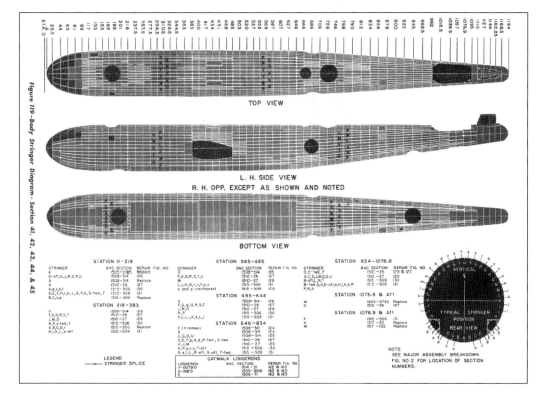

LEFT B-29 body stringer diagram for sections 41, 42, 43, 44 and 45. (USAAF)

Chapter One

The B-29 story

Years ahead of its time, the B-29's development suffered considerably as change upon change was added to its design. However, the result was a superb and versatile bomber that greatly outclassed its peers and allowed it to continue in service in many guises for several years after the Second World War.

OPPOSITE B-29-1-BWs in Boeing's giant Wichita Plant II. Note the camouflaged planes partway along the far production line. *(USAF)*

Strategic bombing effectively began on 13 June 1917 when Germany sent 14 Gotha bombers from occupied Belgium to bomb London. Although they caused only a few casualties, these were mainly civilians and the fact that the enemy could fly over the massed armies and fleets to attack civilians in their homes caused widespread panic. The political impact of this was enormous and, despite a relatively effective air defence system being quickly created around London, the idea took hold that defence was not possible against bombers. Consequently, Britain set out to create its own independent bomber force and thus was born the Royal Air Force, initially tasked solely with the strategic bombing of Germany.

During the early 1930s, despite opposition from the Army and Navy, certain people within the US Army Air Corps (AAC) began to push for their air arm to become an autonomous service and the strategic bomber was seen as the way for this to happen, even if existing bombers had limited range and payload and could scarcely be called strategic. However, on 14 April 1934 the AAC initiated 'Project A', a feasibility study into a 'Long Range Airplane Suitable for Military Purposes' and on 12 May 1934 the AAC began negotiations with Boeing and Martin. Boeing responded with their model 294 that was originally designated XBLR-1 (Experimental Bomber Long Range 1) but changed to XB-15 in July 1936 before construction was complete.

At the time of its first flight on 15 October 1937 it was the largest bomber ever tested in the USA, although it was grossly underpowered and never had a realistic chance of forming a viable strategic bomber. Its development and production did, however, teach Boeing a great deal about large aircraft design. After the 'Project A' experiment the US turned its attention to developing smaller, if still heavy, bombers such as the Boeing model 299 (B-17) that had more chance to get into production, and it was not until the threat of war once more arose that they looked again to long-range 'super-bomber' designs.

In 1937, President Roosevelt was concerned about the apparent paralysis of Britain and France in their dealings with the Nazi regime. Realising that this was largely due to fear of possible Luftwaffe bombing raids on their cities, he became intent on preventing a similar situation arising in America so asked Congress for some $300 million to allow the AAC to build its strength. This was granted on 3 April 1937 when AAC planners were given the go-ahead and the acting chief of the AAC, Major General Henry 'Hap' Arnold, formed a study board under the direction of General Walter Kilner to determine the air corps' needs.

Specification

General Kilner's board reported in June 1939 and recommended the development of several medium and heavy long-range bombers. Following submission of this report, on 10 November 1939 General Arnold requested authorisation to study a 'Very Long Range' bomber. This was granted on 2 December and a team of AAC engineers under Captain Donald Putt of Air Material Command at Wright Field began to prepare the specification. Once complete, this called for a 'super-bomber' that could fly at 400mph with a 5,333-mile range and be able to deliver a 1-ton (2,000lb) bomb load to a target at the halfway point.

Suitable companies were given the requirement on 29 January 1940 as Request for Data R-40-B and Specification XC-218, with responses to be submitted within 30 days. Despite the advanced requirements and almost impossible timescales, all six companies – Boeing, Consolidated, Douglas, Lockheed, Martin and Sikorsky – responded to the challenge and returned bids by the end of February 1940.

Boeing was in a good position having been in discussions with the AAC on potential super-bombers since early 1939. Not surprisingly these discussions concluded that any such super-bomber would have to exhibit great range coupled with an ability to carry a heavy bomb load. Convinced that the AAC would need such a bomber, in August 1939 Boeing privately began working on a design. To attain high speed and long range the design had to be as aerodynamically clean as possible. All external rivets were flush, all fuselage panels butt joined and all vents, drains or scoops were deleted or streamlined.

Critical as streamlining was, of even greater importance was the wing. Initially Boeing was attracted to the Davis wing developed by Consolidated and used on their B-24 Liberator. This high aspect ratio, laminar flow aerofoil offered low drag and hence long range. However, negotiations bogged down leaving Boeing to develop its own wing. This culminated in the Boeing 117 aerofoil, a slender wing with the extremely high aspect ratio that became one of the B-29's defining characteristics. This provided great efficiency and hence offered long range and high speed, although a downside was very high wing loading. This resulted in higher take-off and landing speeds and concerns over the wing's strength. The take-off and landing speed issue was solved by the inclusion of large fowler flaps which, when lowered, extended out the rear of the wing, expanding its area by 20% and adding a third to the lift when fully deployed. Adequate strength in such a slender wing was attained by increasing the thickness between the two wing spars that were connected by ribs to create a number of rigid cells.

Building on this design, Boeing's bid, designated model 341, was for a mid-winged, four-engined monoplane with an overall length of 85ft 6in, a wingspan of 124ft 7in and a gross weight of 85,672lb. Armed with six flexible 0.5in machine guns and able to carry 2,000lb of bombs, the design met the specification with a theoretical top speed of 405mph and range of 5,333 miles at 25,000ft.

In April, however, following early feedback from the European war, the AAC revised the specification to incorporate several modifications, including increased defensive armament, armour plating and self-sealing fuel tanks, and all companies were asked to resubmit.

Candidate responses

Boeing responded by modifying their model 341, adding four more 0.50in machine guns, a 20mm cannon, armour to all crew positions and self-sealing fuel tanks in the wings. Drag reduction was still paramount so when the armament was increased Boeing opted for a revolutionary remote-controlled turret system, designed by Sperry and recommended by engineers from Air Material Command. In this system ten machine guns were mounted, two each in five turrets, two above and two below the fuselage and a tail turret, which also held the 20mm cannon. The gunners were located away from their turrets, sighting via periscopes looking through teardrop-shaped blisters on the outside of the fuselage. The four fuselage turrets were retractable, aiding the obsession with drag.

These changes met the new specification but at a price. The improved armament weighed 2,507lb more than the model 341's and the self-sealing tanks another 3,000lb. This increased weight required an extra 3,680lb of fuel to allow the plane to achieve the same range. In turn this extra fuel needed bigger tanks in larger wings and hence yet more weight in a spiral of weight and fuel gain. Eventually the final design had a wingspan of 141ft 3in and a length of 93ft 0in. In total these changes added 17,794lb, which included 8,834lb of extra fuel. The added weight also affected the top speed, which dropped by 23mph to 382mph. Designated the model 345 this new design was submitted to the AAC in May 1940.

With the revisited designs ready, the AAC set up a special board at the Air Corps' technical centre at Wright Field in Dayton, Ohio, under Colonel Oliver Echols of Air Material Command to assess them. Martin and Sikorsky elected not to resubmit, leaving just four competing companies. The board ranked their submissions and assigned designations in order of preference. Boeing's

THE B-32 DOMINATOR

The B-32 suffered far more development problems than the B-29 and only a handful saw combat in the final weeks of the Second World War. Originally called the 'Terminator', the name had changed to 'Dominator' by the time the first production B-32 was accepted. The only combat missions were flown by three B-32s assigned to the 386th BS, 312th BG and 5th AF at Clark Field, Luzon, on a combat evaluation. The evaluation was a success and the 386th BS began to convert to B-32s in July 1945. However, in August the unit moved to Okinawa just as the war ended. After this they flew photoreconnaissance missions during the uneasy ceasefire that existed from 15 August until the formal surrender of Japan on 2 September.

Despite its brief operational history, the B-32 did gain the, perhaps dubious, distinction of being involved in what was probably the last aerial combat of the Second World War. On 18 August, Japanese fighters jumped two B-32s that were conducting photoreconnaissance missions. The B-32s claimed two fighters but although one B-32 escaped unharmed the other was badly shot up, with one photographer and a gunner badly wounded while another photographer, Sergeant Anthony J. Marchione was killed.

In total, 118 B-32s were completed – 3 XB-32s, 75 B-32s and 40 TB-32s – and all but one were made at Consolidated's Fort Worth, Texas, factory with the one being built at their San Diego, California, plant. No complete B-32 survives.

BELOW A B-32 shows off its high wing and cylindrical fuselage as it takes on fuel while on Okinawa. The B-32 was to have been pressurised but this was dropped to simplify the design. Hence the standard manned turrets rather than the remote-control turrets of the B-29. Note the Curtis Electric propellers – fitted as standard to the B-32's Wright R-3350 engines. *(USAF)*

model 345 was the favourite so got the lowest designation, XB-29. Next came Lockheed's (model 51-81-01) as XB-30, then Douglas's (model 332F) as XB-31 and lastly Consolidated's (model 33) was given XB-32.

Because of the advanced requirement, AAC policy needed two sources for the design in case the first choice proved to be unworkable and so, on 4 June 1940, General Arnold authorised $85,000 each to Boeing and Lockheed to allow them to continue refining the design and produce mock-ups for wind tunnel testing.

In August Lockheed withdrew and when Douglas declined to take it on, the 'back-up' contract passed to Consolidated and the XB-32.

Having been awarded the contract, Boeing set about converting the theoretical model 345 into a design that could actually be built. The engineering calculations were tested in wind tunnels and resulted in further changes. It was discovered that the inboard engine nacelles affected the airflow so Boeing added a small extension to the trailing edge of the wing between the inboard nacelle and fuselage. This extension was not included in aerodynamic calculations, nor the wing area figures, and was nicknamed 'Yehudi' by the engineers after the popular 1940 song 'Who's Yehudi?' or 'The little man who wasn't there'.

When wind tunnel tests also discovered that the engine nacelles created too much drag these were redesigned. The new design hugged the engine, halving the drag but causing untold problems with overheating for the rest of the B-29's service. Yet more wind tunnel tests resulted in changes to the rudder and also to the lengthening of the fuselage by some 5ft to enlarge the bomb bays, allowing twice as many 500lb bombs to be carried.

Boeing's preliminary designs were completed on 24 August 1940, allowing the AAC to present Boeing with a contract for two flyable and one static test prototypes. Awarded on 6 September 1940, contract AC-15429 stipulated that the first prototype, now designated XB-29, was to be delivered in April 1942 with the second to follow in June. Encouragingly, in late November 1940 AAC engineers inspecting Boeing's full-scale mock-up were so impressed that on 14 December the contract was amended to add a third flyable XB-29.

Despite the prototype having not yet flown, on 1 May 1941 the AAC ordered 250 B-29s, increased to 500 after Pearl Harbor and an impressive 1,665 were on order before the first XB-29 took to the air.

Development

As Boeing worked to create the prototypes, the AAC insisted on over 900 design changes to accommodate lessons learned by witnessing the air war raging over Europe. Essential though these were they slowed progress such that the first prototype was not ready until early September 1942. After initial taxi tests and a few small test 'hops' that reached 15 or so feet in altitude, the first true flight finally took place on 21 September 1942 when Boeing's chief test pilot Eddie Allen took off for a 75-minute flight. Somewhat surprisingly it went flawlessly but was a false dawn. The airframe met all expectations, leading Donald Putt to comment 'unbelievable for such a large plane to be so easy on the controls … easier to fly than B-17 … faster than any previous heavy bomber … stall characteristics remarkable for such a heavy plane …'.

Unfortunately the engines were a different matter and soon engine failures began to decimate the test programme. Fires were frequent and when the second XB-29 joined the programme on 30 December it suffered a fire on its maiden flight followed by several more. Indeed, by 17 February 1943 it had only managed eight flights totalling a paltry 7 hours 27 minutes. Eddie Allen considered the plane dangerous but with the pressure on testing it could not be grounded. Consequently he took it up again on 18 February on a flight that ended in disaster when a catastrophic engine fire caused it to crash, destroying the plane and killing all on board. This was a massive setback that placed the entire B-29 programme in jeopardy. The USAAF could not allow this. The US government had committed over $1.5 billion to the project and the USAAF needed their super-bomber not only to help beat Japan but also as the instrument to grant them independence from the Army. To get the programme back on track the USAAF took a more active role. General Arnold set up the 'B-29 Special Project' to oversee testing, production and crew training, with the aim of getting the

ABOVE **The first XB-29. Note the three-bladed propellers and lack of armament.** *(USAF)*

BELOW **The third XB-29 in flight.** *(USAF)*

BELOW **Two YB-29s in flight. Nearest is the seventh YB-29 (41-36960). Note the silver strips on the leading edges of the wings and tail where the de-icer boots should be.** *(USAF)*

B-29 into combat by the start of 1944. Although this did not quite happen (the B-29's first combat mission was flown on 5 June 1944), the influx of technical support, and especially the reduction in design changes needing to be introduced, worked wonders. Testing continued steadily, initially with the two XB-29s (the third XB-29 having joined the programme in late May), then with the 14 YB-29 service test planes when they became available from late June onwards. The first YB-29 (41-36954) had been ready on 15 April but was grounded until 29 June following the Eddie Allen accident.

Production

The massive number of aircraft on order was far too great for Boeing to handle alone and the contract was split between four companies at four newly built government-owned Aircraft Assembly Plants:

- 765 by Boeing at Plant II in Wichita, KS;
- 300 by North American Aviation (a part of General Motors) at Aircraft Assembly Plant No 2, Kansas City, KS;
- 400 by the Bell Aircraft Corp. at Aircraft Assembly Plant No 6, Marietta, GA;
- 200 by the Fisher Body Division of General Motors at Aircraft Assembly Plant No 7, Cleveland, OH.

With an eye to post-Second World War aeroplane production Boeing considered North American a potential commercial threat so, when the opportunity presented itself they were removed from the B-29 contract. In August 1942 a deal was struck whereby the US Navy would relinquish their control of Boeing's plant in Renton, WA (made possible because of the cancellation of the Boeing PBB-1 Sea Ranger seaplane), in return for a share of B-25 production that would now be made by North American at Aircraft Assembly Plant No 2 in Kansas City. This allowed Boeing to convert the Renton plant for B-29 production and led to some lengthy and acrimonious legal wrangling.

Also, in July 1943 the B-29 contract with the Fisher Body Division of GM was transferred to the Glenn Martin Co., allowing Fisher to concentrate on the development and production of the XP-75 'Eagle' fighter.

RIGHT A diagram showing the component parts of Martin-produced B-29s with the companies who made them. Although the B-29 was a Boeing-designed plane there are no Boeing built items shown in this diagram and, apart from the inner wing that was built by Martin, practically every other component was supplied by the US automobile industry. Boeing and Bell-produced B-29s and B-29As had a similar number of subcontractors, also predominantly from the automobile industry. (USAAF)

THE GLENN L. MARTIN - NEBRASKA B-29 PROGRAM

B-29 CONTRACTORS LEGEND

- BALTIMORE
- CHRYSLER
- GOODYEAR
- HUDSON
- OMAHA
- A.O. SMITH
- BRIGGS

CODE	TITLE	DWG. NO.	CODE	TITLE	DWG. NO.	CODE	TITLE	DWG. NO.	CODE	TITLE	DWG. NO.
ALL	FINAL ASSEMBLY	15-8045	62	NOSE GEAR INST. A.O.S.	15-13418	41-B	DOOR ASS'Y-NOSE WHEEL BRIGGS	14-2281	17	WING TIP INST. HUDSON	15-7304
75	ENG.INST.R.H.- OUTBD. CHRYSLER	3-14374	62-A	WHEEL- NOSE GEAR G.F.E.	530033	41-C	STAND ASS'Y-ENGINEERS SHAKESPEARE	15-8802	16	WING L.E. INST.- OUTBD. HUDSON	15-7249
75	ENG.INST.R.H.- INBD. CHRYSLER	3-14373	62-B	TIRE & TUBE - NOSE GEAR G.F.E.		41-D	STAND INST-PILOT'S AISLE SHAKESPEARE	15-8565-5	12	WING INST.- OUTBD. HUDSON	15-10184
75	ENG.INST.L.H.- INBD. CHRYSLER	3-14372	61	LANDING GEAR INST. A.O.S.	15-13446	41-E	STAND INST-PILOT'S CONTROL SHAKESPEARE	15-7226	15	WING L.E. INST.- INBD. CHRYSLER	15-7246
75	ENG.INST.L.H.-OUTBD. CHRYSLER	3-14371	61-A	WHEEL & BRAKE ASS'Y-LDG.GR. G.F.E.		41-F	STAND ASS'Y-BOMBARDIER'S SHAKESPEARE	15-857 1	14	WING L.E. INST.- INBD. CHRYSLER	15-7247
107	MOUNT ASS'Y - ENGINE MARTIN, O.	15-7157	61-B	TIRE & TUBE - LDG. GR. G.F.E.		41-G	STAND ASS'Y-CO-PILOT'S CONTROL SHAKESPEARE	15-7276	13	WING INST.- INBD. CHRYSLER	15-7248
602	ENGINE G.F.E.	SPEC.670-H	45	BODY INST.- TAIL. HUDSON	3-14335	106	COL. ASS'Y-AIL & ELEV CNTRL G.F.I.FISHER	15-7203	11	WING INST.- INBD. OMAHA	15-7150
603	PROPELLER G.F.E.	SPEC.ID04-M	44	BODY INST. - REAR HUDSON	3-14334	105	NACE ASS'Y	15-8497	11-B	CHORD-WING SPAR-UPPER FR. G.F.I. BELL	*
105	MANIFOLD G.F.I.FISHER	6-11105-1	44-A	OILO & YOKE ASS'Y-SKID ASS'Y A.O.SMITH		87	RUDDER INST. GOODYEAR	15-9857	11-C	CHORD-WING SPAR-LOWER FR. G.F.I. BELL	**
72	NAC.INST.R.H.-OUTBD. G.F.I.FISHER	3-14344	43	BODY INST.-WING GAP GOODYEAR	3-14333	85	FIN INST. GOODYEAR	15-8032	11-D	DOOR ASS'Y-LDG.GR. WHEEL BRIGGS	14-2275
72	NAC.INST.L.H.-OUTBD. G.F.I.FISHER	3-14341	42	BODY ASS'Y-CENTER GOODYEAR	3-14332	84	DORSAL FIN INST. GOODYEAR	15-7205	11-E	CHORD-WING SPAR-UP.REAR G.F.I. BELL	***
72-A	CELL ASS'Y-ENG.OIL TANK G.F.I.FISHER	9-4539	42-B	DOOR ASS'Y-FWD.BOMB BRIGGS	14-2199	82	ELEVATOR INST. GOODYEAR	15-70717	11-F	CHORD-WING SP.-LOWER REAR G.F.I. BELL	****
71	NAC.INST.R.H.-INBD. G.F.I.FISHER	3-14343	42-C	DOOR ASS'Y-REAR BOMB BRIGGS	12-508	81	STABILIZER INST. GOODYEAR	15-7200	606	TANK ASS'Y-WING FUEL FIRESTONE	9-4261
71	NAC.INST.L.H.-INBD. G.F.I.FISHER	3-14342	604	TANK ASS'Y-AUX. FUEL GOODRICH	15-10765	36	FLAP INST. BRIGGS	15-8489	607	TANK ASS'Y-WING AUX.FUEL FIRESTONE	
71-A	CELL ASS'Y-WING.OIL TANK G.F.I.FISHER	9-4539	41	BODY INST.- NOSE CHRYSLER	3-14331	33	AILERON INST. HUDSON	15-7301	101	TURRET ASS'Y-TAIL GUNS G.F.I.FISHER	15-10190

15-11835, 15-11834, & 15-11835
15-11836, 15-11837, 15-11636, & 15-11839
AN-C-55 TYPE I & 26563

AN-C-55 TYPE I & 26546-D TYPE II A
H-3-101M-1, H-2-258-1, & H-2-259-1

* 2-778 & -1, 2-777 & -1, 2-1813 & -1
** 12-466 & -1, 14-2204 & -1, 14-2205 & -1, 8-2695 & -1

*** 14-2160-266 & 267, 2-1006 & -1, 2-1814 & -1
**** 14-2827 & -1, 8-1396 & -2, & -3, 8-2694 & -1

ABOVE B-29 assembly plants and modification centres. *(mark@chidgeyacres.demon.co.uk)*

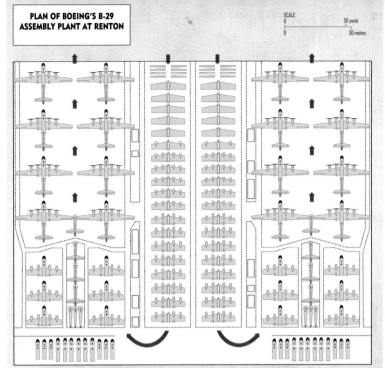

ABOVE The layout of Boeing's Renton plant showing how B-29s progressed through the building. *(mark@chidgeyacres.demon.co.uk)*

BELOW The layout of Martin's Omaha plant showing how B-29s progressed through the building. Huge though this plant was, it was the smallest of the B-29 plants, having been converted from B-26 production and having only a single production line for B-29s. Bell's plant operated two parallel lines, while both of Boeing's operated four. *(mark@chidgeyacres.demon.co.uk)*

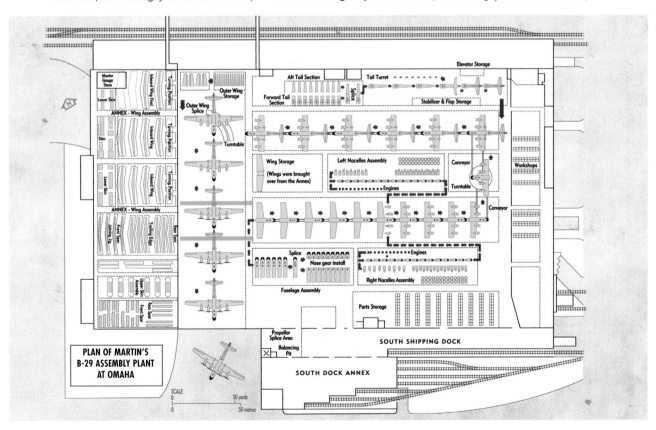

PLAN OF MARTIN'S B-29 ASSEMBLY PLANT AT OMAHA

These changes created the last distribution of production to four prime airframe assembly plants with final production figures at each being:

- 1,630 by Boeing at their Plant II at Wichita, KS;
- 1,119 by Boeing at their plant in Renton, WA;
- 531 by Glenn L. Martin Co. at Aircraft Assembly Plant No 1 at Fort Crook (Omaha), NE;
- 663 by Bell Aircraft Corp. at Aircraft Assembly Plant No 6 at Marietta, GA.

In addition, a vast network of subcontractors was set up throughout the country for B-29 components and sub-assemblies, notably:

- Hudson produced 802 B-29 rear fuselages, bulkheads, outer wing panels and wingtips in Detroit;
- Fisher Body Division of GM produced 13,772 B-29 engine nacelles plus 566 nose sections at Aircraft Assembly Plant No 7 at Brookpart Village (Cleveland), OH;
- Dodge (Chrysler) produced most Wright R-3350 engines for B-29s at Chicago, IL;
- Frigidaire Division of GM produced all the B-29 Hamilton Standard propellers at Dayton, OH.

Production blocks

Although changes to the specification of the B-29 were reduced to what were considered essential, they still amounted to a phenomenal number. This was not a problem that was in any way unique to the B-29, and the USAAF reduced the impact of these changes on the manufacturers by using a production block system for all aircraft types. At the manufacturing site all planes in a given production block (normally 50 or 100) would be produced to the same specification agreed to at the start of the block. In this way the workers could maintain a steady throughput of finished planes. Specification Change Notices authorised while the block was being produced were grouped together and introduced into the production line at the start of the next block.

Production blocks for each aircraft type were typically incremented by 5, eg 1, 5, 10 etc, and had a code for the manufacturing site added to the end, eg B-29-15-BW refers to the 50 B-29s produced by Boeing at their Wichita plant in production block 15. Block numbers were individual to manufacturing sites so B-29-15-BA and B-29-15-BW need not have been manufactured at the same time nor would they necessarily contain the same modifications. The manufacturing sites relevant to the B-29 were:

Code	Description
BO	Boeing Seattle, WA. Only the three XB-29s were built here although many B-17s were and so have the BO suffix to their production block.
BW	Boeing Wichita – Boeing at Wichita, KS.
BN	Boeing Navy – Boeing at Renton, WA. The Navy descriptor arose because the Renton plant was originally built to produce seaplanes for the US Navy.
MO	Martin Omaha – Glenn L. Martin Co. at Omaha, NE.
BA	Bell Atlanta – Bell Aircraft Corp. at Marietta, GA.

The plane's production block was added to the Technical Data Block (TDB) stencilled on the left side of the nose.

Modification centres

After acceptance by the USAAF (against the specification used for the block) the planes went to a modification centre where the latest upgrades were added, bringing the new planes to the most up-to-date standard. This two-stage approach, although seemingly inefficient, worked well and allowed huge volumes of planes to be produced. In total there were nineteen modification centres with three of these modifying B-29s:

- No 8 – Fort Crook (Omaha), NE, operated by the Glenn L. Martin Co.;
- No 13 – Denver, CO, operated by Continental Airways;
- No 14 – Birmingham, operated by the Betchel-McCone-Parsons Corp.

Additionally the Bell Aircraft Corp. ran a B-29-only modification centre at their B-29 production plant in Marietta, GA.

BELOW B-29 production blocks, serials and major changes.

Date	BO Block	First Serial	Last Serial	No built	BW Block	First Serial	Last Serial	No built	BA Block	First Serial	Last Serial	No built	BN Block	First Serial	Last Serial	No built	MO Block	First Serial	Last Serial	No built	
Jul-41	XB-29	41-002	41-003	2																	
Apr-42	XB-29	41-18335		1																	
May-42					YB-29	41-36954	41-36967	14													
Sep-43					B-29-1-BW	42-6205	42-6254	50													
Oct-43																					
Nov-43																					
Dec-43					B-29-5-BW	42-6255	42-6304	50	B-29-1-BA	42-63352	42-63365	14									Lorenze blind landing equipment
Jan-44					B-29-10-BW	42-6305	42-6354	50													Elimination of bunks
Feb-44					B-29-15-BW	42-6355	42-6404	50					B-29A-1-BN	42-93824	42-93843	20					Fuel in wing centre section
Mar-44					B-29-20-BW	42-6405	42-6454	50	B-29-5-BA	42-63366	42-63381	16									4 gun upper forward turret
Apr-44					B-29-25-BW	42-24420	42-24469	50													20mm deleted
May-44					B-29-30-BW	42-24470	42-24519	50	B-29-10-BA	42-63382	42-63401	20					B-29-1-MO	42-65202	42-65204	3	De-icer boots deleted
Jun-44					B-29-35-BW	42-24520	42-24569	50	B-29-15-BA	42-63402	42-63451	50					B-29-5-MO	42-65205	42-65211	7	Pneumatic bomb bay doors
Jul-44					B-29-40-BW	42-24570	42-24669	100					B-29A-5-BN	42-93844	42-93873	30	B-29-10-MO	42-65212	42-65219	8	Cowl flap shortening
Aug-44					B-29-45-BW	42-24670	42-24769	100									B-29-15-MO	42-65220	42-65235	16	
Sep-44													B-29A-10-BN	42-93874	42-93923	50	B-29-20-MO	42-65236	42-65263	28	
Oct-44									B-29-20-BA	42-63452	42-63501	50									
Nov-44					B-29-50-BW	42-24770	42-24869	100	B-29-25-BA	42-63502	42-63551	50									
					B-29-55-BW	42-24870	42-24919	50													
					B-29-55-BW	44-69655	44-69704	50													
Dec-44					B-29-60-BW	44-69705	44-69804	100	B-29-30-BA	42-63552	42-63580	29	B-29A-15-BN	42-93924	42-93973	50	B-29-25-MO	42-65264	42-65313	50	
									B-29-30-BA	42-63581	42-63621	41									
Jan-45													B-29A-20-BN	42-93974	42-94023	50	B-29-30-MO	42-65315	42-65383	69	
Feb-45					B-29-65-BW	44-69805	44-69904	100	B-29-35-BA	42-63622	42-63691	70	B-29A-25-BN	42-94024	42-94073	50	B-29-35-MO	42-65384	42-65401	18	
																	B-29-35-MO	44-27259	44-27325	67	
Mar-45					B-29-70-BW	44-69905	44-70004	100	B-29-40-BA	42-63692	42-63751	60	B-29A-30-BN	42-94074	42-94123	50					
									B-29B-40-BA	44-83890	44-83895	6									
Apr-45					B-29-75-BW	44-70005	44-70104	100	B-29-45-BA	44-83896	44-83962	67	B-29A-35-BN	44-61510	44-61609	100					
May-45					B-29-80-BW	44-70105	44-70154	50	B-29-50-BA	44-83963	44-84008	46	B-29A-40-BN	44-61710	44-61809	100	B-29-40-MO	44-27326	44-27358	33	
					B-29-80-BW	44-87584	44-87633	50									B-29-40-MO	44-86242	44-86276	35	
																	B-29-45-MO	44-86277	44-86315	39	
Jun-45					B-29-85-BW	44-87634	44-87683	50	B-29-55-BA	44-84009	44-84056	48	B-29A-50-BN	44-61810	44-61909	100	B-29-50-MO	44-86316	44-86370	55	
					B-29-86-BW	44-87684	44-87733	50													
Jul-45					B-29-90-BW	44-87734	44-87783	50	B-29-60-BA	44-84057	44-84103	47	B-29A-55-BN	44-61910	44-62009	100	B-29-55-MO	44-86371	44-86425	55	
					B-29-90-BW	45-21693	45-21742	50													
Aug-45					B-29-97-BW	45-21743	45-21757	15	B-29-65-BA	44-84104	44-84139	36					B-29-60-MO	44-86426	44-86473	48	
					B-29-95-BW	45-21758	45-21792	35	B-29-65-BA	44-84141	44-84149	9									
					B-29-96-BW	45-21793	45-21812	20	B-29-65-BA	44-84151	44-84152	2									
					B-29-95-BW	45-21813	45-21842	30	B-29-65-BA	44-84155	44-84156	2									
Sep-45					B-29-100-BW	45-21843	45-21872	30					B-29A-60-BN	44-62010	44-62109	100					
Oct-45																					
Nov-45																					
Dec-45																					
Jan-46																					
Feb-46													B-29A-65-BN	44-62110	44-62209	100					
Mar-46																					
Apr-46																					
May-46													B-29A-70-BN	44-62210	44-622309	100					
Jun-46																					
Jul-46																					
Aug-46																					
Sep-46													B-29A-75-BN	44-62310	44-62328	19					
Oct-46																					
Nov-46																					
Totals				3				1630				663				1119				531	3960

B-29 variants

XB-29

Prototype aeroplanes.

YB-29

Service test aeroplanes. Built to near production
standard but still with three-bladed propellers,
although these were quickly swapped for four-
bladed propellers in the field.

B-29

Standard production version. See Chapter
Three – Anatomy of the B-29 – for details. Later
planes had a formation stick added to the C-1
autopilot to facilitate formation flying.

B-29A

Similar to the B-29 in all respects except in
wing construction and manner of attachment
to the fuselage. The inboard wing of the B-29
is continuous through the fuselage whereas
the inboard wing of the B-29A is joined at
the centre section, which is a complete and
separate assembly and the wings are bolted to
this at station 47.75. The different construction
means that only three fuel cells can be fitted
in the wing centre section, being able to hold
1,120 gallons. Outboard of station 510 the B-29
and B-29A wings are identical. This reduction
in fuel capacity by some 200 gallons was not
popular and prompted General LeMay to tell
Colonel Irvine (XXI BC Deputy Chief of Staff for
Supply and Maintenance) to 'write Washington
and tell them that we don't like the Renton
airplane'. Despite these reservations B-29As
continued to arrive and made up a sizeable
proportion of all B-29 types in the Pacific
theatre. Many publications state that because
of the differing method of connecting the wing
to the fuselage the B-29A had a wingspan 1ft
greater than the B-29. This is a fallacy, with all
official USAAF documentation quoting only a
single wingspan for both the B-29 and B-29A.
All B-29As were produced by Boeing at the
Renton plant. Early planes were equipped with
the transfer fuel system while subsequent ones
had the manifold system. These later aircraft
also had a formation stick added to the C-1
autopilot to facilitate formation flying. The very
latest planes (in blocks 70 and 75) had the
upper forward four-gun turret redesigned as

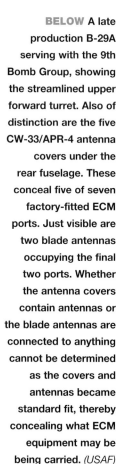

RIGHT The forward bomb bay and wing centre section of B-29A *It's Hawg Wild*.

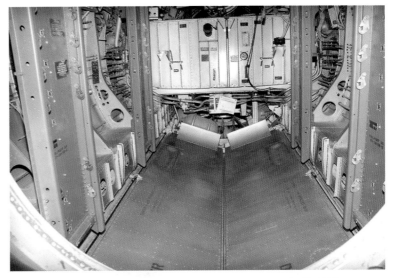

a streamlined teardrop shape similar to those fitted to B-50s.

B-29B

Similar to the B-29 apart from having all turrets, fire control, crew equipment and accessories removed except for the tail guns. Smooth closures were installed for all turret and sight openings. AN/APQ-7 radar was supplied instead of the AN/APQ-13. The AN/APQ-7 used a scanner mounted in a 16ft streamlined vane beneath the fuselage. This 'Eagle Wing' antenna contained an array of 250 dipoles mounted on the leading edge of the antenna fed by a waveguide of variable width. Operating at a wavelength of about 3cm the beam width was about 0.4° to 0.5° in azimuth and about 30° in elevation. The antenna was fixed with the beam being scanned 30° left and right electronically by varying the width of the waveguide.

The tail turret was equipped with the AN/APG-15B gun-laying radar. All new build B-29Bs were produced by Bell. The changes reduced the basic weight of the B-29B to 72,318lb, a saving of 3,466lb from the B-29A's basic weight, allowing the B-29B to fly higher, faster and further than the B-29s or B-29As.

Later, B-29Bs were created from standard B-29s or B-29As by removing the guns and turrets. Many were converted in this way during the GEM project.

ABOVE The AN/APQ-7 'Eagle Wing' radar antenna is clearly visible between the two bomb bays as this B-29B climbs away. *(USAF)*

LEFT B-29Bs line up on the apron at Bell's Marietta plant, showing the spherical AN/APG-15B gun-laying radar mounted below and between the two tail guns. Operating at 4in the 12in dish gave a conical beam width of about 25°. *(USAF)*

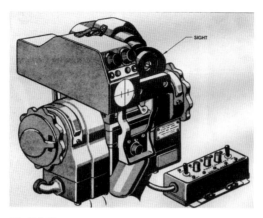

B-29C

Similar to the B-29 but with upgraded engines.
Some 5,000 planes were projected but the
order was cancelled and none was made.

B-29D (XB-44)

Similar to the B-29A but with Pratt & Whitney
R-4360 engines replacing the Wright R-3350.
One B-29A (42-93845) was converted, being
redesignated XB-44. Although 200 B-29Ds
were on order, they were cancelled at the
end of the Second World War. The order was
revived post-war with a redesigned airframe
under the new designation B-50, with 371
being produced.

B-29E

A single B-29 converted in 1946 to test revised
fire control systems.

B-29F

Six B-29s modified for cold-weather trials in
Alaska.

B-29G

A single B-29B modified to carry General
Electric jet engines on a retractable mount in
the rear bomb bay.

B-29L

Proposed B-29 version capable of accepting
in-flight refuelling.

B-29-MR

Some 74 B-29s were converted as B-29
Modified Receivers (also known as the
B-29B GEM). Similar to the B-29B apart from
modifications to allow in-flight refuelling from a
KB-29M tanker using the British looped hose
system and to carry a nuclear bomb. Refuelling
equipment comprised a contoured fuel tank in
the rear bomb bay capable of holding 2,193
gallons, a refuelling operator's station in the aft-
unpressurised compartment and a windlass,
containing approximately 350ft of line for pulling in
the hose from the tanker, located in the right side
of the fuselage under the tail plane. To help the
receiver find the tanker both tankers and receivers
carried AN/APN-2B and AN/APN-68 location
equipment. To accommodate an auxiliary crew
member – essentially a minder for the 'special'
bomb (as the nuclear bombs were termed) – the
radio operator and all his equipment were moved
to the rear pressurised compartment opposite the
radar operator while the auxiliary crew member
occupied the vacated radio operator's station at
the right rear of the forward pressurised section.

The GEM (Global Electronic Movement)
project was the code name for a programme to

RIGHT A B-29MR of the 353rd Bomb Squadron, 301st Bomb Wing, 2nd Air Force. Note the refuelling receptacle under the horizontal stabiliser. *(Charlie Harlow)*

CENTRE The forward bomb bay in *Enola Gay* showing the modifications made to allow the single large atomic bomb to be carried. Similar modifications were made to the B-29MRs. Of note is the single shackle mounted just under the tunnel and the sway braces. Also observe the cut-out in the tunnel with the round viewing ports. This is to allow the shackle to be viewed when the bomb is in place to ensure it is properly connected. *Enola Gay*, and the other Second World War Silverplate conversions, had two sets of sway braces – one set for the 'Little Boy'-type bomb (the braces mounted on the roof) and one for the 'Fat Man' type (the braces on the side bomb racks). It is probable that the B-29MRs only had the 'Fat Man' type since the Mk IV bombs carried were essentially of the same design. *(Scott Willey)*

BELOW LEFT The early 'special' bombs were complex and needed near constant attention, a situation that resulted in an 'auxiliary crew member' monitoring the condition of the batteries and various circuits in the bomb via a flight test box (FTB). This is the FTB in *Enola Gay*, mounted on the forward end of the radio operator's table. In B-29MRs the radio operator was moved to the rear pressurised compartment, giving the auxiliary crew member more space. *(Scott Willey)*

BELOW RIGHT To help with refuelling at night the B-29MR was fitted with an array of spotlights to illuminate the upper surfaces and fin, as shown in this diagram. *(USAF)*

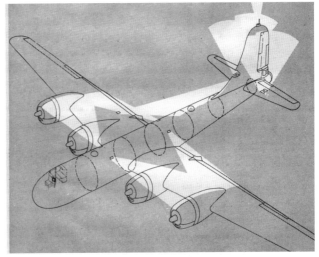

ABOVE The diminutive XP-85 'Goblin' parasite fighter hanging on its trapeze under EB-29 44-84111. The XP-85 was not for use with the B-29, being intended to be carried in the bomb bay of the massive B-36. *(USAF)*

upgrade B-29s to be able to carry and drop an atomic bomb. This was essentially a conversion similar to that carried out during the Second World War for the Silverplate B-29s, but by the time GEM came into being the code word Silverplate had been replaced by Saddletree but the conversion remained the same. The GEM conversion added all Saddletree modifications as well as in-flight refuelling capability.

CB-29K

A single B-29 converted to a transport in 1949.

DB-29/QB-29

Drone-directing B-29. This aircraft was a stripped-down B-29 devoid of armament but with additional radio control equipment installed to allow drones to be operated.

EB-29

E stood for Exempt and denoted a number of one-off conversions for specific trials.

F-13/F-13A (FB-29/FB-29A, RB-29/RB-29A)

Similar to the B-29/B-29A but with the addition of cameras for photographic reconnaissance

LEFT EB-29 45-21800 with the Bell X-1-2 high-speed research plane. The sister X-1-1 became the first aircraft to break the sound barrier when piloted by USAF Captain Chuck Yeager and dropped from this EB-29 on 14 October 1947. Note the appropriate Bell nose art. This EB-29 was also used to launch the Bell X-1A and X-1B aeroplanes, although by then the black undersides had been removed leaving the EB-29 in overall natural metal. *(NASA)*

LEFT EB-29 44-62093 during 'Project Tip Tow' designed to test the feasibility of a bomber carrying its own fighter protection. Several successful cycles of attachment and detachment were carried out with the F-84's engines shut down during the 'tow' and restarted before detaching. In these trials the F-84 pilot had to maintain manual control and Republic were tasked with developing an automatic flight control system. When this was tested on 24 April 1953 the F-84 immediately flipped over on to the wing of the EB-29, causing both to crash with the loss of all in both planes. *(USAF)*

work. They retained all bombing and defensive armament. Given that the B-29 would be operating at far greater ranges than any other aeroplane in the USAAF, the only way that mission planning photographs and post-strike damage assessment photographs could be obtained was by another B-29. In March 1944 Boeing worked with Fairchild to develop a photoreconnaissance version of the B-29.

F-13s carried a suite of six cameras located in the rear pressurised compartment. Because of the need to withstand the pressure differential when flying pressurised at high altitude the camera windows were made of ¾in thick glass. Making the holes and fitting the glass involved considerable structural work that was carried out by Continental Airlines at the Denver modification centre. Some 118 F-13s were created.

The cameras carried were: a vertically mounted Fairchild K18 for general photographic reconnaissance work as well as close-ups of specific areas; two K-22s on a split vertical mount that could cover a strip about 2 miles wide from 20,000ft in altitude; and three K17 cameras in a trimetrogon arrangement that covered a 30-mile-wide strip for photo mapping work.

In late 1945 the F-13 was redesignated the FB-29 and in 1948 it was reassigned again, this time to RB-29. RB-29s also took on Electronic Intelligence (ELINT) responsibilities,

being fitted with various signal analysers and recorders at the expense of the cameras. A typical ELINT fit could comprise two HF/VHF communication intercept positions (AN/ARR-5), one metric radar intercept position (AN/APR-4), one metric intercept and DF position (AN/APR-4, AN/APA-17) and two centimetric (X-band and S-band) radar intercept and D/F positions (AN/APR-9, AN/APA-11). Wire recorders were also carried to capture signals for later analysis.

Guardian Angel/Porcupine

Not an official designation but rather a descriptor for any B-29 derivative fitted with additional ECM equipment with the intention of jamming enemy radios and radars that might interfere with a mission. The term Porcupine originated from the profusion of antennas that such planes carried, normally outside the rear pressurised section. Porcupines were fitted with ten pre-tuned APT-1 or APT-3 barrage jammers untended in the bomb bay and three spot-tuned APT-1 or APT-3 jammers tended by two ECM operators to target specific radar threats. Porcupines also carried 2,000 bundles of RR-2/U or RR-3/U (Rope) with automatic dispensers. They were first deployed on 1 July 1945 when four flew racetrack patterns over the target stacked up from about 12,000ft, the lowest flying clockwise, the next anticlockwise and so on up the stack.

LEFT F-13A. Note the window in the fuselage side; this is the port for the left-hand K-17 camera in the trimetrogon. The three vertical camera ports can just be seen under the fuselage. The camera is the vertical K-18. *(USAF)*

LEFT A KB-29M looped hose tanker refuelling B-50A 46-0010 *Lucky Lady II* while training for the first non-stop round the world flight that took place between 26 February and 2 March 1949. The B-50A was a standard bomber version and flew 23,452 miles in 94 hours 1 minute, being refuelled four times by KB-29Ms. The flight was used by SAC to demonstrate their global reach. *(USAF)*

KB-29K

An interim designation for the looped hose tanker project. Became the KB-29M.

B-29L

An interim designation for the B-29 receiver intended to work with the KB-29K. Became the B-29MR.

KB-29M

Looped hose system

Boeing reopened their Wichita plant and converted 92 B-29s (no B-29As) by removing all defensive armament and associated systems and installing refuelling equipment. The refuelling equipment consisted of two contoured fuel tanks in the bomb bays: 2,660 gallons in the forward and 2,299 gallons in the rear. These were plumbed into the aircraft's fuel system allowing the tanker to use this fuel or to provide fuel from its own tanks to the receiver. All fuel tanks were fitted with nylon non-self-sealing

RIGHT An extract from AN 01-20EJA-1 describing the method used to connect and disconnect with the looped hose system. *(USAF)*

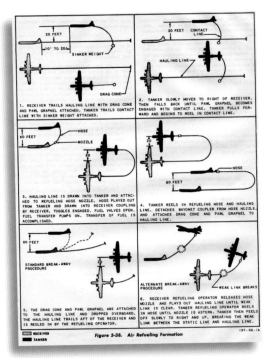

RIGHT A KB-29M of the 43rd Air Refuelling Squadron. Note the two antennas under the outer wing. These, and a similar pair under the right-hand wing, plus the one visible under the forward nose, are the AT-96 and AT-97 stub antennas for the AN/APN-2B and AN/APN-68 location equipment fitted to both the tankers and receivers. *(USAF)*

fuel cells instead of the usual self-sealing cells, allowing a greater load to be carried: 1,400 gallons in each outboard tank, 1,500 in each inboard and 1,400 in the wing centre section tank. Planes were equipped with either the fuel transfer or manifold system. A large hydraulically operated drum containing 240ft of 3in hose was located where the rear lower turret would have been. The end of the hose had a brass nozzle with a centre-fitting receptacle able to receive a 'bayonet fitting' on the end of a cable released by the receiver.

The drum was connected to the bomb-bay tanks via an array of pipes, cut-off switches and pumps. Adjacent to the hose drum was a second, smaller drum, containing 350ft of ⅛in hauling cable, and an operator's station from which the system was controlled. Behind the drums a hole in the fuselage floor allowed the hose and cable to exit. Initially fuel transfer was simply by gravity allowing a mere 95 gallons per minute to flow. Later a pump was added to the

tanker increasing the flow rate to 200 gallons per minute – an important increase when the receiver could need 2,000 gallons in a single refuelling.

Probe and drogue system

Oddly the KB-29M designator remained unaltered when some of the looped hose tankers were modified into the more efficient probe and drogue system where the tanker reeled out a hose fitted with a cone-shaped drogue at the end. The receiver was equipped with a probe on its nose or wingtip that the pilot had to fly into the drogue. Once a firm contact had been made fuel was pumped to the receiver. This system was much simpler than the original looped hose and could be used by single-seat fighters as well as multi-crew bombers.

KB-29P

Similar to the B-29 (only 2 B-29As were converted compared to 114 B-29s) apart from having all defensive armament removed

ABOVE A probe and drogue-equipped KB-29M refuels an F-84. The F-84 could only fill the tip tanks and could fill just one at a time, requiring two hook-ups per refuelling. *(USAF)*

and in-flight refuelling equipment installed. A manoeuvrable, telescopic boom with an articulated nozzle, attached to the bottom of the rear fuselage, provided the means to connect to and transfer fuel to the receiver. Hydraulic and aerodynamic controls for the boom were in the boom operator's compartment (formerly the tail gunner's compartment). All planes had Curtiss-Wright electric constant-speed, feathering and

reversing propellers and a manifold fuel system for normal operation and a high-capacity pump system for refuelling. Two contoured bomb-bay tanks were installed capable of holding 2,573 gallons in the forward bomb bay and 2,181 gallons in the rear. By using nylon non-self-sealing fuel cells instead of the standard self-sealing cells additional fuel could be carried in the wing and wing centre section tanks: 1,400 gallons in

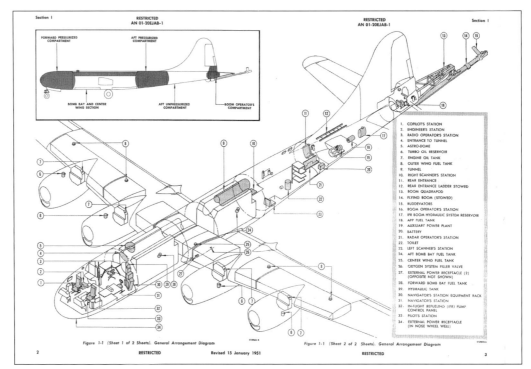

each outboard tank, 1,500 in each inboard and 1,400 in the wing centre section tank; however, structural limitations restricted the total fuel load to 10,017 gallons. Fuel could be transferred at a selective rate up to 600 gallons per minute. A signal amplifier sensed contact and controlled the equipment according to aeroplane positions, rate of change of positions and fuel line pressure. If any of the pre-set limits were exceeded the system automatically initiated an involuntary disconnect. Voluntary disconnects could be set in motion by either the boom operator or receiver pilot. A manually controlled nitrogen system purged the boom.

KB-29T

A single prototype three-point tanker using the probe and drogue system (45-21734). Instantly christened the 'Triple Nipple', this plane had three hoses, one on each wingtip and one in the fuselage so could refuel three aircraft at the same time. It became the prototype for the KB-50 three-point tankers.

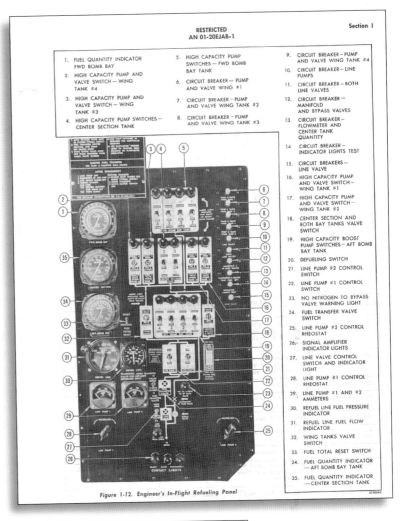

Figure 1-12. Engineer's In-Flight Refueling Panel

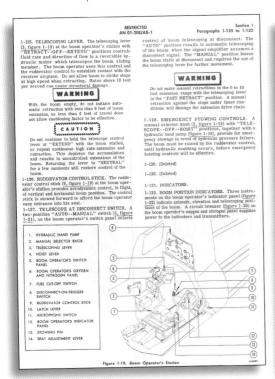

Figure 1-19. Boom Operator's Station

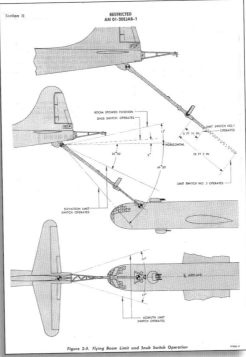

Figure 2-5. Flying Boom Limit and Snub Switch Operation

all defensive armament was removed. Two became P2B-1Ss while the other two, due to internal modifications, became P2B-2Ss. One of the P2B-1S planes (44-84029) was later further modified as the drop plane for the US Navy's high-speed research Douglas D-558-II Skyrockets. Achieving over 100 successful drops the P2B-1S obtained the name *Fertile Myrtile*.

SB-29/SB-29A

Twenty-two B-29s and three B-29As were modified at Tinker AFB between 1950 and 1952. Their mission was air search and rescue of personnel stranded in water. Search was visual and by radar (AN/APQ-13A) while rescue was accomplished by a droppable A-3 lifeboat.

SB-29s retained the full capability of the B-29/B-29A including all armament with the exception of the forward lower turret. This turret was replaced by the AN/APQ-13A radar that was displaced from its usual location between the bomb bays by the lifeboat. The radio operator was moved to the rear pressurised compartment where he occupied a position opposite the radar operator.

The 30ft A-3 lifeboat was installed on the underside of the fuselage by using a suspension truss with boat displacement arms secured on the exterior of the forward bomb-bay doors. The lifeboat was attached to the suspension

ABOVE P2B-1S *Fertile Myrtile* jacked up to receive a D-558-II prior to a test flight. The tally board on the fuselage side is split into two sections, one each for the two D-558-IIs, NACA 144 at the front and NACA 145 at the rear. This photo is taken partway through the test programme and both sections of the tally board were full by the end. *(NASA)*

P2B-1S and P2B-2S

In March 1947 the US Navy took delivery of four B-29s as long-range search and patrol planes, redesignating them as P2Bs. The P stood for Patrol while 2B denoted it as the second patrol plane from Boeing. Although they retained their sighting blisters (useful for visual searching)

LEFT SB-29s undergoing depot level maintenance at Tinker AFB. Note the pods under the wings of the second and third planes from the camera. These are flare pods as fitted to some SB-29s, allowing illumination flares to be dropped during the search or rescue procedures. *(USAF)*

BELOW Antenna locations for the SB-29. *(USAF)*

An S-3 lifeboat nestles against the underside of an SB-29 of the 5th Air Rescue Squadron. Note the antenna for the AN/URW-4 remote-control equipment under the nose. Not visible are the stub antennas for the AN/APN-2 rendezvous radar and AN/ARA-8A homing adapter as located under the outer wing. (USAF)

truss with a type U-1 bomb shackle, which engaged a ring set in the centre of the lifeboat's deck, while four displacement arms were mounted symmetrically on the interior side of the gunwales.

The lifeboat was dropped by means of a manual release controlled by the pilot. The displacing arms caused the boat to move first downward and then away from the fuselage. During this operation the bomb doors remained closed. The lifeboat's fall was slowed by a parachute and once on the water was guided to the survivors by the navigator using the AN/URW-4 remote-control equipment.

An outside filler permitted the centre-wing fuel tank to be serviced without removing the lifeboat.

TB-29/TB-29A

B-29s normally devoid of turrets and used for pilot, co-pilot and flight engineer training as

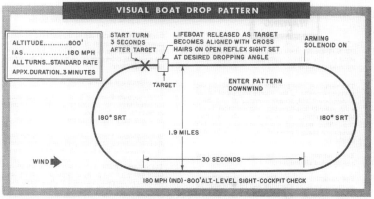

ABOVE The recommended visual boat drop pattern. (USAF)

LEFT A TB-29 trainer assigned to Maxwell AAF for transition training. (USAF)

tow reel operator's control console

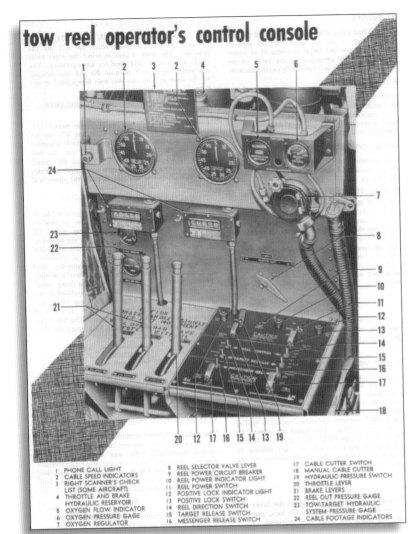

1 PHONE CALL LIGHT	8 REEL SELECTOR VALVE LEVER	17 CABLE CUTTER SWITCH
2 CABLE SPEED INDICATORS	9 REEL POWER CIRCUIT BREAKER	18 MANUAL CABLE CUTTER
3 RIGHT SCANNER'S CHECK	10 REEL POWER INDICATOR LIGHT	19 HYDRAULIC PRESSURE SWITCH
LIST (SOME AIRCRAFT)	11 REEL POWER SWITCH	20 THROTTLE LEVER
4 THROTTLE AND BRAKE	12 POSITIVE LOCK INDICATOR LIGHT	21 BRAKE LEVERS
HYDRAULIC RESERVOIR	13 POSITIVE LOCK SWITCH	22 REEL OUT PRESSURE GAGE
5 OXYGEN FLOW INDICATOR	14 REEL DIRECTION SWITCH	23 TOW-TARGET HYDRAULIC
6 OXYGEN PRESSURE GAGE	15 TARGET RELEASE SWITCH	SYSTEM PRESSURE GAGE
7 OXYGEN REGULATOR	16 MESSENGER RELEASE SWITCH	24 CABLE FOOTAGE INDICATORS

LEFT The tow reel operator's control console as located at the right scanner's station. *(USAF)*

well as serving as radar targets to help develop intercept tactics for USAF continental defence fighters in the early and mid-1950s.

TB-29 and TB-29A also denoted B-29s or B-29As modified for tow-target operation at medium or high altitude. Tow-target TB-29s had all turrets removed and two separate hydraulically operated cable reel mechanisms with 6,500ft of ³⁄₁₆in armoured cable positioned in the rear bomb bay. The cables ran through externally mounted tubes to two tow-target pods under the tail compartment. The pods were each designed to hold a 9ft by 45ft cloth flag target. As target towing was a non-tactical use, many B-29s ended their careers as TB-29 target tugs, resulting in a large proportion of surviving B-29s having been TB-29s.

BELOW LEFT The tail compartment looking forward. *(USAF)*

BELOW The aft bomb bay looking forward, showing the cable reels and associated equipment. *(USAF)*

tail compartment – looking forward

1 HANDLE	6 CABLE GUIDE EXTENSION
2 MESSENGER RELEASE BLOCK	7 FISH
3 RELEASE SOLENOIDS	8 TARGET POD
4 MESSENGER	9 FLAG TARGET
5 CABLE ROLLER	10 TARGET KEEPER

aft bomb bay – looking forward

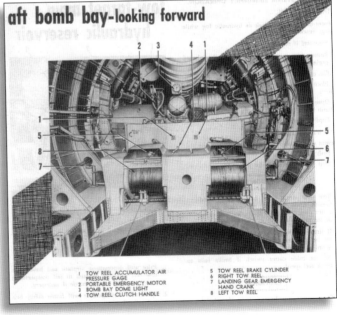

1 TOW REEL ACCUMULATOR AIR	5 TOW REEL BRAKE CYLINDER
PRESSURE GAGE	6 RIGHT TOW REEL
2 PORTABLE EMERGENCY MOTOR	7 LANDING GEAR EMERGENCY
3 BOMB BAY DOME LIGHT	HAND CRANK
4 TOW REEL CLUTCH HANDLE	8 LEFT TOW REEL

WB-29

Initially the USAAF weather squadrons flew standard B-29s or B-29As with the rear lower turret replaced by an airborne particulate filter assembly. However, from 1950 onwards specially modified WB-29s arrived on the squadrons from depots in the US. The WB-29 conversion involved removing all defensive armament; shifting the radar operator from the rear to the forward pressurised compartment where he sat in front of the navigator on the left-hand side; moving the radio operator from the forward to the rear pressurised compartment where he sat facing the right-hand fuselage wall; and providing a station for the radiosonde operator where the radar operator's station had been. A weather observer station was added in the extreme nose replacing the bombardier's station. A radiosonde ejection airlock was installed in the floor of the rear pressurised compartment and the nuclear particulate filter assembly – universally referred to as the 'bug catcher' or 'crackerbox' – was mounted where the CFC sighting blister would have been. Having the crackerbox in the rear pressurised compartment made operating it much easier since the filters needed changing every few hours, and with the crackerbox in the rear unpressurised section the plane needed to be depressurised to reach it.

Specialised weather recording equipment

ABOVE A WB-29 clearly showing the bug catcher mounted where the CFC sighting blister would have been. Note the ghost of the Triangle V on the fin, denoting the WB-29's previous existence as a B-29 bomber with the 301st BW, 8th Air Force. *(Bernie Barris)*

LEFT A close-up of a bug catcher, this time mounted where the rear lower turret would be in a standard B-29. *(Bernie Barris)*

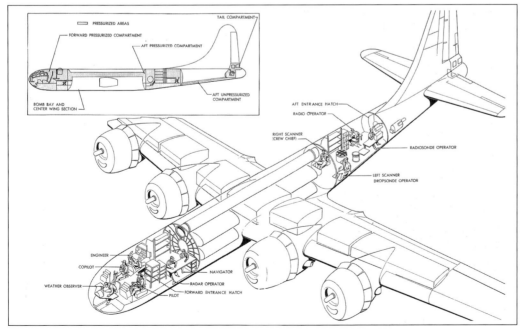

LEFT Diagram showing the general arrangement of the WB-29. Note the radar operator sitting next to the navigator in the forward pressurised compartment and the radio operator and radiosonde operators in the rear pressurised compartment. Observe also the bomb-bay fuel tanks. WB-29s generally flew with a full set of bomb-bay tanks, giving maximum range. *(USAF)*

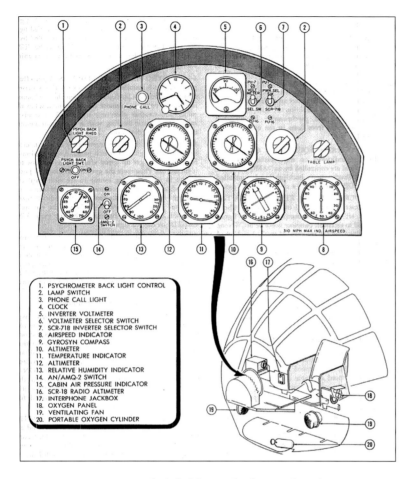

1. PSYCHROMETER BACK LIGHT CONTROL
2. LAMP SWITCH
3. PHONE CALL LIGHT
4. CLOCK
5. INVERTER VOLTMETER
6. VOLTMETER SELECTOR SWITCH
7. SCR-718 INVERTER SELECTOR SWITCH
8. AIRSPEED INDICATOR
9. GYROSYN COMPASS
10. ALTIMETER
11. TEMPERATURE INDICATOR
12. ALTIMETER
13. RELATIVE HUMIDITY INDICATOR
14. AN/AMQ-2 SWITCH
15. CABIN AIR PRESSURE INDICATOR
16. SCR-18 RADIO ALTIMETER
17. INTERPHONE JACKBOX
18. OXYGEN PANEL
19. VENTILATING FAN
20. PORTABLE OXYGEN CYLINDER

ABOVE The weather observer's instrument panel mounted in the very nose. *(USAF)*

installed for use by the weather observer included a ML-313/AM psychrometer to measure water vapour in the air, an ID-271/AMQ-2 aerograph temperature indicator, an ID-272/AMQ-2 aerograph relative humidity indicator, an SCR-718 radar altimeter and an AN/APNQ-52 Pulse Doppler Drift attachment to the AN/APQ-13A radar. A number of AN/AMT-3 radiosonde units were carried that could be dropped via the radiosonde ejection airlock and

RIGHT The dropsonde airlock as fitted to the floor of the rear pressurised compartment. *(USAF)*

contained instruments to record temperature, humidity and pressure as they parachuted to earth, this information being radioed back to the plane since the unit was lost.

WB-29s flew regular weather recording tracks as well as penetrations of typhoons to gain knowledge of these severe weather systems.

Eventually 39 B-29s and 65 B-29As were converted to WB standard.

Silverplate/Saddletree

Code names for the conversion of B-29s to carry the early US atomic bombs. Silverplate B-29s were operated by the 509th Composite Group to drop the bombs on Hiroshima and Nagasaki that ended the Second World War. Just after the war Silverplate was compromised and replaced by the code name Saddletree. The conversion was the same. The GEM project (see B-29MR above) incorporated the Silverplate/Saddletree conversions as well as others.

Washington B Mk 1

The name given to the B-29 by the RAF who received 84 B-29As and 3 B-29s between 1950 and 1952 as part of the Mutual Defense Assistance Programme (MDAP). Identical to the American B-29 and B-29As apart from the LORAN set being replaced with Gee. Eight main force bomber squadrons (Nos XV, 35, 44, 57, 90, 115, 149 and 207) traded their Avro Lincolns for Washingtons, with each squadron operating eight planes while three specially modified B-29As were used as electronic intelligence gathering aircraft. The bomber Washingtons operated from RAF Marham (35, 90, 115 and 207 Squadrons) and RAF Coningsby (XV, 44, 57 and 149 Squadrons), while the ELINT Washingtons operated from RAF Watton (192 Squadron). No Washington was nuclear capable, all being standard conventional bombers. All the bomber squadrons converted to English Electric Canberras by 1954, while 192 Squadron continued to operate the special B-29s until 1958 when serviceability issues forced their retirement just before the de Havilland Comet R Mk 2 took over. The 192 Squadron specials had all gun turrets apart from the tail guns removed and were fitted with a comprehensive suite of ELINT equipment installed into the rear pressurised compartment with six operators; equipment – AN/ARR-5, AN/APR-4, AN/APR-4 + AN/APA-17, AN/APR-9 + AN/APA-11 and ARI 18021.

In 1952 two Washingtons were converted by Vickers into trials support planes and transferred to the RAAF for use in guided weapons trials such as 'Blue Boar', 'Red Rapier' and 'Green Cheese' at the Woomera weapons test range. These were retired in 1957 and scrapped in Australia.

Tupolev Tu-4

Given the reporting name 'Bull' by NATO's Air Standards Co-ordinating Committee, the Tupolev Tu-4 was an unauthorised copy of the B-29. In late 1944 three B-29s (42-6256, 42-6365 and 42-6358) made emergency landings in Russia and were interned (a fourth, B-29A 42-93829, crashed). The Russians, having failed to obtain B-29s under the Lend-Lease policy and with no bomber of such sophistication, decided to reverse engineer the aircraft and produce a Russian copy. The process took two years, with the first Russian version taking to the air on 19 May 1947. Eventually three factories produced over 1,200 Tu-4s between 1949 and 1953: Plant No 18 at Kuibysher (about 480), Plant No 22 in Kazan (644) and Plant No 23 in Moscow (160).

To get the Tu-4 into service as quickly as possible very few changes were authorised from the interned B-29 'pattern' planes and the only significant changes were to the engines and defensive armament, with Russian Shvetsov ASh-73K engines being used rather than Wright R-3350s, and 20mm Berezin B-20 cannons, later succeeded by 23mm Nudelman Rikhter NR-23 cannons, replacing the 0.50-calibre Brownings, although the B-29's sights and computers were retained.

The Tu-4 remained in front-line service until the early 1960s with a number having been adapted to carry nuclear bombs as Tu-4As. Other variants were the Tu-4K stand-off missile carriers and 300 Tu-4s converted into Tu-4Ds as transports. The last Tu-4 variants in service were a few Tu-4s operated by the Chinese People's Liberation Army Air Force. In the 1970s the remaining airworthy examples were re-engined with Shanghai WJ-6 turboprops and operated well into the 1980s as 'Turbo Bulls'.

An interesting trial use of Tu-4s was 'Burlaki'

ABOVE Three Washington B Mk 1s fly over Queen Elizabeth II's coronation review at RAF Odiham on 15 July 1953. The Washington nearest the camera, WF552, served with XV Squadron and was originally 44-62326, the third last B-29A made and one of two Washingtons with the streamlined upper forward turret. The other is WF547 of 149 and 44 Squadrons (44-62328, the very last B-29A made). *(Jeff Brown)*

a towed fighter concept. Unlike the US Tip Tow idea, as tested with the EB-29, the Russians tested towing a fighter with a Tu-4 using a probe and drogue system that looked remarkably similar to the probe and drogue aerial refuelling system of the KB-29M. The fighter (a MiG 15) had a telescopic probe that connected to a drogue. Once contact was made the fighter was towed with the engine off. A later adaptation allowed the fighter to refuel as well as to be towed. The system proved to be workable but was overtaken by new planes and never went into service.

BELOW A Tu-4 Bull at Monino Central Air Force Museum, Moscow. Note the longer barrels of the 23mm cannons in the turrets.

Chapter Two

B-29 at war

Destined for use against the Japanese, the world's most advanced bomber tentatively began operations from the most primitive of airfields but became devastatingly effective when bases on the Mariana Islands became available. After the Second World War the B-29 formed the core of the newly created SAC, carrying the US's nuclear capability before ending its service somewhat unsatisfactorily over Korea, where political limitations relegated it to little more than a tactical role.

OPPOSITE Hundreds of 100lb M-47A2 incendiary bombs tumble from 39th BG B-29s. The bombs were conveyed multiply suspended, 6 per each 500lb bomb rack with 12 bundles per bomb bay, allowing some 144 of the bombs to be carried. Note how they exit the plane in a tight group before separating in the airstream. P 36 is 44-69870 *City of Aurora/The Caboose*. She suffered an engine fire and was abandoned over Gifu on 9 July 1945. *(Andy Kerzner)*

Training and XX BC missions from India and China

When the USA entered the Second World War their earliest war plans had 2,040 B-29s (24 groups of 85 planes each) based in Northern Ireland, from where they could pummel Germany. However, by 1943 it had been agreed

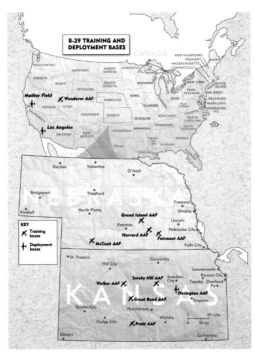

that the B-29 would only be used against Japan. Unfortunately, even with the B-29's great range, there were no Allied bases from which the B-29 could reach Japan. The US Joint Chiefs of Staff had ordered the main islands in the Mariana's chain to be seized, primarily for use as B-29 bases. Although still distant from Japan, bases on the Marianas would bring much of the country within range and they could be supplied directly by sea. Regrettably, the expected date of capture was too late for the USAAF so the B-29's introduction to combat would be in the China–Burma–India (CBI) theatre, operating out of India but with forward bases around Chengtu in China from where they could just reach the southern tip of Kyūshū.

This was far from ideal. The B-29 was the most complex bomber ever produced and operating it from the primitive bases available around Calcutta in India would be difficult. Worse, the infrastructure in China was non-existent and with no land route available all supplies would have to be flown over the Himalayas from India. Still, with no alternatives to hand the decision was made and Chinese labourers, directed by US engineers, began building four bases around Chengtu.

All of this was yet in the future and before any planes could deploy, both their air and ground crews needed to be trained. Initially four airfields in Kansas were chosen for this purpose, with tutors at each airfield teaching a single bombardment group (BG), allowing a full bombardment wing (BW) to train at the same time. Later, four airfields in Nebraska joined the B-29 programme, allowing two full BWs to receive instruction concurrently.

Originally it was expected that two BWs, the 58th and 73rd, would deploy to India under the direction of General Wolfe and XX Bomber Command (BC). However, the capture of the Mariana Islands was brought forward, allowing the 73rd BW to deploy there, leaving only the 58th BW to operate in the CBI. Consequently, on 1 March 1944 the 73rd BW transferred out of XX BC to a newly created XXI BC, leaving XX BC with only the 58th BW. Commanded by Brigadier General Haywood Hansell Jr, XXI BC was the organisation intended to command the bomber forces on the Mariana Islands, while on 4 April a new numbered air force, the 20th

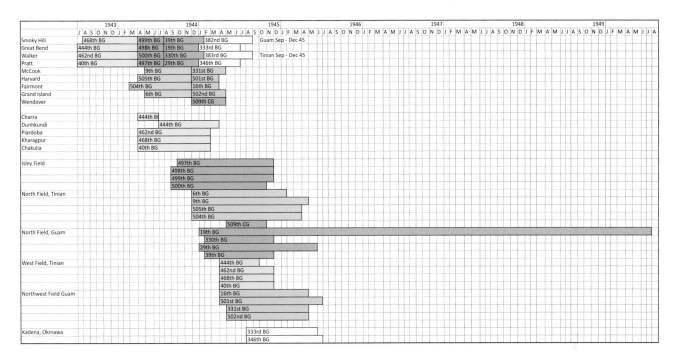

	1943	1944	1945	1946	1947	1948	1949
Smoky Hill	468th BG	499th BG 39th BG 382nd BG	Guam Sep - Dec 45				
Great Bend	444th BG	498th BG 19th BG 333rd BG					
Walker	462nd BG	500th BG 330th BG 383rd BG	Tinian Sep - Dec 45				
Pratt	40th BG	497th BG 29th BG 346th BG					
McCook		9th BG 331st BG					
Harvard		505th BG 501st BG					
Fairmont		504th BG 16th BG					
Grand Island		6th BG 502nd BG					
Wendover		509th CG					
Charra		444th BG					
Dunhkundi		444th BG					
Piardoba		462nd BG					
Kharagpur		468th BG					
Chakulia		40th BG					
Isley Field		497th BG 498th BG 499th BG 500th BG					
North Field, Tinian		6th BG 9th BG 505th BG 504th BG					
North Field, Guam		509th CG 19th BG 330th BG 29th BG 39th BG					
West Field, Tinian		444th BG 462nd BG 468th BG 40th BG					
Northwest Field Guam		16th BG 501st BG 331st BG 502nd BG					
Kadena, Okinawa		333rd BG 346th BG					

AF, came into being to command both XX and XXI BCs. This was a unique organisation within the USAAF, being the only numbered air force created to operate a single type of aeroplane and reflected the great importance placed upon the B-29 by the USAAF hierarchy. The commander of the 20th AF was also unique. General Henry (Hap) Arnold, the head of the USAAF, wanted to ensure that the 20th AF was not diverted from its strategic aim so appointed himself as its leader, commanding it from Washington DC.

The XX BC planes were scheduled to deploy to India in early March 1944. Unfortunately, when Arnold visited Salina (Smoky Hill) on 9 March to witness the first B-29 depart he found chaos. To his disgust, not a single bomber was combat ready and none was likely to be in the near future. Arnold suspended the impending deployment and ordered immediate remedial action, appointing one of his assistants, Major General Bennett Meyers, to supervise it. Thus began a month of frantic activity, known as the 'Battle of Kansas', where every available technician – including several hundred drafted in from the B-29 production factories and modification centres – worked round the clock, mostly outdoors and in freezing conditions, to ready the planes. Despite the atrocious weather the maintainers worked wonders, replacing hundreds of training engines for war-rated ones, correcting wiring faults and performing many other vital

remedies before the first B-29 was ready by the end of the month. Others quickly followed and in early April the 58th BW B-29s started deploying to the four airfields around Calcutta. One of the first B-29s to set off deviated from the route to visit England in an unsuccessful bid to fool the Axis powers into thinking the B-29 was destined for Europe. After a few days it continued on to India, being the only B-29 to visit England during the Second World War.

ABOVE Timeline showing what groups trained and operated from what base, when.

BELOW Map showing the two deployment routes to India. *(mark@ chidgeyacres.demon.co.uk)*

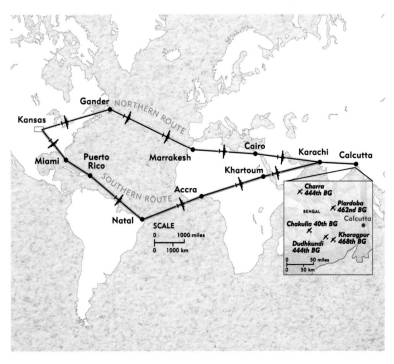

FIRST AND THE LAST

First B-29 in Britain

The first B-29 (or more accurately YB-29) to land in England arrived on 6 March 1944. This plane was diverted from its deployment to India in an attempt to convince the Japanese that the B-29s were to be used against the Germans in Europe. As a ruse the operation failed completely and the Japanese remained fully aware of the B-29 force being readied against them. However, the YB-29 did visit several bases to test their suitability for handling the heavy B-29 and this information was used in the post-war development of bases for the USAF's Strategic Air Command and for the RAF's use of the B-29.

BELOW *Hobo Queen*
after arriving in India.
Note the bomb-bay
fuel tanks. These were
the normal method
for B-29s to carry fuel
over the 'Hump' to the
Chinese bases.

The following diary covers the visit by YB-29 41-36963 *Hobo Queen* to Britain on the 'Pathfinder Project':

Date	Operation
26 Feb 1944	Left Marietta, Georgia, to deploy to India via the southern route.
1 Mar 1944	Ordered back to Marietta to take northern route to England.
6 Mar 1944	Left Gander for St Mawgan.
8 Mar 1944	Arrived Bassingbourn. Flew to various British and American bases testing runways for weight-carrying capacity. Plane shown to many important visitors including Churchill, Eisenhower, General Carl Spaatz, Air Chief Marshal Tedder.
1 Apr 1944	Left St Mawgan for Marrakech flying west for two hours before heading south to Marrakech.
2 Apr 1944	Left Marrakech for Cairo.
5 Apr 1944	Left Cairo for Karachi.
6 Apr 1944	Left Karachi for Kharagpur and met by K.B. Wolfe, commander of XX BC.

Following its arrival in India *Hobo Queen* was used for several 'Hump' flights (across the Himalayas), being the only YB-29 to deploy overseas.

Last B-29 in Britain

The last ever flight of a B-29 into Britain ended at Duxford on 2 March 1980 (almost 36

years to the day after the first YB-29 landed at St Mawgan!) when *It's Hawg Wild*, B-29A 44-61748, landed. The B-29 was flown from the USA after the Imperial War Museum (IWM) rescued it from the US Navy's China Lake proving ranges. *It's Hawg Wild*, a 307th BG Korean War veteran is now substantially restored and on permanent display in the American Air Museum at Duxford.

In 1979 the US Navy had donated this aircraft to the IWM who contracted Aero Services of Tucson to recover it and deliver it to Duxford. After surveying the airframe they came to the unexpected conclusion that it would be cheaper to fix the machine and fly her over than it was to take it apart and ship it. After much restoration

work *It's Hawg Wild* eventually took off for her first flight on 16 November 1979, flying to Tucson where Jack Kern and his company readied her for the 6,500-mile flight to England.

Sporting the UK civil registration G-BHDK, the delivery flight began on 16 February 1980 with a flight from Tucson to Flint, Michigan, and then to Loring AFB, Maine. After a delay at Loring AFB unsuccessfully trying to cure the No 3 engine's insatiable appetite for oil the flight continued via Gander, Sondrestrom and Keflavik before arriving at RAF Mildenhall on 1 March. The next day *It's Hawg Wild* flew to Duxford where she landed at about 2pm on Sunday 2 March, almost certainly being the last B-29 to fly into Britain.

ABOVE The Indian bases were far from finished when the first B-29s arrived. Here Indian women carry away dirt and stones in baskets balanced on their heads as construction continues. The B-29 is 42-6229 of the 793rd BS, 468th BG. She was lost on 15 June 1944 when she ran off the end of the runway while taking off at Pengshan, China, for the mission to Yawata, the first operation flown from China. *(USAF)*

BELOW No 44-42994 *Our Gal* of the 458th BG showing off her nose art, bombing symbols and camel 'hump' symbols. Note the blister above the 'L' of *Gal*. This is the drift recorder sight blister for the early type B-5 drift recorder. *(Sparky Corradina)*

Although much work had been done to ready the planes, the deployment did not run smoothly and during the week starting 15 April 1944, five take-off accidents at Karachi resulted in flights being suspended. The cause was traced to engine overheating. Engines that worked in America failed in the heat of India. The overheating burned the oil off the exhaust valves on the rear row of cylinders. These then stuck causing the engine to fail. Wright quickly introduced modifications to give greater cooling and better oil distribution and only when these modified engines arrived did the deployment restart.

Despite this setback the XX BC flew its first mission on 5 June against the Makkasan railway yard at Bangkok; 98 B-29s took off from India with 77 of these bombing, although later assessment showed that a mere 18 bombs had landed on the target. The first mission from China was delayed by problems in getting sufficient stores stockpiled at the forward bases. With no land or sea supply routes, everything from food to fuel and bombs had to be flown the 1,200 miles from India to the Chinese bases over the Himalayas, or 'the Hump' as it was more commonly known. This was extremely inefficient, requiring an enormous effort to mount each raid. So acute were the supply problems that even B-29s were used as transports to carry bombs, fuel or stores over the Hump. The B-29s had sufficient range to reach the forward bases direct from India

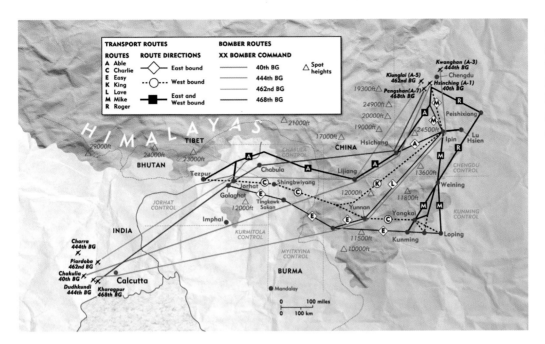

LEFT Map showing the routes taken by transport planes and bombers across the Hump to China. *(mark@ chidgeyacres.demon. co.uk)*

but even so the round trip generally took three days. The main cargo plane, the Curtiss C-46 Commando, had less range so needed to refuel en route, making the round trip for these planes even longer. These Hump flights were also dangerous and B-29 crews were awarded a mission credit for each, this being recorded on the plane with a camel symbol to differentiate it from the more normal bomb image. Paul Hunter, an FE with the 40th BG recalled the Hump flights: 'About May 1 we started hauling gasoline to China ourselves. A typical flight would leave India with 6,500 gallons of gas, fly to A-1 [Hsinching airfield, China], off-load 600 gallons, then fly back to India the next day with just enough reserve fuel so that the engines would not run out of gas when the nose was pointed down on final approach. The Hump was known for having the world's worst flying conditions. We had to fly between the higher peaks. We couldn't fly over them. Most of the time we flew in clouds or just above them. When in clouds we could only hope we were on course and flying between the mountains and

LEFT Consolidated C-109 44-49059 of the 2nd Air Transport Squadron having suffered an undercarriage failure while landing – a common problem for C-109s. Although B-29s were used to transport fuel and bombs across the Hump, the great majority of fuel transport fell to the C-109s and no B-29 amassed anywhere near the number of Hump missions as this C-109 veteran with 150 camels to show for it. *(USAF)*

LEFT The Hump offered few safe landing places should bad weather or mechanical problems affect a plane. *(USAF)*

CENTRE Although B-29s and C-109s did sterling work, it was the Curtis C-46 Commando that took the bulk of material from India to China. Here C-46 42-96689 of the 2nd Air Transport Squadron flies over mountains in western China. This plane was lost on 27 February 1945 after overshooting the runway at Yangkai. *(USAF)*

not into one. We all learned to have a fear of and respect for the Hump. On only two or three occasions were the clouds broken enough to see the ground. Then we could look down or around at the rugged, spectacular beauty.'

Eventually sufficient stores were in place and the first mission from China took place on

BELOW Final preparations by 40th BG personnel for the 15 June 1944 mission to Yawata, the first to be launched from the Chinese bases, are watched by the Chinese workers who prepared the airfield at Hsinching (known as A-1). The B-29 nearest the camera is 42-6289 *Nippon Nipper* of the 44th Bomb Squadron. *Nippon Nipper* did not survive long, being destroyed by an electrical fire when on the ground at Chakulia, India, on 7 July 1944. *(USAF)*

the night of 15/16 June 1944 when 68 B-29s took off to bomb the Imperial Iron and Steel Works at Yawata on Kyūshū. Some 47 aircraft reached the target area but the bombing was again ineffective, with only one bomb landing near the target. Although unproductive, Yawata was hailed as a great achievement, marking as it did the first time that American land-based bombers had attacked Japan.

These first missions were fruitless trips and although larger and more positive ones followed, logistical problems dominated operations from China. The small number and weight of missions did not impress the 20th AF commander, who needed successful missions to justify the USAAF's political aspirations almost as much as he needed them to help win the war. He therefore demanded results despite the difficulties and when these were not forthcoming replaced Wolfe with Brigadier General Curtis LeMay, a commander who had excelled with the 8th AF in Europe and who would soon become almost synonymous with B-29 operations against Japan. Immediately upon arriving in India, on 29 August 1944, LeMay set about revamping the tactics of the 58th BW by intensifying training (especially formation flying), revising the formation and introducing lead crews.

Even with LeMay's reorganisation, XX BC was never going to be as efficient as XXI BC. It was therefore decided that once a suitable base

ABOVE No 42-24442 *Wichita Witch* of the 793rd BS, 468th BG on its way to bomb Rangoon on 3 November 1944. *Wichita Witch* completed 20 combat operations in the CBI theatre and 8 Hump missions before being returned to the US as war weary on 23 February 1945. *(USAF)*

BELOW Chinese soldiers carrying the traditional tandem baskets troop past 42-6331 *Gone with the Wind* as they continue the construction of Hsinching (A-1). She was mistakenly shot down by a British Beaufighter on 21 December 1944. *(USAF)*

ABOVE No 42-24471 *Chattanooga Choo Choo* on the way back to Pengshan (A-7) after bombing Anshan, Manchuria. *Chattanooga Choo Choo* completed 16 combat operations in the CBI, 3 Hump missions and 15 combat missions from Tinian before returning to the US as war weary on 7 April 1945. *(USAF)*

was available on the Marianas, the 58th BW would redeploy there. Before this, however, with XXI BC starting operations against Japan from the Marianas, XX BC abandoned its forward bases in China, the 21st and final mission from China being flown on 17 January 1945. Almost at the same time, LeMay left XX BC to take over XXI BC from Hansell. Colonel Roger Ramey took charge of XX BC, continuing operations from the Indian bases against targets in and around Malaysia until a base was ready on the Marianas. The XX BC's 49th and last mission occurred on the night of 29/30 March 1945,

after which the 58th BW moved to the Marianas and XXI BC; XX BC then became redundant and was disbanded.

Much criticism has been heaped upon XX BC, with detractors pointing out the low number of missions flown and the small tonnage of bombs dropped. Although this is true, it hides the fact that XX BC operated the world's most advanced bomber – and a design that still suffered many teething problems – from airfields with some of the most primitive facilities imaginable and with huge logistical problems. To fly any missions under these conditions was a considerable feat and the knowledge gained, especially by LeMay, greatly aided XXI BC in their operations.

XXI BC and missions from the Marianas

The XXI BC had been created to operate from airfields constructed on the newly captured Mariana Islands of Guam, Tinian and Saipan. Unlike in the US, India or China, where the abundance of suitable land allowed each BG to occupy a different airfield, the shortage of land in the Marianas required the fewer bases to be large enough to hold and operate all four groups (180 B-29s) of a complete BW.

RIGHT No 42-65226 of the 677th BS, 444th BG en route to bomb Ōmura on 21 November 1944. This plane was lost with her entire crew during a mission to Singapore on 11 January 1945. *(USAF)*

Isley Field[1] on Saipan was finished first and the B-29s of the 73rd BW began arriving there on 12 October 1944.

On 28 October the 73rd BW flew the XXI BC's first mission when 18 B-29s took off to attack the submarine pens on Truk; 14 of these reached the target, dropping some 42 tons of bombs. Other missions to Truk and Iwo Jima

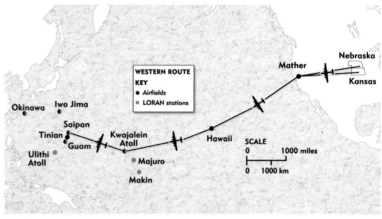

ABOVE Map showing the deployment route to the Mariana Islands. *(mark@chidgeyacres. demon.co.uk)*

1   The field was actually named in honour of US Navy commander Robert H. Isley, who was killed on 13 June 1944 when his Grumman Avenger was shot down while strafing the airfield (then in Japanese hands and called Aslito Field) during the invasion of Saipan. Unfortunately, an early misspelling of his name was never corrected.

LEFT B-29s of the 500th BG, 73rd BW rest at their hardstands made of crushed coral on Isley Field, Saipan. In the background are the accommodation Quonset prefabricated huts. *(USAF)*

followed, before, on 24 November, the XXI BC mounted a maximum-effort mission against Tokyo: 111 B-29s took off but only 24 managed to reach the primary target where they dropped 58 tons of bombs but inflicted only minor damage (a further 59 attacked the secondary target). Disappointing though the result was, the raid was significant as it marked the first time that US bombers had assaulted Tokyo since the Doolittle raid of 1942. Mechanical and navigational problems accounted for most of the B-29s that failed to reach the primary target, although only two were lost.

Navigation for the B-29s was such a concern because to avoid Japanese fighters based on Iwo Jima they were routed well to the west, meaning a 1,500-mile flight over water with no radio or radar checkpoints until close to Japan

LORAN

The word LORAN is derived from LOng RAnge Navigation. It is a US development of the British pulse transmitting navigation aid Gee (and its post-Second World War derivative DECCA). Whereas the British opted for very high-frequency (VHF) radio waves, providing high accuracy but over relatively short distances, the vast extent of the Pacific required the US to develop a high-frequency system, sacrificing some accuracy for greatly increased range.

To work, LORAN required three radio transmitters. For convenience one was normally termed the Master station with the other two being Slave A and Slave B. Normally there was a monitoring station present as well that could ensure the pulses were being transmitted correctly. The three transmitters and the monitor were grouped in what was called a 'chain'. In operation the Master transmitted a pulse. This pulse radiated out and was received by the two Slaves. These waited a predefined amount of time and then they transmitted a pulse. The delay was important since this meant that any user of the system would always, regardless of where they were, receive the pulses in the order Master, Slave A, then Slave B. At an interval that meant all pulses would have passed beyond their useable range, the sequence repeated.

To use the system, a navigator tuned his receiver to the published frequency of the chain. On an oscilloscope the pulses would appear as blips. By measuring the distance between the blips it was possible to determine the time difference between the arrival of the pulses. A given time difference between the Master's blip and Slave A's blip would place the user on a hyperbolic arc that passed through the baseline between the two stations. The second time difference (between the Master and Slave B) placed the user on a second hyperbolic arc. Where these two arcs crossed was the user's position. To plot the position the user employed special LORAN lattice charts produced for each LORAN chain that showed where the hyperbolic arcs for each time difference lay.

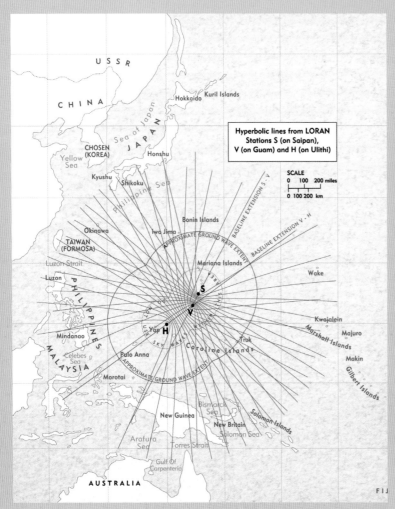

itself, a huge distance for crews to navigate using only dead reckoning (DR) and celestial fixes. This had been anticipated and as the US forces advanced from island to island the US Coastguard rushed LORAN transmitting stations into service on suitable islands almost as soon as they were cleared of enemy forces. The first of the stations for the B-29s was built on Saipan, with the second on Cocos Island

2 miles off the south coast of Guam. The third station in the chain, at Potangeras Island in the Ulithi atoll, went on air on 13 December 1944, and the chain was pronounced operational on 1 March 1945. Later, once the islands had been secured, additional stations would be built on Iwo Jima and Okinawa.

During December 1944 the 313th BW deployed to the Marianas, occupying the newly

ABOVE B-29s of the 497th BG, 73rd BW queue up to take off at the start of a mission. *(USAF)*

LEFT Despite extensive and generally effective defences, the USAAF did not have it all their own way. Here three B-29s from the 499th BG at Isley Field, Saipan, burn after an attack by 11 Mitsubishi A6M Zero fighters from Iwo Jima on 27 November 1944. *(USAF)*

LEFT North Field, Tinian. When this photo was taken on 8 July 1945 this was the largest airfield in the world, with four parallel 8,500ft runways. *(Earl Johnson)*

completed base at North Field on Tinian. The 313th BW flew its first mission on 21 January 1945. This was XXI BC's 21st sortie and was a return to Truk, this time with 33 B-29s. It was also the first mission that XXI BC carried out under LeMay, who had transferred from XX BC on 20 January.

As the 73rd and 313th BWs began operating together, the 20th AF's fourth BW, the 314th, finished training and deployed to North Field on Guam. The 314th BW's initial mission was also the XXI BC's first three-wing raid and took place on 25 February when 229 B-29s took off to attack Tokyo.

With the Marianas secure, the Americans turned their attention to Iwo Jima. This tiny volcanic island, of only just over 8 square miles in area, lay almost exactly halfway between the Marianas and Japan on the most direct route. Radar stations on Iwo Jima gave Japan warning of impending raids, while aircraft from the airfields were able to launch attacks against the airbases on the Marianas as well as harass the B-29s on their way to and from Japan. Iwo Jima was therefore selected for capture, to remove the threat of its Japanese garrison, provide airbases for long-range fighters to escort the B-29s over Japan and to offer an emergency landing ground for damaged or fuel-starved B-29s returning from Japan. Elements of the 4th and 5th Marine Divisions landed on 19 February

CENTRE North Field, Guam. B-29s took off towards the camera where, just out of view, 200ft-high cliffs fell away to the sea, giving the heavily loaded bombers some free altitude to help ease their engines. *(Earl Johnson)*

LEFT A newly arrived B-29 of the 29th BG, 314th BW sits on its hardstand while a bulldozer clears vegetation as North Field, Guam's, construction continues. The B-29 will become Square O 41 of the 29th BG, 314th BW. She survived the war to be reclaimed at Tinker in 1954. *(USAF)*

RIGHT Approaching Iwo Jima from the south, although seldom used on the outward flight; seeing Iwo Jima while returning was often a lifesaver for crews of damaged or fuel-starved B-29s. Mount Suribachi is at the centre of the photo with the fighter field visible to the right. The bomber field is off the photo to the right. *(Steve Smisek)*

1945 with the 3rd Marine Division disembarking the next day. All predictions were that it would be a quick battle. Unfortunately the predictions were wrong and ferocious fighting continued for 36 days (the famous photo of Marines raising the US flag on Mount Suribachi occurred on day four of the battle). Although the 21,000-strong Japanese garrison did not expect to survive, they intended to kill sufficient numbers of Marines so that America would baulk at further invasions of Japanese-held islands.

Even with Iwo Jima captured, the B-29s had to make long flights over open ocean. Consequently, air-sea rescue was given a high priority with both the 20th AF and US Navy devoting a considerable number of assets to it. By way of example, the support for the mission flown during the night of 9/10 March 1945 (before Iwo Jima was secure) consisted of four US Navy submarines, three US Navy surface ships (the US Navy called this lifeguard duty),

ABOVE Landing on 4 March 1945 after bombing Tokyo, *Dinah Might* of the 9th BG, 313th BW was the first of over 2,200 B-29s to land on Iwo Jima during the Second World War. *(USAF)*

LEFT B-29s from many BGs line the sides of Iwo Jima's taxiways, testifying to the usefulness of this small volcanic island. *(USAF)*

ABOVE No 42-24614 *Joltin Josie* T Sq 5 leads P-51s of the 45th Fighter Squadron, 15th Fighter Group, 7th Fighter Command from Saipan to their new base on Iwo Jima, March 1945. Based on Iwo Jima and equipped with extra-long-range fuel tanks, the P-51s of the 7th FC had just enough range to escort B-29s to Japan. However, the fighters needed a B-29 to help them navigate across the 800 miles of featureless ocean. The B-29 orbited offshore to mother them home after the mission. *Joltin Josie* was lost on 1 April 1945 while taking off for an operation to Tokyo. *(USAF)*

BELOW Streaming smoke from her feathered No 4 engine, a 29th BG B-29 limps home. The vast distances from Japan to the safety of their home bases or even Iwo Jima meant that any damage picked up over the target could easily become fatal. *(USAF)*

two dumbo and four super dumbo planes,[2] in addition to numerous picket and crash boats operating just offshore of the airfields. The northernmost submarine was stationed a mere 20 miles off the Japanese coast. The 20th AF also produced ditching guides to inform crews of which islands in the Marianas chain were secure and where the best conditions for ditching could be found. Despite these preparations, rescue from the sea was still no means assured and only about a third of the men who went into the water were recovered.

The results of the early raids were disappointing and fell far short of the USAAF leadership's requirements. The long climb to 25,000ft needed around 900 gallons of fuel that at 6lb per gallon weighed 5,400lb, reducing the bomb load by a similar amount. The climb also substantially increased wear on the engines, causing many failures, while at the high altitude the planes encountered very strong winds (the jet stream) and lower-level clouds often hid the target, making accurate bombing difficult.

Faced with these problems and now with three BWs on the Marianas, LeMay introduced a new tactic that would dramatically alter the fortunes of the 20th AF and Japan. He ordered the B-29s to bomb from low altitude, at night with incendiary bombs, attacking not a pinpoint target but the entire city. By needing less fuel, this change allowed nearly double the bomb load to be carried, but the crews were horrified,

---

2   Dumbo was a term used to denote air-sea rescue duty. Dumbo planes were normally Boeing B-17s fitted with extra life rafts. Where B-29s were so fitted they were termed super dumbos.

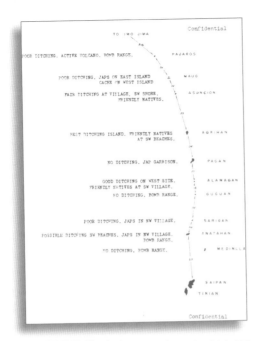

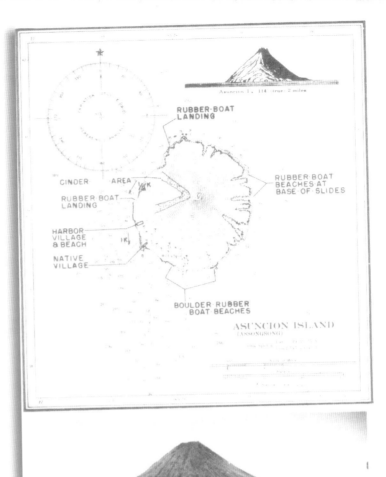

ABOVE The index page from the 20th AF's 'Ditching Guide' detailing which of the Mariana Islands were safe.

RIGHT One of the descriptive pages from the guide showing where it was safe to land around Asuncion Island. The guide held similar pages for all the islands in the chain.

fearing that flying low would expose them to intense flak, and rumours of 75% losses circulated around the squadrons. However, on the night of 9/10 March LeMay sent every available B-29 to Tokyo. Some 325 aircraft took off, the first time that more than 300 had been airborne (and only eight days after the 20th AF had first sent up over 200), with 270 of these bombing Tokyo.

It was a spectacular success. Losses, although heavy (14 B-29s failed to return), were far lighter than anticipated, and the devastation caused was enormous with later analysis revealing that this had been the most destructive bomb raid in history, greatly surpassing the earlier European firestorms in area destroyed and casualties on the ground. The 270 B-29s dropped 1,667 tons of incendiaries, totally destroying 16.8 square miles

RIGHT V Sq 50, 42-63447, ditched 60 miles from Saipan out of fuel. In this instance the crew, who can be seen in the life rafts, were all rescued by a US Navy PBY-5 Catalina on lifeguard duty. *(USAF)*

of Tokyo with casualties of over 84,000 dead and a million people wounded or displaced. By way of comparison, the destruction of Hamburg in 1943 took four separate missions, totalling 3,095 sorties over a ten-day period, to destroy just less than 8.5 square miles. Direct comparisons cannot be made between raids on Japan and Germany due to differing circumstances. Japan had wooden buildings, narrow streets and a poor firefighting organisation, while Germany had tile and brick buildings, wide streets and excellent firefighting capabilities. However, the destruction wrought to Tokyo on a single night by a mere 270 B-29s clearly showed the potential power of the 20th AF that, by the end of the war, possessed three times the number of B-29s that were available to bomb Tokyo on this occasion.

Four more such raids quickly followed (Nagoya, Osaka, Kobe and Nagoya again) before the 20th AF paused to rest fatigued air and ground crews and replenish its stocks of incendiary bombs. The supply chain had been unable to adjust to the rapid increase in usage and the latter raids were flown with increasing quantities of high explosives as the incendiary supplies dwindled. The five raids destroyed slightly more than 32 square miles of Japan's largest cities for the loss of 21 B-29s (14 of which were on the first mission). Although the attempted precision raids had given way to area attacks it was a major breakthrough for the 20th AF and a catastrophe for Japan.

After this the 20th AF settled into a pattern of flying low-level night-time incendiary raids against urban targets, interspersed with medium- to high-altitude precision attacks that, apart from two significant diversions (at least from the 20th AF leadership's point of view), generally remained true for the rest of the war.

The first of the diversions was a demand by Admiral Chester Nimitz that the 20th AF attack airfields on Kyūshū to support the US Navy as it prepared for, and undertook, the invasion of Okinawa, set for 1 April 1945. The Navy was under a heavy assault by kamikaze pilots and wanted the airfields bombed to reduce this

MEDAL OF HONOR RECIPIENT MASTER SERGEANT HENRY 'RED' ERWIN

Henry Erwin was born in May 1921 in Adamsville, Alabama. Enlisting in the Army Air Corps he became a radio operator with the 52nd Bombardment Squadron, 29th Bombardment Group based at North Field, Guam. Known as 'Red' to his crew he was the radio operator on *City of Los Angeles*, the lead ship in a daylight formation mission to the chemical plant at Koriyama on 12 April 1945.

As radio operator Red had the task of dropping coloured flares through a chute in the floor to help the other planes find them at the rendezvous point. When instructed by the A/C Red pulled the pin and dropped the flare into the chute. However, the flare malfunctioned, igniting the phosphorous immediately. The flare flew out of the chute into Red's face, burning at 1,100°, blinding him and filling the compartment with smoke. Red, aware that the flare could destroy the plane, picked it up and felt his way round the gun turret and navigator's desk to throw it out of the co-pilot's window. While carrying the flare the phosphorous ignited his body, burning his flesh to the bone. The other crew members extinguished the fire and administered first aid while the A/C turned for Iwo Jima where Red could obtain emergency treatment.

At Iwo Jima the medics did not think he could pull through and senior AAF officers, led by Major General LeMay, approved the award of the Medal of Honor in a matter of hours so the presentation could be made while Red was still alive. However, Red surprised everyone by surviving, was flown back to the US and after 30 months and 41 operations his sight and the use of one arm were restored. He lived until 16 January 2002, the only recipient of the Medal of Honor from a B-29 crew.

SMOKE AND THERMALS OVER KAWASAKI

J. Brasfield, navigator, 28th BS, 19th BG, 314th BW

After lunch, they briefed us for tonight's incendiary raid on Kawasaki, located on Tokyo Bay. We are going in at just 7,600 feet. It should be quite a fiery place as they say that there are many industrial plants in our target area. Merrily the fires will burn!

The town of Kawasaki was red hot when we got there. It seemed like that whole town was a mass of flames. Bishop took over and dropped our bombs visually. I watched terrific flames from the fires out of my window. What a Hell on Earth it was down there! One Jap AA crew, completely surrounded by flames, kept firing their gun until completely devoured in flames. You hate them but you still admire them for that kind of courage in the face of sure death. The AA was very heavy, but for some reason it just was not directed at us. B-29s seemed to be everywhere, to the right and to the left of us.

After bombs away, Bishop called over [the] interphone to say we were going to hit a column of smoke. About ten seconds later, we came the closest in all our experiences to meeting our end. This thermal, a column of hot air and smoke rising above the fires had more force than any stream of compressed air ever could. It tossed us around like a cork in a creek. I did not have my safety belt fastened so I was thrown up against the roof of the navigator's compartment. All of my papers, maps, and instruments went in different directions. We gained 2,500 feet in 15 seconds. Those wings must have flexed their maximum of 12 feet, but they held together. That was all that mattered just then.

Joe Simmons later told us that he lost all control of the ship while we were caught in that thermal. He had everything set to dive the ship, but we still ascended at a rate of better than 3,000 feet per minute. He said that all he could do was to try to hold the wings level and hope that the ship would hold together. The fact that I am now writing this account proves that it did just that.

ABOVE Not Kawasaki but a similar conflagration in Toyama captured during the raid by 173 B-29s from the 73rd BW during the night of 1/2 August 1945. *(USAF)*

BELOW On 5 June 1945, B-29s with bomb doors open approach Kobe and the immense mass of smoke caused by the incendiaries from earlier waves. The towering thermals created by the fire bombs often extended above the B-29s' bombing altitudes, forcing them to fly through them as recounted by J. Brasfield for the night mission to Kawasaki. *(USAF)*

J. Handwerker, pilot, 28th BS, 19th BG, 314th BW

We took off Friday the 13th at 5.34pm and each ship was on its own. We were all right until about 350 miles from Japan when the No. 3 engine started throwing oil. We lost 15 gallons in about 15 minutes, so we feathered the engine before it was all pumped out. We had enough oil left to run the engine at that rate for a half hour and the time we would be over Japan was only to be 23 minutes. We figured to have enough power to get in there and get out.

When we hit the coast and started in on Tokyo we started the engine up and she ran good. The only trouble was that the damn thing left a trail of smoke that made us look like we were laying a smoke screen. The searchlights picked us up about 20 miles from Tokyo and they must have seen the smoke coming from the engine and thought we were having trouble because we had searchlights all the way on our bomb run and for 10 minutes after we made our turn to leave Tokyo. While we were in the searchlights the flak batteries were pounding [the] hell out of us. The flak was bursting under us and shaking us up pretty badly and we could hear it going into the ship. Sure is a funny sound! Sounds like somebody had a pop-corn machine under the seat. The searchlights covered the tail gunner and the bombardier and they couldn't see anything.

The first thing I knew I looked up and saw a long burst of tracers shooting by the co-pilot's window about even with him. There were fighters on us and one of the fellows who was further in [the] back of us said he could see us framed in the searchlights with the flak bursting all around us, our No. 3 engine smoking like hell and three or four fighters buzzing around shooting at us. The tough part about it was that we were on our bomb run and couldn't turn to get away from them. This fellow in [the] back said they were so busy with me that they didn't fire a shot at him. That's the way it goes. It's rough as hell for some guys and again it's easy for another. We dropped our bombs and started to climb and turn and just about turned that plane inside out trying to get out of the searchlights, but they stuck with us. Some would follow us as far as they could and then another bunch would pick us up. After we broke away and climbed, the engineer was watching the oil and sure enough, it was being pumped out just about like we said and the pressure dropped to zero and lights were still on us. The engine wasn't going to be worth a damn anyway, so I let it run for about a minute longer and God must have been on our side because as I was hitting the feathering button, the searchlights went out. We still had the fighters and they followed us for about 30 miles before we shook them.

RIGHT B-29s of the 19th BG, 314th BW disgorge high-explosive bombs over an airfield on Kyūshū during the raids against the kamikazes. Note the forward bomb bays have 16 x 500lb bombs while the rear hold only 4. It is probable that the planes each have a bomb-bay fuel tank in the rear bay. See also the plane furthest away dropping 4 x 2,000lb bombs. *(Andy Kerzner)*

threat. The 20th AF leadership was unhappy, feeling that this was a waste of their capability. However, higher authority prevailed and the airfield raids began on 27 March, remaining a significant part of 20th AF operations until the middle of May. Whether the raids had any significant effect remains open to debate. What is clear is that the kamikazes were inflicting terrible losses on the fleet operating off Okinawa and any help was urgently needed. During the course of the Okinawa battle, even with the B-29 support, kamikazes sank 36 and damaged nearly 400 ships.

The second diversion, which started on the same day as the airfield raids, was the aptly named 'Operation Starvation'. This was the

ABOVE LEFT No 44-69985 *Jake's Jalopy* of the 9th BG, 313th BW drops aerial mines over the Japanese inland sea during 'Operation Starvation'. *Jake's Jalopy* survived to be scrapped at McClellan in 1948. *(USAF)*

ABOVE West Field, Tinian, home to the 58th BW when they moved from India to the Marianas. *(Earl Johnson)*

mining of the coastal waters around Japan. All of these missions were flown by the 313th BW who, in the course of some 46 missions, dropped over 12,000 mines and sank 63% of all Japanese shipping lost between 27 March 1945 and the end of the war.

BELOW No 44-61555 *Miss Judy* of the 462nd BG, 58th BW landing on Tinian and still carrying the CBI markings. *Miss Judy* survived the war to end her days at the China Lake weapons test range. *(USAF)*

The Japanese had some rudimentary gun-laying and searchlight-directing radar capability – largely based on older US and British radars captured in the early battles of the Second World War. To counter these, B-29s began to carry electronic countermeasures (ECM) equipment, or Raven as the B-29 crews called it. Later B-29s were fitted for (but not with) ECM in the factory but, even so, getting sufficient sets into theatre was a problem and, although the standard Raven rack was capable of holding three units, B-29s normally carried only a single APT-1 barrage jammer pre-set to 185–205 MHz, the primary range of the Japanese anti-aircraft gun-laying radars. The policy was that each of the normal 11-plane squadron formations would be electronically self-sufficient with most carrying the APT-1 while a few were fitted with two APQ-2 spot jammers and an ECM operator to tune them. The barrage jammers were normally operated by the radio operator since apart from being turned on they needed no further attention. The radio operator also had the task of dispensing the rolls of RR-2/U or RR-3/U untuned Rope, effective in the low-frequency range between 25 and 350Mc, through the vertical camera port or rear entry door in the rear unpressurised section. Initially the ECM gear was seen as unnecessary, but once crews saw flak become erratic and searchlights lose their track everyone wanted it. It was the XXI BC's intention to modify half their B-29s to carry spot jammers but the war ended before any unit attained this level. Also better and more powerful jammers were coming into service such as the AN/ARQ-8, but only a handful of these sets arrived in theatre before the end of the war.

RIGHT RR-2/U and RR-3/U untuned Rope. Untuned Rope comprised 0.5in 400ft-long strips of aluminium foil suspended from a small parachute (RR-2/U, left) or simple card (RR-3/U, right).
(Mike Hanz)

Meanwhile, the 20th AF continued to grow, with the 58th BW, having redeployed from their bases in the CBI, arriving at their base of West Field, Tinian, during April 1945. The unit took part in its first mission from the Marianas on 5 May.

The 20th AF now had over 700 B-29s on the Marianas and mounted its first four-wing raid on 14 May 1945 when 524 B-29s took off to attack Nagoya. This was the second highest number of B-29s airborne on a single mission during the war. The largest operation took place ten days later when 558 B-29s took off to bomb Tokyo during the night of 23/24 May. The raid on this date also holds the record for the greatest number of tons dropped on one mission by the USAAF. The 3,646 tons that fell beat the previous record of 3,609 tons released by the 20th AF on Nagoya during the night of 16/17 May. By comparison, the greatest tonnage dropped by the 8th AF was 2,917.2 tons from 1,250 planes on Cologne on 17 October 1944. Remarkably the 20th AF had beaten this maximum with one-third the number of bombers and at over four times the distance.

The 20th AF had been created to bomb Japan into submission and now, with four wings at his disposal, LeMay began the task in earnest with an almost constant stream of maximum-effort operations that often had 600 or sometimes as many as 800 B-29s in the air every two or three days. By this stage in the war there were few targets left that warranted multi-wing missions, so generally LeMay split his force, sending each wing, or even individual groups, to a different target and thereby devastating three, four or even five cities simultaneously. Five months earlier, on hearing of the loss of Saipan, Fleet Admiral Osama Nangana had reported to the Japanese senate: 'Hell is now upon us.' Although there had been a pause while the US built up their forces and refined their tactics, his words were now proving to be true.

The last of the 20th AF's BWs, the 315th, arrived at North West Field, Guam, in late April 1945. The 315th BW flew the B-29B with its highly precise AN/APQ-7 radar allowing them, it was hoped, to attack targets with accuracy at night even if obscured by cloud. During May and early June the first two planes flew radar reconnaissance missions to Japan, mapping the AN/APQ-7 radar signatures of suitable targets. The main force arrived in June and flew their first mission on the night of the 26th/27th against the Utaube oil refinery at Yokkaichi and completed 14 more before the end of the war. All of the 315th BW operations were flown at night against the Japanese oil industry, dropping their bombs by radar.

As June drew to a close, the 509th Composite Group (CG) began to arrive at West Field, Tinian. Although called a group, it contained only 15 specially modified B-29s. These 'Silverplate' B-29s were able to carry the atomic bombs. Administratively linked with the 313th BW, the 509th CG used the circle symbol of that wing with a group symbol of a forward-pointing arrow. However, to avoid letting the Japanese know that a special unit was operating, the unit painted markings from other groups on its planes. Consequently, the 509th CG planes only flew with their correct tail markings after the war had ended.

With the war in Europe over, Churchill, Truman and Stalin met at Potsdam in Germany to decide the post-war fate of the conquered and, to some extent, the liberated countries. The ongoing war against Japan was also covered and this resulted in a declaration being issued by Britain, USA and China covering the terms of surrender and post-war status of Japan. This was given out on 26 July 1945 and concluded with an ultimatum to Japan either to surrender unconditionally or face what was described as 'prompt and utter destruction'. The Japanese found the terms

unacceptable so, despite being all but beaten militarily, chose to disregard the declaration and pinned their hopes on being able to inflict sufficient losses on American forces during the inevitable invasion of Japan to force a negotiated peace.

Perhaps to reinforce the warning in the Potsdam declaration, the day after it was issued, the 20th AF demonstrated their complete air supremacy by dropping leaflets over twelve Japanese cities proclaiming that over the next few days four or more would be bombed and encouraging their populations to flee. Although the B-29 crews were, understandably, unhappy at this warning of the enemy beforehand, two days later, during the night of 28/29 July, the 20th AF launched attacks against six cities, all of which had been notified of the strikes in the leaflets. The fact that no B-29s were lost clearly showed how weak the defences had by now become.

ABOVE North West Field, Guam, home to the B-29Bs of the 315th BW. *(Earl Johnson)*

BELOW B-29Bs of the 315th BW. *(USAF)*

LEFT One of the leaflets warning the Japanese that 12 of their cities would be destroyed over the coming days. The cities are: Tokyo, Ujiyamada, Tsu, Koriyama, Hakodate, Nagaoka, Uwajima, Kurume, Ichinomiya, Ogaki, Nishinomiya and Aomori. Of these Ujiyamada, Tsu, Uwajima, Ichinomiya, Ogaki and Aomori were attacked during the night of 28/29 July. The reverse of the leaflet warned the population to flee the city. *(Andy Kerzner)*

RIGHT The mushroom cloud from the Hiroshima atomic bomb rises to over 20,000ft, while the surface cloud has extended 10,000ft around the point of impact. *(USAF)*

BELOW *Enola Gay* landing back on Tinian after dropping the atomic bomb on Hiroshima. *(USAF)*

Although the 509th Composite Group was the last B-29 unit of the 20th AF to deploy to the Pacific, they were not the last B-29 unit to go there. This honour fell to the B-29Bs of the 316th BW that started to deploy in July and August 1945 as part of the 8th AF. With their arrival the Strategic Air Forces came into being. Led by General Carl Spaatz, this included LeMay's 20th AF and the 8th AF commanded by Lieutenant General Doolittle.

Only the 333rd and the 346th BGs had arrived in theatre by the end of the war and the B-29s of the 8th Air Force operated on only one occasion during the conflict. This was against the oil storage yard at Akita when its B-29s operated from Okinawa during the night of 14/15 August 1945.

Before this, however, on 6 August the *Enola Gay* of the 509th CG dropped the first atomic bomb on Hiroshima. The bomb, calculated as having an explosive yield equivalent to 15,000 tons of TNT (nearly four times greater than the highest tonnage dropped on a mission by the USAAF in the war), wiped out Hiroshima and over 70,000 of the inhabitants. Although not as destructive as the earlier Tokyo fire raids, this devastation was wrought by a single plane and bomb, a situation that could not be defended against. Despite the debate that has been ongoing since, it was not seen as controversial on the squadrons at the time. Although the power of the weapon was awesome it was considered just another weapon in the arsenal and if it helped them to get home quicker, and alive, then so much the better. After the attack, rumours started, the foremost being that the B-29 force would be stood down while peace negotiations went ahead. LeMay quashed these by laying on heavy raids on both the 7th and 8th.

Silverplate was the code name for the USAAF's project to modify B-29s to deliver the atomic bomb, although it later also included the training and operational aspects of the programme as well. Silverplate was a part of the larger 'Project Alberta' or 'Project A' that was responsible for developing the means to deliver the atomic bomb. This included designing the bomb shape, the radio altimeters and pressure sensors required to allow the bomb to explode at the optimum altitude, modify the bomber to be able to carry it, and train the air, ground and special ordnance crews needed to support the mission when it deployed overseas. 'Project Alberta' was, in turn, a part of the overarching 'Manhattan Project' that covered all work relating to the design and delivery of the atomic bomb.

The prototype Silverplate B-29 was a standard B-29, B-29-5-BW, serial 42-6259, that was delivered to Wright Field, Ohio, on 2 December 1943 where it was modified, largely by hand, to carry the dummy atomic bomb shapes then being evaluated. At that time, one of the anticipated designs was a long, thin 'gun-type' plutonium (Pu-239) bomb of about 17ft in length code named 'Thin Man'. To be able to support this shape, extensive modifications were required to the B-29's bomb bays since the bomb, although carried in the rear bay, extended into the forward one. The modifications included the removal of all four bomb-bay doors and the outer fuselage section between the two bomb bays. Even with these alterations, it was a tight fit as the existence of the main wing spar between the bomb bays only allowed a 2ft-diameter bomb to be carried. Twin release points adapted from glider tow and release mechanisms were fitted in the rear bomb bay to secure the bomb.

The other shape of bomb considered was for an implosion-type device and this, largely spherical bomb (code named 'Fat Man'), would fit into the forward bomb bay where it was fastened to another twin set of modified glider tow and release mechanisms.

Testing of the bomb shapes started when a 'Thin Man' was dropped on a bombing range near the US Army airfield of Muroc, California, on 6 March 1944. On 14 March two further drops were made, both of these being of the 'Fat Man' variety. All these trials were successful, although in all cases the bomb failed to drop immediately, which frustrated many of the calibration tests being run on the ballistic properties of the shapes. When the fourth test resulted in a 'Thin Man' type dropping prematurely and seriously damaging the aircraft the release mechanism was changed to the British system of using a single release mechanism for large bombs. Consequently a British Type G single-point attachment and Type F release mechanism were obtained and installed in the B-29.

As the bomb development advanced, it became evident that 'Thin Man' would not work. This design was based upon the fissibility

LEFT 'Thin Man' (foreground) and 'Fat Man' (background) casings rest before being used during the testing of the atomic bomb release mechanism. *(USAF)*

of pure Pu-239 but, at that time, it was not possible to create pure Pu-239 as traces of Pu-240 kept creeping in and the increased fissibility of this mixture made it impossible to merge two pieces of Pu before fission would start, which would have resulted in a fizzle. So, on 17 July 1944, the Pu gun-type weapon was abandoned and work pressed on with a Uranium (U-235) gun-type weapon. Due to U-235's slower fission rate the length of this gun-type bomb (code named 'Little Boy') was significantly less and it too could fit wholly into the forward bomb bay, simplifying the modifications needed and leaving the rear bomb bay free for the carriage of long-range fuel tanks.

With the B-29 proving to be capable of carrying the atomic bomb, in August 1944 a batch of 17 'production' Silverplate B-29s was ordered – to be taken from the production lines at Martin's assembly and modification centre at Omaha, Nebraska. These were delivered, essentially as standard B-29s, to Wendover AAF where the turrets were removed and the planes used to train the crews of the newly formed 393rd Bomb Squadron of the 509th Composite Group (CG). Commanded by Lieutenant Colonel Paul Tibbets – a veteran of the European and North African campaigns and, as a former B-29

test pilot, one of the most knowledgeable B-29 pilots in the AAF – the 393rd BS was the unit that would eventually take the Silverplate B-29s into combat.

Although somewhat primitive, Wendover AAF was ideal for instruction, being near the Salton Sea bombing range, yet was remote, greatly assisting the obsession with secrecy: 'What you hear here, What you see here, When you leave here, Let it stay here!' was repeated on ever-present billboards and backed up by ever-watchful guards. One of the things that had to be devised was how the bomber could survive the explosion and this resulted in the crews practising a full power turn through 155° as soon as they had dropped their bomb. Such a turn would place the plane as far from the point of explosion as possible, a necessity given the immense shock wave that the bomb was expected to generate.

The intensive training programme effectively wore out these aircraft and consequently a third batch of 20 Silverplate B-29s was ordered. The first 5 of these went to the test unit (216th Base Unit) for continued development work, while the next 15, so-called combat models, were delivered to the 393rd Bomb Squadron with the first arriving in April 1945. These were all altered to Silverplate standard at the Martin modification centre at Omaha (having also been built at the same facility) before being transported to Wendover. Subsequently, they were flown to North Field, Tinian, by their crews, appearing in theatre in June and July 1945. *Enola Gay* was one of these planes (in fact the 31st Silverplate B-29) and reached Tinian on 6 July.

Although the 509th CG was an independent unit, when at North Field it came under the resident conventional B-29 bomb wing (the 313th BW) for administrative purposes. Shortly after coming to Tinian the 509th CG aircraft were painted with an arrow in a circle tail marking to denote them as belonging to the 509th CG. However, to try and confuse the Japanese, these group markings were soon removed and replaced with markings from other B-29 units as shown in the table opposite:

Colonel Paul Tibbets, CO, 509th CG

Paul Tibbets was born in Quincy, Illinois, on 23 February 1915. He received his initial flight training in 1937 and quickly rose through the ranks to become CO of the 340th BS, 97th BG, 8th AF, with which he led the first US daylight heavy bomber mission over occupied Europe. In February 1943 Tibbets was recalled to the US to assist with the development of the B-29, becoming a test pilot; he also helped to train the first combat crews and set up a school for B-29 flight instructors. When the 509th CG formed in December 1944 Tibbets was selected to command it, being promoted to full colonel in January 1945. After training at Wendover AAF the 509th CG deployed to Tinian where it continued to refine the tactics needed to safely drop the atomic bomb. After successfully releasing the first atomic bomb on Hiroshima on 6 August, Tibbets was awarded the Distinguished Service Cross and became a national hero as the man who 'ended the war with Japan'.

After the war Tibbets continued to command the 509th when it took part in the Bikini atoll nuclear tests and retired in 1966 as a brigadier general.

509th tail markings				
A (497th BG)			**Circle R (6th BG)**	
71	44-27303 *Jabit III*		82	44-86292 *Enola Gay*
72	44-27302 *Top Secret*		89	44-27353 *The Great Artiste*
73	44-27300 *Strange Cargo*		90	44-27354 *Big Stink*
84	44-27296 *Some Punkins*		91	44-86291 *Necessary Evil*

Triangle N (444th BG)			**Black Square P (39th BG)**	
77	44-27297 *Bockscar*		83	44-27298 *Full House*
85	44-27301 *Straight Flush*		94	44-86346 *Luke the Spook*
86	44-27299 *Next Objective*		95	44-86347 *Laggin' Dragon*
88	44-27304 *Up an' Atom*			

BELOW 509th CG 'Operation Order 35' sending *Enola Gay* to Hiroshima. *(USAF)*

Having arrived in theatre the crews of the 509th CG began an intensive period of training with practice bombing missions, using standard 500lb and 1,000lb bombs, being carried out against the small island of Rota in the Marianas chain that was still held by Japanese forces. As the crews grew more proficient they began to range further afield to bomb other Japanese-held islands. Truk was attacked on 5 July 1945 with an assault on Marcus Island the following day. Marcus Island counted as an operational mission and became a regular destination although, much to the disgust of the crews who bombed it after 20 July, it had by then been reclassified as only a training mission.

On 20 July the 509th crews finally got to bomb mainland Japan when ten Silverplate B-29s each dropped a single 'pumpkin' bomb that simulated the size, shape and weight of the 'Fat Man' type of atomic bomb but contained 5,500lb of conventional explosives. Because of the large diameter of the 'pumpkin' and nuclear bombs, and the low clearance of the B-29, loading them required special bomb-loading pits. The bomb was placed in the pit, the B-29 pulled over it, then the bomb raised into the bomb bay with a hydraulic jack. Three further missions to Japan took place on subsequent days (23, 26 and 29 July), resulting in a total of 37 pumpkin bombs being dropped. To simulate the planned atomic mission, each plane was given an individual target so only one or sometimes two planes would be above each city as it was bombed. It was hoped that the Japanese would become used to the sight of the solitary B-29s and their single bomb and they would not consider them a worthy target for interception.

ABOVE The crew of *Enola Gay* for the Hiroshima mission. Left to right, standing: Lieutenant Colonel John Porter, ground maintenance officer; Captain Theodore J. ('Dutch') Van Kirk, navigator; Major Thomas Ferebee, bombardier; Colonel Paul Tibbets, 509th CG, CO and pilot; Captain Robert Lewis, co-pilot; Lieutenant Jacob Beser, RCM. Left to right, kneeling: Sergeant Joseph Stiborik, radar operator; Staff Sergeant George Caron, tail gunner; Private First Class Richard Nelson, radio operator; Sergeant Robert Shumard, assistant engineer; and Staff Sergeant Wyatt Duzenbury, flight engineer. *(USAF)*

One unusual worry for the mission planners was the small possibility that Japanese radars may inadvertently prematurely trigger the bomb's radar proximity fuses designed to detonate it at the optimum distance above the ground. To counter this threat, First Lieutenant Jacob Beser, RCM officer (and the only man to fly on both atomic missions), monitored Japanese radar transmissions. The bombs had four separate air-burst fuses and as Beser explained: 'We had the option of switching off one, two or even all four of the fusing radars if it looked as if there were transmissions from enemy radars which might interfere with those fitted in the bomb. We were not worried about the deliberate jamming from the Japanese – that would have required extremely detailed a priori knowledge of our mission. The real problem was inadvertent jamming from radars.'

Clearance for the atomic mission was given on 25 July 1945 with a message to General Carl A. Spaatz, commander of the US Strategic Air Forces in the Pacific, that authorised the 509th CG to 'deliver its first special bomb as soon as weather will permit visual bombing after about 3 August 1945'. On 2 August LeMay issued Special Bomb Operational Order No 13 to the 509th CG to carry out the attack and when, on 5 August, the weather forecast for the next day was suitable the mission was set for the 6th. Later that day Tibbets named his B-29 *Enola Gay* after his mother and the plane was then towed to the special bomb-loading pit where the 'Little Boy' bomb was lifted into the forward bomb bay. The load was completed by 16:00hrs that afternoon.

Briefings for the special mission were held at around 12am then at 1.30am on 6 August the three weather-reporting planes, *Full House*, *Jabit III* and *Straight Flush* took off. These would detail the weather over the three potential target cities that were, in order of priority, Hiroshima, Kokura and Nagasaki. At 2.45am the *Enola Gay* started her take-off run accompanied by three other Silverplate B-29s. *The Great Artiste* would carry special instruments to assess the strength of the explosion and V-91, later named *Necessary Evil*, would act as the photo plane accompanying *Enola Gay* to Japan, while the unnamed V-90 would go as far as Iwo Jima where she would wait as a reserve in case *Enola Gay* developed a fault. A special bomb-loading pit, similar to the ones on Tinian, had also been built on Iwo Jima to cater for this possibility.

As history has recorded, *Enola Gay* did not develop any faults and, after *Straight Flush* radioed a coded message to confirm that the weather over Hiroshima was suitable, the fate of the city was sealed.

At 9.15am the 'Little Boy' bomb dropped from *Enola Gay* at 31,600ft above Hiroshima. The instant the bomb had left the plane Tibbets began the maximum-rate turn through 155° that would place them as far from the point of blast as possible. The bomb fell for some 45 seconds before detonating at 1,900ft above the city. The shock wave, expanding away from the epicentre at the speed of sound, caught up with *Enola Gay* less than a minute later. Despite being an estimated 15 miles 'slant range' away at that time *Enola Gay* still suffered two severe jolts in quick succession (the direct shock wave and a reflected one), although no damage was done to the aircraft.

After turning back over Hiroshima to survey the damage Tibbets turned *Enola Gay* for home, landing back on Tinian at 2.58pm – a mission of 12 hours 13 minutes. The earlier deception seems to have worked for the three planes on the atomic mission went unchallenged by the Japanese defenders.

With no surrender from the Japanese the second special bomb, this time of the 'Fat Man' type, was readied. The plan was to drop it on 11 August but weather reports stated that the 9th would be better. Kokura was the primary target with Nagasaki as the secondary. The crew for this mission was led by Major Charles Sweeney, the 393rd BS commanding officer flying *Bockscar*, although the nose art and name had not been painted on before the mission. Unfortunately this operation did not start well. Shortly before the crew boarded, the ground crew discovered that a fuel transfer pump for the rear bomb-bay fuel tank had failed, meaning the 600 gallons in the tank were unavailable. Worse, the fuel, weighing 3,600lb, could not be offloaded, so that it would have to be carried to Japan and back. After a hurried discussion it was decided to go anyway, using Okinawa as a potential diversion should fuel become critical.

As with the Hiroshima mission two weather planes took off first (*Enola Gay* and *Laggin' Dragon*) to report the conditions over the primary and secondary targets. Then, at 03:49hrs, *Bockscar* and the three supporting planes *The Great Artiste* (the only plane to be at both atomic missions), V-90 and *Full House*, launched. *Full House* went only to Iwo Jima in case of emergency but was not used. V-90 was the camera plane and also carried observers from the UK: Group Captain Leonard Cheshire and William Penney. The weather planes reported both targets as clear but when Major Sweeney approached Kokura the weather had deteriorated and after expending valuable fuel making two runs they headed to Nagasaki.

Fuel was now becoming short and the weather was also quickly closing in on Nagasaki. The approach was made using

ABOVE The crew of *Bockscar* for the Nagasaki mission. Left to right, standing: Major Charles Sweeney, 393rd BS, CO and pilot; Lieutenant Charles Albury, A/C; Lieutenant Fred Olivi, co-pilot; Captain Kermit Beahan, bombardier; Captain James Van Pelt, navigator; and Lieutenant Jacob Beser, RCM. Left to right, kneeling: Staff Sergeant John Kuharek, flight engineer; Sergeant Abe Spitzer, radio operator; Sergeant Ray Gallagher, assistant flight engineer; Staff Sergeant Ed Buckley, radar operator; and Staff Sergeant Albert Dehart, tail gunner *(USAF)*

radar but at the last moment the bombardier, Captain Kermit Beahan, spotted their aiming point through a gap in the clouds and they released their bomb from 31,000ft at 11:58hrs. 'Fat Man' exploded 1,650ft above the city with a yield of 21 kilotons. Making their escape turn, five shock waves buffeted the planes but they survived, heading straight to Okinawa as fuel was now critical. However, they made it safely – having just enough fuel to taxi off the runway – and after refuelling landed back on Tinian at 23:39hrs. As with the Hiroshima mission *The Great Artiste* dropped three instrumented canisters known as 'Bangometers' that drifted down on parachutes measuring the force of the explosion and radioing this back to the plane. But on this mission Luis Alvarez, one of the physicists readying the bomb, taped a handwritten message to Professor R. Sagane,

LEFT 509th CG 'Operation Order 39' that set the second atomic mission in progress. *(USAF)*

the Japanese physicist at the University of Tokyo, to each canister. The message read:

Headquarters
Atomic Bomb Command
August 9, 1945
To: *Prof. R. Sagane*
From: *Three of your former Scientific Colleagues during your stay in the United States*

We are sending this as a personal message to urge that you use your influence as a reputable nuclear physicist, to convince the Japanese General Staff of the terrible consequences which will be suffered by your people if you continue in this war.

You have known for several years that an atomic bomb could be built if a nation were willing to pay the enormous cost of preparing the necessary material. Now that you have seen we have constructed the production plants, there can be no doubt in your mind, all the output of these factories working twenty-four hours a day, will be exploded on your homeland.

Within the space of three weeks, we have proof fired one bomb in the American desert, exploded one in Hiroshima and fired the third this morning.

We implore you to confirm these facts to your leaders and to do your utmost to stop the destruction and waste of life which can only result in the total annihilation of all your cities if continued. As scientists, we deplore the use of which a beautiful discovery has been put, but we can assure you that unless Japan surrenders at once, this rain of atomic bombs will increase manifold in fury.

This second atomic attack finally did convince the Japanese that the war was lost and they surrendered on 14 August.

After the war a further 27 Silverplate B-29s were supplied, bringing the total (including the prototype) to 65 nuclear-capable B-29s delivered between 1943 and 1946. The code name Silverplate was replaced with Saddletree post-hostilities but the modifications were the same.

BELOW The atomic physicists on Tinian with one of the 'Bangometer' instrumented canisters dropped by *The Great Artiste* immediately prior to both atomic bomb drops. Left to right, standing: Harold Agnew, Luis Alvarez. Left to right, kneeling: Lawrence H. Johnston, Bernard Waldman. *(Los Alamos National Laboratory)*

Despite the damage caused by the first atomic bomb, the Japanese government still did not sue for peace. Consequently, on 9 August 1945 a second bomb was dropped, this time on Nagasaki, and on the same day the Russians launched a huge, and very successful, land invasion in Manchuria. Once more, rumours spread that Japan had surrendered and many celebrations started up – prematurely as it happened, since further missions were flown on the 10th.

Having used both of the atomic bombs located in the Marianas and with still no capitulation from the Japanese, the 509th CG sent one of their planes back to the USA to collect the third (and only remaining) atomic bomb. As this plane made its journey and the diplomatic process ground on, the conventional bombing stopped. However, with no concrete surrender LeMay wanted to resume the pressure and so, over the next few days, the 20th AF crews were briefed and then stood down a number of times before, on 14 August, they were briefed for what would be their final bombing missions of the Second World War.

Eventually the Japanese emperor recognised that the nuclear bombs meant that the 'prompt and utter destruction' promised in the Potsdam declaration was upon them and so, after several meetings with his senior officials, accepted the Allies' terms for surrender. This was announced on 14 August 1945 and many B-29 crews

returning from their last operation heard of the submission before landing.

Although there was an initial wariness by the Allies, preparations for the occupation of Japan went ahead rapidly and on 19 August the Japanese sent a 16-strong mixed diplomatic and military delegation to Manila to receive the Allies' surrender instructions and initial occupation plans. These flew from Japan to Le Shima, Ryukyu Islands, in two specially marked Mitsubishi G4M-1 'Betty' bombers where they boarded a Douglas C-54 Globemaster that took them to Manila for the talks.

After the ceasefire of 14 August the B-29 force was stood down. Now, however, several hundred B-29s were readied for a new type of undertaking: to drop supplies to prisoners

ABOVE The Mitsubishi Steel & Arms Works in Nagasaki was nearly 100% destroyed by the atomic blast despite lying half a mile from ground zero. *(USAF)*

LEFT Chaplain Paul Schade of the 330th BG gave a victory wave to each returning B-29 after the final mission of the Second World War. The ceasefire came when the B-29s were returning home and, for many crews, this was their first ever peacetime landing. *(Steve Smisek)*

ABOVE Supplies for POW camps are loaded into a B-29B of the 315th BW. All BWs contributed planes to the massive humanitarian effort to supply the POWs until they could be liberated and repatriated. Here cardboard boxes are used. *(USAF)*

ABOVE Where bombs once hung, 40-gallon oil drums, now full of food and medicines, are loaded into the forward bomb bay of a B-29 prior to a POW supply drop. *(USAF)*

BELOW A leaflet describing the contents of a supply drop. The reverse said the same, but in Dutch. *(Andy Kerzner)*

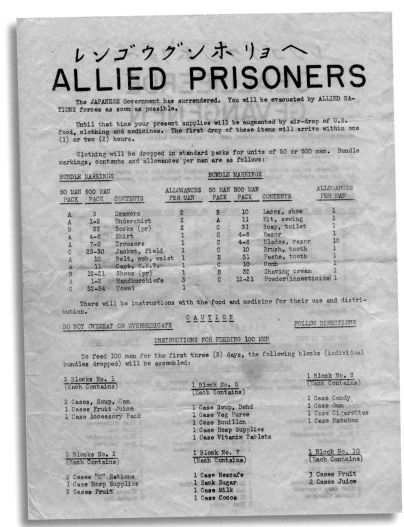

of war (POWs) awaiting liberation from their camps. The first POW missions were flown on 27 August and the last on 20 September, during which the B-29s flew 900 effective sorties and delivered nearly 4,500 tons of food to 63,500 POWs.

The war officially ended on 2 September 1945 with the signing of the Instrument of Surrender by representatives of both Japan's military and government on board the battleship USS *Missouri* at anchor in Tokyo Bay. To complement the fleet of Allied warships a massive fly-past was arranged involving some 1,500 US Navy planes and 462 B-29s from both the 20th and 8th AFs.

With the arrival of new BWs to fill airfields, and replacement planes being delivered to make good losses in the operational wings, B-29s poured into the Marianas at an average rate of about 120 aircraft per month from when the first B-29 arrived at Saipan until the end of the war almost ten months later. This increasing strength was remorselessly brought to bear on Japan by ever-larger raids inflicting ever-greater damage until, as stated in the US Strategic Bombing Survey: 'The bombing offensive was the major factor which secured agreement to unconditional surrender without an invasion of the Home Islands, an invasion that would have cost hundreds of thousands of American lives ... even without the atomic bombing attack, air supremacy over Japan could have exerted sufficient pressure to bring

RIGHT B-29s fly over USS *Missouri* as part of the show of force that accompanied the surrender signing ceremony. Some 462 B-29s took part but orbited and flew over twice, giving the impression of some 800 bombers. After the second pass the formation dispersed, with several B-29s buzzing Tokyo, an action that earned them a reprimand for 'unmilitary-like behaviour' from General LeMay upon their return to their bases. *(USAF)*

about unconditional surrender and obviate the need for invasion.'

With the Second World War over almost all servicemen thought about getting home as quickly as possible. For the B-29 crews this was usually achieved through 'Operation Sunset'. Crews were selected on a points system, with points being awarded for time overseas and missions completed. Successful crews were then teamed with a B-29 – potentially from a different BW – and flew this back to the US, often with numerous members of ground crew as passengers. Normally the air crew left the plane as soon as they arrived in the US with a ferry crew then taking the plane on to one of the great storage depots established to cope with the problem of returning aircraft.

Storage

Unlike other Second World War combat planes, the B-29 was not considered obsolete, so aircraft returning home from the Pacific or, in some cases, straight from the production lines gathered at Victorville, California, Pyote, Texas, Warner Robins Army Air Depot, Georgia, and Davis-Monthan,

RIGHT A happy Crew 12, 19th BG, 314th BW flying home as part of 'Operation Sunset'. Taken on Hawaii just before the final leg of their homeward journey. Their B-29, Z-15, had completed 20 missions as *Fire Bug*, with the 500th BG, 73rd BW, but Vern Chandler, the A/C with Crew 12, renamed her *Princess Pat IV* for this journey home, continuing his policy of naming all the B-29s allocated to him after his daughter Pat. She retained *Fire Bug* on the port side. *(Andy Kerzner)*

Arizona, for long-term storage. The problem of storing aircraft had never occurred before and there were no technical orders so base personnel devised their own. Initially all removable items, bombsight, guns etc were taken to secure storage locations. The spark plugs were replaced by special silica gel sealed plastic ones and silica gel packs were positioned in the engine nacelles to keep them dry. At Pyote, B-29s so preserved were said to be 'pickled'. At Warner Robins and Davis-Monthan more elaborate plans saw contracts given out to cocoon B-29s (250 at Warner Robins and 486 at Davis-Monthan) by inserting bags of silica gel in the engine nacelles and fuselage, then sealing all openings and spraying four layers of insulmatic, a plastic compound, over the entire airframe. To ensure all areas were covered, the layers were

different colours: yellow, red, black then silver. Effective though this was at preserving the plane, removing it was troublesome, taking on average 3,600 man-hours to ready the machine for flight, and at Davis-Monthan the original contract was terminated after 455. Many stored B-29s eventually returned to service although others were 'reclaimed', the term for being stripped of useable parts to keep the planes in service flying.

Strategic Air Command and the Cold War

Strategic Air Command (SAC) came into being on 21 March 1946 charged with delivering the US's atomic weapons.

Soon after this, on 18 September 1947 the USAAF finally gained its independence, becoming the US Air Force and an equal partner with the Army and Navy. Initially SAC was a paper tiger for although in 1947 it had 11 BGs, most of these were devoid of personnel or planes and only the 33 Silverplate B-29s of the 509th and 43rd BWs were considered combat effective. The rest, where they had any aircraft at all, were capable of only limited operations. Worse, even the B-29 with its great range was incapable of reaching the likely target nations (notably the USSR) from US soil. To counter these difficulties the USAF initiated the Global Electronic Movement (GEM) programme, intended to increase the number of nuclear-capable bombers available while also enlarging their range by including aerial refuelling. To support this, SAC converted 92

Projects 'Ruby' and 'Harken'

Towards the end of the war in Europe the Allies developed some giant bombs. Although these were effective they proved incapable of penetrating the massively reinforced structures that Germany was building – even though the mathematical theories implied that they should. Germany's defeat gave the Allies access to these structures and hence allowed tests of the penetration of these large bombs. In a trial called 'Project Ruby' the USAAF teamed with the RAF and released inert bombs of varying designs against the U-boat fabrication plant at Farge near Hamburg. Explosive rounds were also aimed against the U-boat pens on the island of Heligoland. The roof at Farge varied in thickness from 14.75ft to 23ft, providing an ideal target for the penetration tests. Between 25 March and 30 October 1946 three B-29s and five Lancasters flew from RAF Marham, dropping over 220 bombs from various altitudes ranging from 4,750ft to 20,000ft. Inert bombs were used at Farge due to the proximity of houses within the 500yd danger area and a power station just outside this. The conclusion of this trial was that none of the bombs tested was capable of perforating the 23ft-thick roof and only the 22,000lb 'Amazon' bomb was capable of penetrating the 14.75ft roof.

Using these results, the bomb casings were redesigned as the 25,000lb T28E1 ('Amazon II') and the 25,200lb T28E2 ('Samson') and the tests were repeated between July and August 1947, this time as 'Project Harken', with unfortunately similar results.

'Operation Crossroads'

The availability of numerous surplus US and captured German and Japanese warships allowed the US to test the effectiveness of nuclear weapons against a fleet. Two tests were planned: 'Able' that used a 23-kiloton air-dropped bomb and 'Baker' that used a submerged bomb. 'Able' took place on 1 July 1946 with the bomb being released by *Dave's Dream* of the 509th BG. The bomb detonated 520ft above the target fleet but missed the aim point by some 710yd. It sank five ships and seriously damaged all others within a 1,000yd

radius. 'Baker' was carried out on 25 July with the bomb suspended 90ft underwater in the centre of the fleet. Ten ships sank. Apart from the bomber for 'Able', B-29s were extensively used during both tests as photographic and weather planes. The operation was controlled by a joint Army/Navy task force called Joint Task Force One with the B-29s being part of Task Group 1.5 operating from the airfield at Kwajalein atoll.

ABOVE One of the 25,200lb T28E2 Samson bombs awaiting loading during 'Project Harken'. *(John Szalay)*

LEFT Able's mushroom cloud climbs above Bikini Atoll. *(Library of Congress)*

B-29s into tankers, designated as KB-29Ms, while 74 bombers were converted to be able to receive aerial refuelling as B-29MRs. Even with the greater range afforded by aerial refuelling it was not practical to launch attacks against the USSR from the US. Consequently, SAC maintained a series of airfields in Europe, primarily in England, to which B-29s would deploy in time of war. Although these bases were several thousand miles closer it was widely thought among crews that should atomic missions be launched they would be one-way only, for even with aerial refuelling the B-29MRs had insufficient range to return home.

Following independence from the Army, SAC adopted what was known as the Hobson Plan or 'Wing-base plan' that organised its forces into wings. A wing consisted of a combat group as well as various support groups. The wing took its number from the combat group within it; hence the 2nd Bomb Wing controlled the 2nd Bomb Group as well as support groups. However, in terms of combat planes the bomb wing held only the aircraft within the combat group. The combat group usually had three squadrons. In the case of the B-29, squadrons were generally authorised between 10 and 20 planes, giving the group 30 to 60 bombers. The use of the term bomb wing by SAC has led to some confusion with the Second World War bomb wing structure. The SAC bomb wing was roughly equivalent in size to a Second World War bomb group but with the support functions making the SAC bomb wing effectively self-sufficient.

The early SAC war plans called for a huge transatlantic movement of nuclear and conventional bombers, tankers and fighters over a five-day period, with massed nuclear attacks starting on day six. Unlike during the war when the atomic bombs were loaded into the B-29 by using a specially constructed pit, SAC adopted a more streamlined method, as described by Charlie Harlow, a B-29MR crew member with the 301st BW at Barksdale: 'We had to practice loading an A bomb on our aircraft every month. We did it on the ramp where the aircraft was normally parked. The whole crew was involved but nobody else. This meant that an unlimited number of aircraft could be loading at the same time and there would be no aircraft waiting in a line for an A bomb loading pit in the event the Emergency War Plan was activated. Loading was accomplished by removing the front left bomb bay door and jacking up the aircraft nose until the tailskid was touching the ground. The bomb was then centred under the aircraft and the aircraft lowered over it. The A bomb was then raised up by a hoist that was part of the aircraft. I recall that we once loaded an A bomb in seventeen minutes.'

For the attacks, formations of nuclear bombers with their tankers and supporting conventional bombers would depart the UK, refuel over the Baltic or Mediterranean before the bombers carried on to penetrate Soviet airspace en route to their target. Conventional bombers escorted the nuclear bombers, providing ECM jamming and simply swamping the defences. Once the nuclear bombers had reached Russia's interior the conventional bombers, which were not able to refuel in flight, bombed their targets then returned home, leaving the nuclear bombers to continue alone. The B-29MRs were soon joined by B-50As, also able to refuel from the KB-29Ms and between them these formed SAC's nuclear capability until joined by the massive Convair B-36 in 1949. SAC's attention now shifted to the new generation of jet bombers, the B-47, and although the B-29s soldiered on as bombers in several of SAC's BWs they were a low priority for new equipment or upgrades, a fact that propelled the B-29 into its second war when North Korea unexpectedly invaded South Korea on 25 June 1950.

BELOW The handover ceremony at Andrews AFB, Maryland, March 20, 1950, for the first four B-29s to the RAF. On the podium stand the US Secretary of State for Defense Mr Louis Johnson (right), and the British Ambassador to the US, Sir Oliver Franks (left). Behind can be seen the 307th BG crews who will shortly fly the B-29s to Britain. B-29 44-61787 became WF435. *(Jeff Brown)*

Washingtons and the RAF

On 27 January 1950 the USA and Britain signed an agreement for the loan of 70 (later increased to 87) B-29s to the RAF. The first four were handed over during a ceremony at Andrews AFB near Washington DC on 20 March before being flown to the UK by crews from the USAF's 307th BW. While in RAF service the B-29s equipped eight main force bomber squadrons while three were converted for ELINT work and used to detect Russian radar emissions. Serviceability, always a problem for USAF B-29s, was worse for the post-war RAF short of experienced personnel and spares and squadrons seldom accomplished their set numbers of flying hours. However, the Washington did represent a quantum leap forward and gave the RAF much needed experience in operating heavy, complex aeroplanes that was a great help as more modern types came into service. In 1953 Canberra bombers began to replace the Washingtons, with all bomber Washingtons having been returned to the US or scrapped in the UK by early 1954. The ELINT planes soldiered on until 1958 when serviceability finally got the better of them and they were retired a few months shy of being replaced by the new Comet R Mk 2s.

The Washington squadrons were part of RAF Bomber Command's main force, intended to operate by night, so formation flying was not regularly practised. However, on 15 July 1953 the RAF massed representatives of all its aircraft types for Queen Elizabeth II's coronation review. By then only four of the original eight Washington squadrons still operated the type (the others having converted to Canberras) and a formation of twelve Washingtons – three from each squadron (35, 90, 115 and 207) – took part in the fly-past, while four more (one from each squadron) stood in the static display. For the event all planes were highly polished, a task that had many a Washington crew member wishing they were in Fighter Command whose diminutive fighters were far easier to polish than the giant B-29s!

John King, former flight engineer on Washingtons with 44 Squadron recalls their bomber squadron use:

The ground school phase lasted for about 10 weeks and crews then moved on to flying. This phase comprised some nine or ten dual sorties varying between four and six hours' duration.

The value of repeated asymmetric sessions was later to become evident as engine failures were not an uncommon occurrence!

Along with the aircraft, Bomber Command adopted many of the USAF operating procedures. Some crewmembers' titles changed – there was now an Aircraft Commander and the waist gunners became 'scanners' and the upper gunner was now a 'central fire controller'. Resistance to complete change meant the signaller was spared being referred to as the 'radioman' and the nav/plotter

LEFT In the pre-health and safety conscious days airmen swarm over RAF Washington WW342 like ants as they polish it in readiness for the Coronation Review in 1953. In the end, despite all the work, this Washington was a spare and did not take part in either the flying or the static displays. *(John Hanby)*

did not have to carry the additional appellation of 'bombardier'.

By far the greatest impact upon Bomber Command procedures was the need to pay considerable attention to aircraft performance. Prior to the introduction of the Washington the Lincoln (descendant of the Lanc) was the heaviest bomber aircraft ever operated by the RAF. With its maximum gross weight of 82,000 lb it was overshadowed by the 140,000 lb B-29. The increase in weight was a quantum leap and called for detailed planning before each sortie. The aircraft operating manual, known as the Dash -1, contained extensive performance data for takeoff, climb, cruise and descent. It was no longer acceptable to use a standard unstick speed for all weights, for example, since higher gross weights would require a more precise calculation. The longer ranges could only be achieved provided particular attention was paid to 'cruise control' – a procedure wherein the cruising RPM were progressively reduced as fuel and war-load were expended so as to maintain the correct speed for maximum range. The consumption of fuel alone could amount to upwards of 40,000 lb on a long 12–15 hr flight.

During the pre-flight planning stage the nav/plotter and the flight engineer would work together to produce a Flight Plan based upon the data from the Dash -1 manual, the engineer extracting the relevant cruise speeds, RPM settings and fuel flows for each weight bracket. Pages of the manual carried coloured edges indicating whether the data was relevant to 'Standard Day' (15°C) or 'Hot Day' (30°C) – this too had a marked impact upon performance. It

was not uncommon for the calculations to take up several hours of the before-flight ritual for crews; during major exercises the initial briefing (navs & engineers) might be held as much as six hours prior to takeoff.

Once the formality of the 'morning prayers' was complete the crew boarded the aircraft and dispersed to their stations. First item of importance was the firing up of the APU or, as it was onomatopoeically referred to – the 'Putt-Putt'. This four-cylinder petrol engine was mounted in the rear unpressurized compartment and was started remotely from the engineer's position. It breathed life into the aircraft electrical system and ensured that the B-29 was independent of the need for separate ground power units. Once the engineer reported, 'Putt-Putt on line', main engine starting got under way. This, too, was effected from the engineer's station and the only other crew members being slightly involved were the two scanners who kept a beady eye open for any sign of an exhaust fire during start up. The engine starting routine was seldom the cause for any problem, provided that during the external pre-flight check each of the prop blades had been hand-pulled through 12 blades. This was no light task and involved as many hands as could be persuaded to help out – two chaps being needed to accomplish this on each blade.

Comfort was the word for the cabin conditions inside the aircraft. In normal flight the pressurization ensured a cabin altitude of 10,000 ft whilst cruising at 30,000 ft. There was a reasonably efficient heating system which could cope with the external temperatures met at about 20,000 ft (and that was a typical cruising altitude) but it was not up to those encountered at the higher levels. An extended cruise at 25–30,000 ft usually called for an extensive amount of warm clothing – not the RAF's strong suit (no pun intended!) at that time. Later, with the advent of the Canberra there would be some excellent cold-weather flying clothing in stores – the trick was to get the 'stores basher' to hand it out!

Although the four Wright Cyclone R-3350 engines pushed out a lot of noise along with their 2,200 hp, the interior noise levels were very low – for a piston-engined aircraft; crew inter-com was via throat-mikes and headsets. Full helmets and oxygen masks were kept close at hand to cope with a pressurization failure or sudden decompression, but were seldom used. For the pilots, perhaps the biggest adjustment was getting used to flying the aircraft visually through the massive structure of the glazed nose. It was a bit like driving a large bus – from the back seat! But like all things once used to it, the framework seemed to vanish.

One of the initial requirements for captaincy (Aircraft Commander) of a Washington was that the pilot had at least 1,000 hours on four-engined aircraft and be a commissioned officer. At this time many captains on the Lincolns which previously equipped the Washington squadrons were NCOs and consequently were posted away and did not attend the conversion process. This avoided a situation where, had they been retained as co-pilots, it would appear to be a demotion. Instead new pilots, some commissioned and many of them just out of training, were posted in to fill these positions. Later several would be returned to the WCU and qualify as Aircraft Commanders in their own right.

Squadron training sorties consisted of a variety of tasks. Typical is one which details a session of ILS approaches at Filton (Bristol) followed by 'Local Flying in S. Wales' (the AC was a Welshman!), air-sea firing off the Leman Bank in the North Sea and then a round-Britain cross-country flight – all in one sortie for a total of 10 hours' flying. A few days later we find the same crew completing a long cross-country flight down to the south of France and back followed by a session of simulated radar bombing runs, code named 'Backchat' (using Southend pier as the target), for another 12 hour sortie. As an aside, it ended slightly prematurely due to an oil leak (surprise!) on No. 3 engine, necessitating the prop being feathered.

August was the month to practice formation flying in readiness for the annual 'Battle of Britain' flypast that took place on the Saturday nearest to September 15th. The formations were representative of all the Commands and the routes and timings were planned by a permanent group based at HQ Fighter Command. With a very large range of cruising speeds to be considered, from the leisurely de Havilland Chipmunk to the Gloster Meteor jet fighter, it was no mean achievement to have them all arrive at the 'gate' with a separation which would result in a continual procession as they passed over Buckingham Palace. The flypast would last for about 15 minutes in those days. A 15-minute flypast today would, in all probability, exhaust the RAF of its total inventory!

Hand-flying the Washington in these formations was tiring. For the handling pilot it was a two-handed effort, with the co-pilot helping out with the power adjustment. B-29 formation spacing reflected the maneuverability (or lack of it) of a large aircraft carrying a goodly amount of inertia. This was no time to try to emulate the crisp formations of Harvards, Vampires and Meteors. Never the less the result looked good (from the air, at least) and the crews enjoyed the respite from the endless routine of bombing, gunnery and navigation exercises.

Autumn saw the arrival of the annual large-scale exercises, involving all of Bomber, Fighter and RAF Germany Commands as well as those of the other NATO partners. The bomber forces were routed out over the North Sea and down through continental Europe before heading back into the British Isles for a simulated attack on a strategic target. Sorties were flown by day and night with the defending fighters doing their level best to obtain cine-gun camera films full of bombers. One B-29 recorded no less than 23 engagements on one sortie.

The use of the Washington was purely as a stand-in until the RAF had sufficient numbers of jet bombers in its inventory. By 1951 the Canberra was entering service and in a few years the Valiant, first of the 'V' bombers, would be arriving. By the end of 1953 and into 1954 the B-29s were returned to the USA.

The Korean War

From the B-29's perspective the Korean War can be divided into three broad phases: daylight operations, night operations and electronic battles.

Daylight operations

When the North Korean army streamed into South Korea the Pentagon was caught completely off guard. Quickly, though, the 22 B-29s of the 19th BG, still stationed on Guam in the Marianas, deployed to Okinawa where, due to the critical situation, they were employed as tactical bombers desperately trying to slow the North Korean advance by attacking troop concentrations, railway yards and any target of opportunity they could. In early July the 22nd and 92nd joined them, with these units being further augmented in early August by the 98th and 307th. It was generally believed in the USA that Korea was simply a prelude to a full-scale war with Russia and it was only the non-nuclear-capable B-29's low priority in the strategic field that allowed them to be deployed to Korea while SAC retained its more able planes (B-29MRs, B-50s and B-36s) for the expected global nuclear war to come. As the war stabilised, the B-29s were released from tactical operations and on 30 July 1950 began a campaign against the North Korean industrial system.

Operating at 15,000ft against no fighter and minimal anti-aircraft opposition, large formations of B-29s systematically wrecked nearly every significant industrial installation in North Korea. By late September 1950 the bombers had effectively run out of targets, partly because of the success of their bombing campaign but also due to the rapid advance of UN troops after the Inchon landings on 15 September meant

that most targets were now under UN control. Thinking the war was nearly over the 22nd and 92nd BWs were released and returned to the US. Unfortunately this was not so and in late October the Chinese joined the fight, rapidly pushing the UN forces back. This intervention also radically changed things for the bombers with much-improved AAA and the first sightings of MiG 15s. The B-29s, having run out of strategic targets in Korea and banned from operating over China, reverted to a largely tactical role with small formations attacking bridges and transport hubs in an ineffective attempt to stem the flow of troops and supplies moving into Korea. Daylight raids continued with increasingly effective harassment by MiGs until on 23 October 1951 the 307th BG sent eight B-29s to bomb the airfield at Namsi. MiGs brought down three aircraft and badly damaged the remaining five. It was now apparent that the B-29 could not survive in the daytime and a few days later B-29s were restricted to operate at night where the darkness temporarily afforded protection.

Night operations

Initially the darkness provided the B-29s with near immunity, while the use of a highly effective form of electronic triangulation known as SHORAN allowed them to accurately hit targets even as small as bridges. Some B-29s had been equipped with SHORAN from June 1951 but with the restriction of the entire force to night operations in October the fitting was increased and SHORAN-guided night operations became the standard from November onward.

To use SHORAN the B-29 flew on an arc a set distance from a transmitter and dropped their bombs when they intersected with a second arc. Accurate though this method was, it did limit the possible approach routes to a target. The North Koreans learned quickly and soon began to group radar-controlled lights and guns along the probable attack routes. To begin with the B-29s did not carry ECM equipment, but when radar-guided lights and guns became evident, the Second World War-era ECM gear was reinstalled and could be effective against the Chinese and North Korean defences – not surprisingly really since they were to all intents and purposes using Russian copies of equipment captured from the Germans during

the war. To be successful, though, the B-29s needed spot jammers and these required dedicated ECM operators to tune them. Unforgivably, ECM operators were in short supply and had to be trained before they could reach the front line. Another problem was that the ECM interfered with the SHORAN signals so could not be used on the bombing run, which was when it was most needed, resulting in several planes being lost or damaged.

The North Koreans also became more tactically astute and began to employ ground-control intercept radars with night fighters in combination with searchlights and anti-aircraft guns. This culminated on 10/11 June 1952 when B-29s attacked the railway bridge at Kwaksan. Two-dozen searchlights caught the bombers, which were then attacked by a dozen or so MiGs. Two B-29s were lost and another made a forced landing. The ECM/SHORAN interference was partly to blame and this disastrous raid marked the end of the 'safe' phase of night operations and ushered in the electronic battles.

Electronic battles

This phase continued until the end of the war. To gather intelligence on the enemy's radars the USAF bolstered its ELINT capability with RB-50s from the 55th Strategic Reconnaissance Wing and these even accompanied the B-29s on missions so as to gather ELINT on enemy radars as they were used in combat. The ECM fit in B-29s was improved and additional ECM operators trained. From September 1952 the prohibition on the use of chaff over Korea was lifted and several dedicated ECM-equipped B-29s accompanied the bombers and would orbit the target area, suppressing enemy radars with ECM and chaff. Finally, in December the B-29s had their undersides painted black as a defence against

ABOVE A 19th BG B-29 rests on its hardstand showing off its black undersides and fin applied in December 1952. *(USAF)*

the ever-more-effective searchlights. These measures reduced losses and after January 1953 no more B-29s were lost to enemy action. During the last phase the B-29s once more returned to strategic targets. However, with a ban on attacking anything in China, strategic strikes were largely irrelevant since all materials could be produced in total safety in China before being carried into Korea for use.

The Korean War was an inconclusive end to the B-29's operational career. Compared to the Second World War losses the B-29 fared well, with only 74 being lost out of 21,000 sorties, a loss rate of less than a third of 1%. When allowed to operate as strategic bombers the B-29s were devastatingly effective, eliminating all strategic targets in North Korea within a matter of weeks. However, the advent of modern jet fighters marked the end of the massed daytime formation, forcing the B-29s

FLYING THE GAUNTLET AND FLAK SUPPRESSION IN MIG ALLEY

Bud Farrell, 19th BG

In the early morning of September 12th, there was a buzz in the air that generally reflected something big – a MAX EFFORT – and the nervous edge adrenaline started early with preflighting the ship, loading EXTRA ammo, cleaning and checking guns and rechecking turret systems, pressure checking engines, etc., an all day job. With late afternoon briefing the Group Briefing Room was 'wired' with tension – the curtain drawn – and the red line went right up to the Yalu near Antung – Manchuria – MIG ALLEY! Right ON the river, Suiho Hydroelectric Power Plant, just below the Dam, at the base – even more difficult than going after the dam itself! There were whistles and sighs upon just seeing the red line ... even before the mission details, and then there were groans and a few heaves ... some got physically sick in the back of the room ... big game jitters!

Takeoff and the trip en-route were routine until our climb through an unpredicted weather front to bombing altitude, we started to pick up ice on the control surfaces which our Aircraft Commander felt in the sloppiness of the ship, and he requested increases in power by the Flight Engineer several times to shake ice and prevent a stall. After several tense minutes we got through and above the front but heard on VHF radio, a 93rd Squadron Sister ship, Major Sanders', crew in some distress from icing and only later learned that they had augured in from approximately 25,000 feet with their full bomb load, with only one out of twelve surviving a last second bailout at 500 feet.

After the anxiety of hearing the breaking ice ricocheting off leading edges with no apparent damage and a clean ship again, we continued for another 200 miles to the IP for our run in on the target – through much clearer than predicted skies. As we approached the IP from the southeast and before our turn to the left on the bomb run, I could see hundreds of anti-aircraft gun flashes, both on the ground and the resultant flak bursts in the air at our altitude and above, and many fingers of searchlights stabbing at the aircraft ahead of us, almost a boulevard of beams lined up along the path.

As we turned on our heading to the target, with no diversion or evasive deviation in our track allowed, our A/C called on interphone and said 'Hang onto your ass – they're catching hell up in front of us' and I felt an exhilaration and adrenaline flow like we were goin' over the top on an amusement park wild roller coaster ride – with breath held and sweating fists clutching the cold metal frame of the blister for some feeling of solidarity – the only time I had the heavy canvas covered lead stripped flak jackets under AND on me! Enemy aircraft were dropping brilliant orange and white parachute flares above the bomber stream to illuminate the B-29s to the orbiting Migs waiting to pounce, with some so intent in pressing their attack that they pursued the B-29s right into their own flak.

From IP, to 'bombs away', there were continuous flak bursts around us, perhaps thousands within sight like a very long string of firecrackers going off in your face and all seeming closer in the dark than they really were. Searchlights scanning from both sides of the river trying to find and lock on, then one huge overwhelming flash reduced all others to nothing – and the B-29 immediately in front of us no longer existed, having taken a direct hit and disintegrated with the explosion of its full bomb load – and twelve men! This has always remained with me as what 'Dante's Inferno' might look like!

As we flew on, I tried to climb inside my flak helmet and make myself even smaller and ducked behind the gun sight reflexively, convulsively, through flashes, searchlights and the rattle of falling spent flak shrapnel against our ship and the ONLY time I ever actually smelled cordite from the flak explosions. At some point we took a direct hit of a major round that miraculously did NOT detonate on contact and went through our horizontal stabilizer VERY close in to the fuselage and Tail Gunner's compartment, went up alongside the vertical stabilizer, grooving it for about ten to hide in the dark. Even the dark eventually held no safety and the war ended with ECM battles that would continue well beyond Korea. Finally, the fallacy of employing strategic bombers in a limited war became evident when all the strategic destruction of industry in North Korea was negated by the simple expedient of building the material in absolute safety just over the border in China.

This was to be the B-29s' last conflict and once over they were quickly removed from front-line service, soldiering on in support roles such as tankers. The last B-29 flight made by the USAF ended at 20:10hrs on 21 June 1960 when Major Clarence C. Rarick of the 6023rd Radar Evaluation Squadron landed B-29 42-65234 at Naha airbase, Okinawa, after a routine radar evaluation mission. The four B-29s of the 6023rd Squadron remained at Naha as fire-training hulks.

---

feet and perhaps detonated above and behind our ship … with no effect on our controls or other equipment – and not discovered until we landed.

A mere two weeks later, and having flown two other combat missions in between, we were briefed to be the flak suppression/ECM lead ship of 45 B-29s on a Maximum Effort to Namsan-Ni, right in the middle of Mig Valley only three miles down river from Suiho and 1,400 feet from the Yalu River. For flak suppression we were loaded with 192 – 100 pounders with VT (Variable Timed) Proximity Fuses set to go off above the ground within range of guns and searchlights for maximum effect on the light and gun crews. After bombs away we were to climb to 28,500ft and orbit, jamming the enemy radars, while the bomber stream came through below us. To operate the ECM gear the group's ECM man, John Lamire, joined our crew and, as we orbited, Marine Corps F-3D Skyknight radar night fighters of VMF(N)-513 would orbit above us to take care of the Mig threat. Also, Douglas B-26 Invaders were to be at low level to take out the lights and guns as soon as they came on.

We arrived in the IP/Target area the boulevard of searchlights bordering the Yalu River started coming on and were almost immediately pounced by the low level '26s and we could see many of the brilliant lights flare up, smoke, and go out, just like a burning out light bulb, hit by the 8 .50s in the hard nosed '26s, strafing, and the gunner at his periscopic sight probably taking a crack at light and gun positions with the 4 more .50s in his two turrets as they flashed by.

Across the target some flak and lights in the same gauntlet bomb run as Suiho but no comparison – ECM and the '26s were really working them over! Maybe it was the element of surprise of one plane being arrogant enough to come over the gauntlet by itself. At 'bombs away', the surge upward created by the sudden dump of 10 tons, 20,000 pounds, was always a point of huge relief, being rid of the bombs and coming off the target, and I always thought of having just gotten rid of the equivalent of 4 or 5 Cadillacs buried in your belly, a higher air and escape speed and no longer riding on 'dynamite'!

After bombs away, we turned to start our climb back to our ECM orbit. Our #1 engine, on my side, started to 'torch' very badly, a bluish engine-exhaust flame trailing almost from the cherry red exhaust stack to past my Plexiglas Blister, and well back toward the horizontal stabilizer. Of no great mechanical consequence or hazard but a very bright beacon for searching Migs! Our Flight Engineer adjusted the fuel mixture, 'leaned it out', but with no significant effect. The A/C decided to shut it down, feather a perfectly good operating engine, and continue the mission, but of course we would have difficulty reaching our briefed altitude of 28,500 feet and finally leveled off at 27,000 or 27,500 feet, enjoying the light show of the Bomber Stream coming through behind and below us.

Well into our orbiting, John Lamire, stashed in the crowded nook behind the upper aft turret, and just behind the amplidyne and dynamotor panel in front of my position, had hollered and then flashed a light to get my attention through the small crescent gap between the fuselage and the panel frame. 'HEY FARRELL … WATCH THIS' … and at about that time it seemed like every scanning searchlight within a 5 mile radius LOCKED on us … CONED us!! 'NOW WATCH' … and the light cone broke up and the beams started scanning again … 'NOW WATCH' … and he did whatever he was doing … AGAIN! 'GODDAMN IT LAMIRE … KNOCK IT OFF!' Frenchy was a crazy Cajun from Beaumont, Texas, and fearless after more missions than I can imagine. He was a master of his art but he aged me about 10 years in TWO minutes!

The Marine F3Ds were there as well and flew almost in our prop wash and God Bless 'Em! We saw no Migs, lost no aircraft, and two hours later headed toward Itazuke AFB at Fukuoka, Japan, for a planned refueling stop and a breakfast layover. 'ITAZUKE HAM AND EGGS 25 CENTS!'

Chapter Three

Anatomy of the B-29

When designed, the B-29 was by far the world's largest and most complex production aircraft, greatly exceeding the other US heavy bombers in every aspect. This leap in capability allowed the B-29 to remain operational well beyond its contemporaries, forming the core of SAC's early offensive power as well as fighting in the war over Korea.

OPPOSITE A view of an R-3350 Wright duplex cyclone engine showing the 'orange peel' air deflectors surrounding the front row of cylinders. Also visible just behind the orange peel are the rocker box crossover oil lines fitted to the top cylinders. *(Dale Thompson)*

The B-29 is a very-long-range, four-engined mid-wing heavy bomber. All models have 18-cylinder Wright Cyclone R-3350 engines driving four-bladed Hamilton Standard full-feathering constant-speed propellers (some later and specialist aircraft had four-bladed Curtiss-Wright electric constant-speed, feathering and reversing propellers). The B-29, B-29A and B-29B are not separate models. The B-29 and B-29B only differ in that the B-29B has all defensive armament apart from the tail turret removed – allowing the B-29B to fly higher and faster than the B-29. The B-29A differs from the B-29 only in having two separate inboard wings instead of a continuous inboard wing. Aerodynamically the B-29 and B-29A wings are identical.

Fuselage

The all-metal fuselage is a semi-monocoque construction where a framework of ribs connected by longitudinal longerons is covered by a stressed aluminium alloy skin. To provide strength for pressurisation the ribs are circular and reinforced near cut-outs by additional structural members (eg the bomb-bay openings are bordered by beams). To reduce drag the skin panels are butt joined and fixed to the underlying frame with countersunk rivets. The exception is around the gun turrets where the skin could be affected by muzzle blast. Here brazier-head rivets are used for greater strength.

The ribs, termed stations, are numbered in inches starting at a datum point 6in forward of

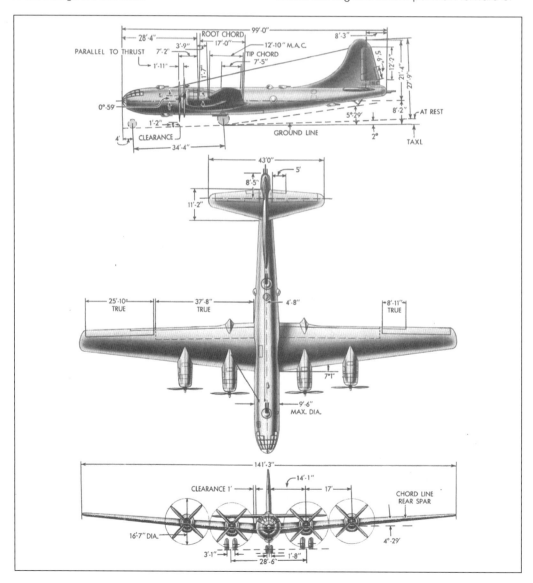

RIGHT General dimensions of the B-29. *(USAF)*

THE B-29'S SKIN

The B-29's stressed aluminium alloy skin used various alloys for different areas: 2S, 3S, 17ST but mainly 24ST a Duralumin core coated on both sides with pure aluminium to a depth of about 5% of the core thickness.

Duralumin is an obsolete trade name for an aluminium alloy where copper (4% approx.) is the main alloying element along with lesser amounts of manganese (1.5% approx.) and magnesium (0.6% approx.). Other elements, notably silicon, zinc, iron, chromium and titanium are present in quantities of less than 0.5%. Depending on the exact mix of alloying elements, the alloy will exhibit different qualities and is designated with a different identifying number. The B-29 skin uses the alloy 24ST. The 24 indicates the composition of the alloy while the S denotes wrought and the T as being heat tempered.

While 24ST has a good strength to weight ratio it is susceptible to corrosion so is generally coated with pure aluminium on both sides to a depth of 5% of the core thickness. Sheets of the coated alloy were made by the Aluminium Company of America (Alcoa) under the trade name of Alclad and by Reynolds as Pureclad. Both were used in B-29 production.

The skin on the B-29 was generally 0.03–0.04in thick, although thicker sheets up to 0.07in were used in locations with the most stress.

The 24ST is still in production under the new designation of 2024 applied by the International Alloy Designation System (the 2000 series denoting Al-Cu alloys with the 24 being the particular composition).

BELOW Bulkheads, spars and ribs within the B-29. Items are located according to a three-dimensional grid: station lines are reference measurements taken cross-sectionally through the fuselage (starting with station 6 at the very nose), nacelles (with 0 at the engine mounting bulkhead and numbered positive behind this and negative in front of this) and empennage (starting with 0 at the centre of the fuselage); water lines are reference measurements taken horizontally through the fuselage (starting with 0 at the lowest point of the fuselage, parallel to the principal centre line) and nacelles (each nacelle has a 0 line 50in below the centre line of the nacelle); and butt lines are reference measurements taken vertically through the fuselage to the left (denoted -) and right (+) of the fuselage centre line. *(USAF)*

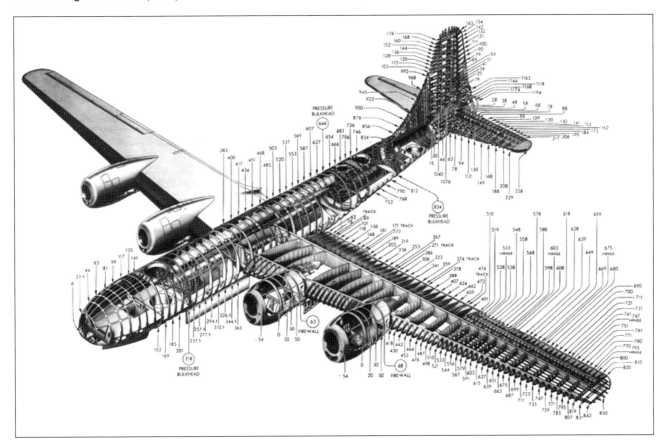

RIGHT The forward
entry hatch in the
rear of the nose-gear
well of *It's Hawg Wild*.
This is the normal
entry point for those
who inhabited the
forward pressurised
compartment. The
hand crank, seen
stowed on the
underside of the hatch,
is for the emergency
operation of the nose
gear. If needed it is
inserted into a gearbox
accessed via a hole in
the forward cabin floor
aft of the central aisle
stand. The gearbox
has a ratio of 3:1 and
257 turns are required
to raise or lower the
wheels. The triangular
item at top centre is
the nose-jacking cone
attached to station
153 and rated for a
maximum 20,000lb
load. *(Author)*

the nose and continuing to station 1194 at the
extreme tip of the tail turret. The longerons are
identified by capital letters left and right of the
lower fuselage centre line. Lower-case letters
denote stiffeners when located between the
longerons. Four of the stations are pressure
bulkheads splitting the fuselage into five
sections: forward pressurised compartment,
bomb-bay compartment, rear pressurised
compartment, tail section (unpressurised) and
tail gunner's compartment.

Forward pressurised compartment

Stretching from the front glazing at station 6
to the pressure bulkhead at station 218, this
compartment accommodates the nose-gear
well, six crew positions – bombardier, aeroplane
commander, pilot, navigator, flight engineer and
radio operator – as well as two of the five gun
turrets and the forward sighting station.

Nose-gear well

Located immediately under the forward
crew compartment this contains the nose
gear, forward entry hatch, engine CO_2 fire
extinguisher bottles, nose jacking cone and the
external power receptacle.

Bombardier station

The bombardier sits in the extreme nose
between the instrument panels for the two
pilots. To his front is the Norden bombsight, to
his left the bombardier's control panel and to
his right the bombardier's desk, gunsight and
control box for the forward sighting station.

CENTRE One of the engine fire extinguisher
bottles in *It's Hawg Wild*. Two bottles are fitted,
one either side of the rear of the nose-gear well.
Each bottle holds 12.6lb of CO_2 at a pressure of
approximately 1,200psi. The system is operated
by controls at the flight engineer's station that
allow either bottle to be directed to any engine.
(Author)

LEFT The hand crank inserted in the gearbox.
The bracing beam for the crank is clamped to
the co-pilot's armour plate and rotated down if
needed. *(USAF)*

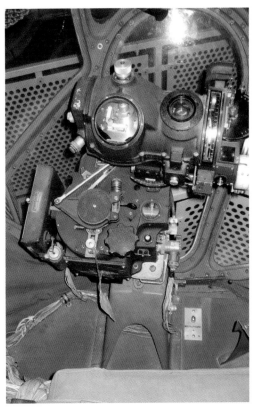

ABOVE The bombardier's station in *It's Hawg Wild*. To the front centre is the Norden bombsight positioned to view through the optically flat panel in the lower centre of the nose glazing. To the left is the bombardier's control panel (hidden by the pilot's control panel). To the right is the forward sighting station. Note the circular parking brake pull button to the right of the pilot's rudder pedals. Also observe the pilot's right brake metering valve between the parking brake and the red label on the instrument panel. The co-pilot's left brake metering valve is in the equivalent location to the left of the co-pilot's left rudder pedal. The device on the nose floor to the right of the bombsight is the SCR-718 radar altimeter that gives a precise altitude below the plane. Note the hydraulic metering valve attached to the near end of the rudder pedals for the brakes on the left main gear. Another valve (for the brakes on the right wheel) is at the far end of the rudder pedal bar. See also, the control wires attached to the quadrants between the rudder pedals and then vanishing under the cabin floor through the ducts either side of the control column. Also notice the Zerk fittings (small yellow-painted pimples on the rudder pedals) that allow the joints to be lubricated.

ABOVE The Norden bombsight in *It's Hawg Wild*. The bombsight comes in two major parts: the detachable sighthead and the fixed stabiliser unit. The optics are all contained in the sighthead and stabilised in the vertical plane (for deviations in pitch and roll) by a gyro mounted under the large glass window to the left. This window allows the bombardier to see the top of the gyro mount, upon which are two spirit levels, one pointing fore to aft the other left to right. A levelling knob allows the bombardier to tilt the gyro in order to make the two spirit levels central. When both are central the gyro is vertical and so too are the optics. The stabiliser unit is actually a permanent part of the Honeywell C-1 autopilot and contains a gyro that acts as a directional reference and stabilises the bombsight in the horizontal plane (for deviations in yaw). Thus the two gyros fix the optics in space regardless of aircraft motion. The rectangular box mounted on the left of the stabiliser unit is the interface to the autopilot, allowing the bombardier to fly the plane via the bombsight when on the bombing run.

LEFT The front of the sighthead in *It's Hawg Wild*. The rectangular window in the centre is the viewing port behind which lie the optics. *(Author)*

RIGHT Diagram from
the bombardier's
'Information File'
identifying the
various parts of the
bombsight. (USAF)

NOMENCLATURE
AND
OPERATION

14. TACHOMETER ADAPTER
15. RELEASE LEVER
16. CROSSHAIR RHEOSTAT
17. DRIFT SCALE
18. PDI BRUSH AND COIL
19. AUTOPILOT CLUTCH ENGAGING KNOB
20. AUTOPILOT CLUTCH
21. BOMBSIGHT CLUTCH ENGAGING LEVER
22. BOMBSIGHT CLUTCH
23. BOMBSIGHT CONNECTING ROD
24. AUTOPILOT CONNECTING ROD

1. LEVELING KNOBS
2. CAGING KNOB
3. EYEPIECE
4. INDEX WINDOW
5. TRAIL ARM AND TRAIL PLATE
6. EXTENDED VISION KNOB
7. RATE MOTOR SWITCH
8. DISC SPEED GEAR SHIFT
9. RATE AND DISPLACEMENT KNOBS
10. MIRROR DRIVE CLUTCH
11. SEARCH KNOB
12. DISC SPEED DRUM
13. TURN AND DRIFT KNOBS

The bombsight has 2 main parts, sighthead and
stabilizer. The sighthead pivots on the stabilizer and
is locked to it by the dovetail locking pin. The sighthead is connected to the directional gyro in the stabilizer through the bombsight connecting rod and
the bombsight clutch.

BELOW The bombardier's panel. The top panel directs the cameras while
the green panel on the right contains all the necessary switches to control
the release of the bombs. Other parts of the panel contain the bomb
indicator lights (black panel at lower right with 40 indicators – one light per
possible bomb location), basic flight controls (large black panel at upper
left) with a remote compass read-out at top, altimeter lower left, airspeed
indicator lower right and clock above. Below the flight instruments is the
intervalometer which, when fed with details of the aircraft's altitude and
speed, provides a method of releasing in train (ie one bomb after the other
rather than salvo when all are released together) a predetermined number
of bombs with a set space interval between successive impacts. It also
controls the drop sequence to ensure that the aircraft's centre of gravity
remains within limits as the bombs drop free. (Dale Thompson)

THE BOMBING PROBLEM

The bombsight is intended to help
the bombardier solve the 'bombing
problem' and so get his bombs on target.
Unfortunately, hitting a target many
thousands of feet below when travelling at
several hundred miles per hour is not trivial
and although the Norden greatly helped it
did not have all the answers.

The bombing problem can be divided
into two parts: the range problem and
the course problem. These are essentially
independent although the solution is
combined within the Norden.

The **range problem** deals with how
far from the target the bombs must be
released so they will carry to it. At the point
of release the bombs are travelling at the
same speed and at the same altitude as
the plane. However, gravity immediately
accelerates them downwards while air
resistance slows their forward motion.
How much they slow depends on their
aerodynamic properties, true airspeed
and how long they fall, which relies on the
bombing altitude (BA) – the difference in
height between the *target* and the *bomber*
when the bombs are dropped. Because
these are constant for any BA and shape
of bomb, they are calculated in tests in
the US and supplied to the bombardier for
every type of bomb and every combination
of BA and airspeed in bombing tables. The
slowing is provided as a term called 'trail',
which is the difference in how far a bomb
will carry forward if dropped in a vacuum
and how far it will travel forward when
dropped in air [A]. How long the bomb falls
for is called 'Actual Time of Fall' (ATF) that,
due to the internal workings of the Norden,
is supplied as a value called 'Disk Speed'
(DS). They are entered into the Norden by
adjusting the trail arm to the indicated value
and by entering the DS on the disk speed
drum.

Although the amount a bomb slows
depends on the airspeed, how far it will
actually carry forward hinges on the ground

speed. This cannot be calculated in advance as it relies on any wind affecting the plane on the bombing run. To calculate this, the bombardier looks through the telescope and brings the target on to the crosshairs by using the search knob. This tilts a mirror under the telescope that deflects the bombardier's view forward or backward. When the target lies on the horizontal crosshair the bombardier keeps it there by adjusting the rate knob. As the plane approaches a target the sight angle decreases. Also, the rate that this decreases changes with both altitude and how near the target the plane is. The DS entered from the bombing tables sets up an initial value and this is refined by the bombardier using the rate knob. When the correct rate is entered the mirror will automatically tilt at an ever-varying speed that keeps the target on the horizontal crosshair. This allows the sight to calculate the ground speed. The sight can now calculate the whole range as the ATF ground speed. This takes no account of the slowing but when the trail is subtracted from this the actual range is obtained. The Norden calculates all these as angles related to the sight angle. The actual sight angle needed to keep the target on the crosshairs is constantly decreasing. The sight has calculated the angle when the bombs need to be dropped and when the sight angle equals the drop angle an electrical connection is made and the bombs are automatically released [B].

The **course problem**. If there is any crosswind the plane must turn slightly into the wind so as to track towards the target. If the plane tracks directly towards the target when the bomb is dropped it will be pushed downwind. This is termed 'cross trail' and to counter this the plane must fly parallel to, but upwind of, the track to the target by the cross trail amount [C]. This is catered for automatically by the sight when the bombardier uses the turn and drift knob to keep the target on the vertical crosshair. When the target remains stationary on the crosshair the sight will have tilted the optics so the plane

is actually tracking upwind of the track by the cross trail amount.

The process worked well when tested in the US but required the wind affecting the plane to be constant all the way to the ground. When the B-29s first bombed Japan, the high altitude used subjected the planes to the jet stream, very strong winds of about 100mph. The Norden calculated the cross trail that this should produce but since the wind did not blow steadily to the ground this was wrong. With no way of determining the wind below the plane bombardiers had to resort to aiming off by what they thought was the right amount, reducing the complex Norden to little more than part of their guesswork!

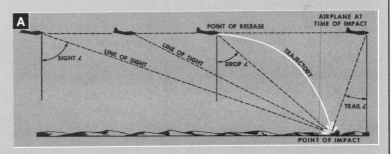

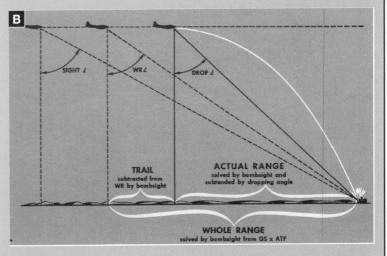

Boeing B-29 Superfortress.

(Mike Badrocke)

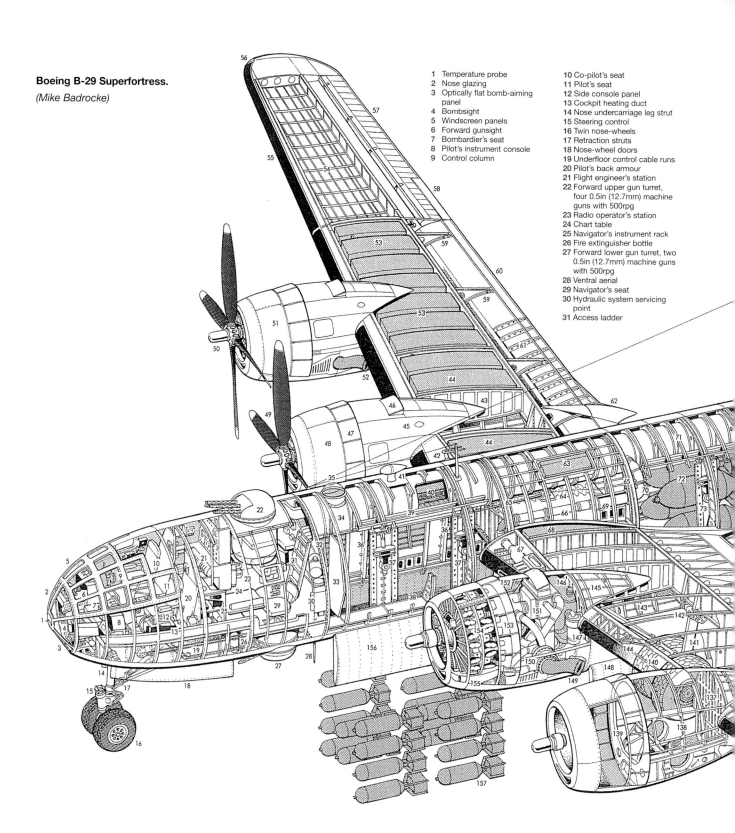

1 Temperature probe
2 Nose glazing
3 Optically flat bomb-aiming panel
4 Bombsight
5 Windscreen panels
6 Forward gunsight
7 Bombardier's seat
8 Pilot's instrument console
9 Control column
10 Co-pilot's seat
11 Pilot's seat
12 Side console panel
13 Cockpit heating duct
14 Nose undercarriage leg strut
15 Steering control
16 Twin nose-wheels
17 Retraction struts
18 Nose-wheel doors
19 Underfloor control cable runs
20 Pilot's back armour
21 Flight engineer's station
22 Forward upper gun turret, four 0.5in (12.7mm) machine guns with 500rpg
23 Radio operator's station
24 Chart table
25 Navigator's instrument rack
26 Fire extinguisher bottle
27 Forward lower gun turret, two 0.5in (12.7mm) machine guns with 500rpg
28 Ventral aerial
29 Navigator's seat
30 Hydraulic system servicing point
31 Access ladder

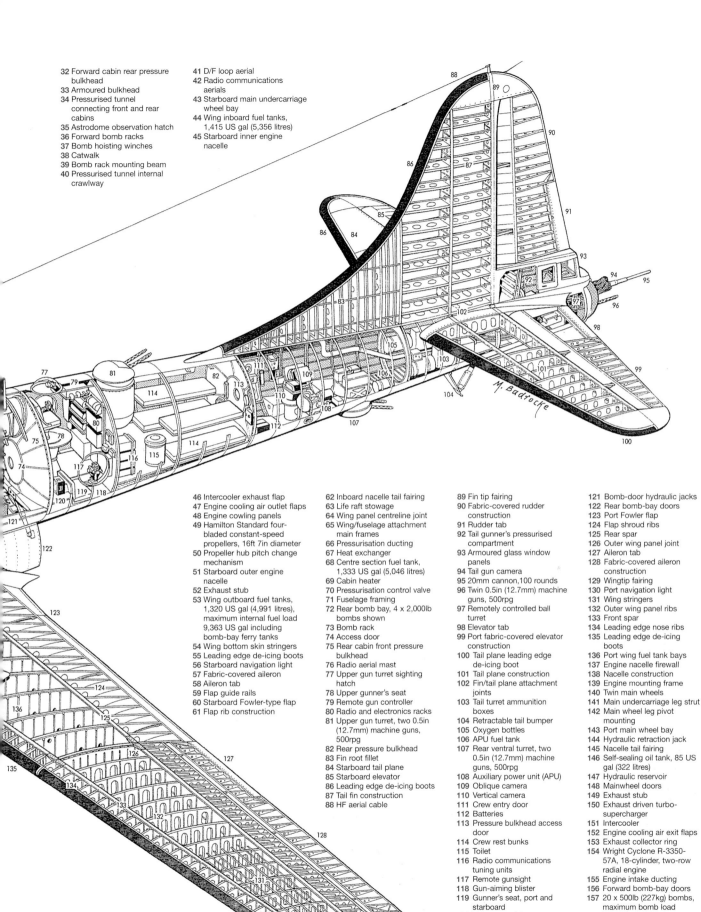

32 Forward cabin rear pressure bulkhead
33 Armoured bulkhead
34 Pressurised tunnel connecting front and rear cabins
35 Astrodome observation hatch
36 Forward bomb racks
37 Bomb hoisting winches
38 Catwalk
39 Bomb rack mounting beam
40 Pressurised tunnel internal crawlway
41 D/F loop aerial
42 Radio communications aerials
43 Starboard main undercarriage wheel bay
44 Wing inboard fuel tanks, 1,415 US gal (5,356 litres)
45 Starboard inner engine nacelle

46 Intercooler exhaust flap
47 Engine cooling air outlet flaps
48 Engine cowling panels
49 Hamilton Standard four-bladed constant-speed propellers, 16ft 7in diameter
50 Propeller hub pitch change mechanism
51 Starboard outer engine nacelle
52 Exhaust stub
53 Wing outboard fuel tanks, 1,320 US gal (4,991 litres), maximum internal fuel load 9,363 US gal including bomb-bay ferry tanks
54 Wing bottom skin stringers
55 Leading edge de-icing boots
56 Starboard navigation light
57 Fabric-covered aileron
58 Aileron tab
59 Flap guide rails
60 Starboard Fowler-type flap
61 Flap rib construction

62 Inboard nacelle tail fairing
63 Life raft stowage
64 Wing panel centreline joint
65 Wing/fuselage attachment main frames
66 Pressurisation ducting
67 Heat exchanger
68 Centre section fuel tank, 1,333 US gal (5,046 litres)
69 Cabin heater
70 Pressurisation control valve
71 Fuselage framing
72 Rear bomb bay, 4 x 2,000lb bombs shown
73 Bomb rack
74 Access door
75 Rear cabin front pressure bulkhead
76 Radio aerial mast
77 Upper gun turret sighting hatch
78 Upper gunner's seat
79 Remote gun controller
80 Radio and electronics racks
81 Upper gun turret, two 0.5in (12.7mm) machine guns, 500rpg
82 Rear pressure bulkhead
83 Fin root fillet
84 Starboard tail plane
85 Starboard elevator
86 Leading edge de-icing boots
87 Tail fin construction
88 HF aerial cable

89 Fin tip fairing
90 Fabric-covered rudder construction
91 Rudder tab
92 Tail gunner's pressurised compartment
93 Armoured glass window panels
94 Tail gun camera
95 20mm cannon,100 rounds
96 Twin 0.5in (12.7mm) machine guns, 500rpg
97 Remotely controlled ball turret
98 Elevator tab
99 Port fabric-covered elevator construction
100 Tail plane leading edge de-icing boot
101 Tail plane construction
102 Fin/tail plane attachment joints
103 Tail turret ammunition boxes
104 Retractable tail bumper
105 Oxygen bottles
106 APU fuel tank
107 Rear ventral turret, two 0.5in (12.7mm) machine guns, 500rpg
108 Auxiliary power unit (APU)
109 Oblique camera
110 Vertical camera
111 Crew entry door
112 Batteries
113 Pressure bulkhead access door
114 Crew rest bunks
115 Toilet
116 Radio communications tuning units
117 Remote gunsight
118 Gun-aiming blister
119 Gunner's seat, port and starboard
120 Voltage regulator

121 Bomb-door hydraulic jacks
122 Rear bomb-bay doors
123 Port Fowler flap
124 Flap shroud ribs
125 Rear spar
126 Outer wing panel joint
127 Aileron tab
128 Fabric-covered aileron construction
129 Wingtip fairing
130 Port navigation light
131 Wing stringers
132 Outer wing panel ribs
133 Front spar
134 Leading edge nose ribs
135 Leading edge de-icing boots
136 Port wing fuel tank bays
137 Engine nacelle firewall
138 Nacelle construction
139 Engine mounting frame
140 Twin main wheels
141 Main undercarriage leg strut
142 Main wheel leg pivot mounting
143 Port main wheel bay
144 Hydraulic retraction jack
145 Nacelle tail fairing
146 Self-sealing oil tank, 85 US gal (322 litres)
147 Hydraulic reservoir
148 Mainwheel doors
149 Exhaust stub
150 Exhaust driven turbo-supercharger
151 Intercooler
152 Engine cooling air exit flaps
153 Exhaust collector ring
154 Wright Cyclone R-3350-57A, 18-cylinder, two-row radial engine
155 Engine intake ducting
156 Forward bomb-bay doors
157 20 x 500lb (227kg) bombs, maximum bomb load 20,000lb (9,072kg)

M. Badrocke

BELOW The aeroplane commander's station. Mounted on the fuselage wall are, from left to right: oxygen distribution panel; radio filter (silver box); instrument landing system (RC-103) control box (the indicator is on the control panel); AN/ARC-8 liaison transmitter control box; moveable light (on spiral wire at top); intercom jack box (grey box below light); and SCR-274N command radio control box behind throttle levers. Note: there should be a Boeing 'hub cap' at the centre of the control wheel. However, these became prized souvenirs and few survived on planes even when in service, let alone when abandoned and awaiting restoration!

Also notice the blue cylinder mounted at the top of the pilot's opening window. This is a tube of silica gel connected to the window via a rubber hose and used to keep moisture out of the gap in double-paned windows.

The silica gel is contained in small glass tubes, allowing the colour to be observed. Blue is OK. If it turns lavender or pink it needs to be reactivated.

Other windows with such tubes are: pilot's and co-pilot's side windows; engineer's escape hatch; navigator's window; bombardier's sighting window; and all five windows in the tail gunner's section. Finally, the radio compass loop is also protected in this way. *(Dale Thompson)*

ABOVE The forward sighting station in *It's Hawg Wild*. The sight is mounted on a moveable arm called a pantograph that allows it to be swung out for use or stowed during the bombing run. The rectangular black box below the gunsight holds the nose gunner's switches (see also page 101). Note the electrical motor on the canopy-framing forward of the gunsight. This is a post-Second World War modification, being the motor for windshield wipers fitted to the panels immediately in front of the A/C and co-pilot.

When not on the bomb run the bombardier is expected to operate the forward sighting station that allows him to control either or both of the forward turrets (see also page 101).

Aeroplane commander (A/C) and co-pilot stations

The A/C sits on the left with the co-pilot on the right. Both have a full set of flying controls but with the flight engineer taking over much of the engine management function they have little in the way of other instruments. This leaves both their instrument panels somewhat simple when compared to other multi-engined planes of the period.

RIGHT Extract from the B-29 Pilot's Handbook detailing the instruments on the A/C's control panel. *(USAF)*

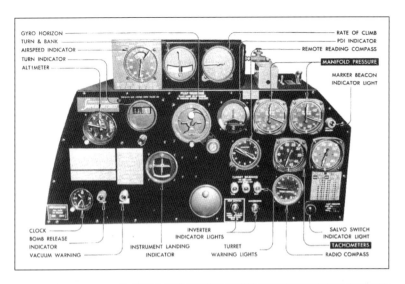

CENTRE The co-pilot's station. On the fuselage wall is the co-pilot's oxygen distribution panel and radio filter box (smaller silver box) next to the intercom jack box. All crew positions have an oxygen distribution panel and an intercom jack box, but only the A/C and co-pilot have the radio filter box.

The oxygen supply dials at the top consist of a blinker that indicates oxygen is flowing by yellow shutters flicking open and shut (they are open in the photo) and a pressure gauge. Below this is the demand regulator. Demand regulators only furnish oxygen when you inhale. No oxygen comes out when you exhale. The switch at the bottom of the regulator can be set to **ON** or **OFF**. When **ON** it automatically dilutes the oxygen with air depending on the cabin pressure – above 30,000ft it delivers pure oxygen. This is termed 'auto-mix' and saves oxygen. When **OFF** it delivers 100% oxygen at all altitudes. The large flexible hose leading from the regulator connects to the user's oxygen mask, while the thinner tube coming from behind the red emergency valve allows a portable bottle to be recharged. Not all crew positions have a recharging tube. The emergency valve bypasses the regulator should this become inoperable, but is very wasteful of oxygen as it is not regulated. Each panel is supplied by two separate supplies in case one should be damaged.

The intercom jack box has a volume control (the circular dial at the top) and five switch settings: **COMP**, to listen to the radio compass receiver; **LIAISON**, which connected the crewman to the long-range radio; **COMMAND**, which linked the crewman to the short-range 'plane to plane' radio; **INTER**, which allowed the crewman to talk to any other crew member without being transmitted outside the aircraft; and **CALL**, an override that let the user be heard on any other station regardless of the setting of their jack boxes.

The switch on the radio filter box can be set to **RANGE**, **VOICE** or **BOTH** and filters the radio input on the **LIAISON** and **COMMAND** jack box settings to voice, coded signals (eg radio compass) or both. *(Dale Thompson)*

BELOW Extract from the B-29 Pilot's Handbook detailing the instruments on the co-pilot's control panel. *(USAF)*

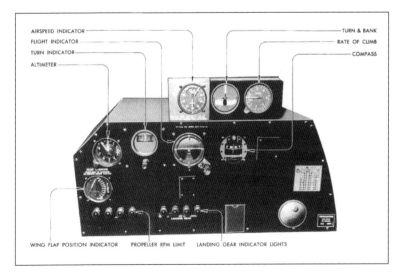

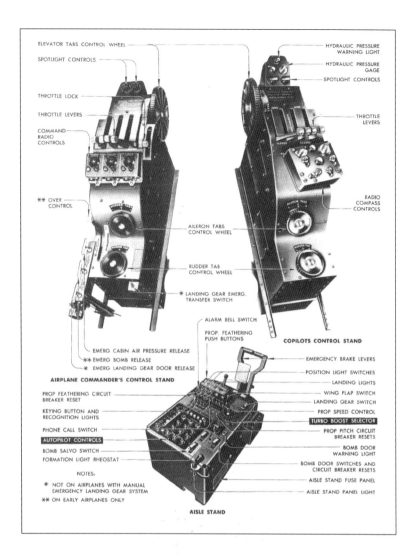

ELEVATOR TABS CONTROL WHEEL

SPOTLIGHT CONTROLS

THROTTLE LOCK

THROTTLE LEVERS

COMMAND RADIO CONTROLS

** OVER CONTROL

HYDRAULIC PRESSURE WARNING LIGHT

HYDRAULIC PRESSURE GAGE

SPOTLIGHT CONTROLS

THROTTLE LEVERS

RADIO COMPASS CONTROLS

AILERON TABS CONTROL WHEEL

RUDDER TAB CONTROL WHEEL

* LANDING GEAR EMERG. TRANSFER SWITCH

ALARM BELL SWITCH

PROP. FEATHERING PUSH BUTTONS

COPILOTS CONTROL STAND

EMERG CABIN AIR PRESSURE RELEASE
** EMERG BOMB RELEASE
* EMERG LANDING GEAR DOOR RELEASE

AIRPLANE COMMANDER'S CONTROL STAND

PROP FEATHERING CIRCUIT BREAKER RESET

KEYING BUTTON AND RECOGNITION LIGHTS

PHONE CALL SWITCH

AUTOPILOT CONTROLS

BOMB SALVO SWITCH

FORMATION LIGHT RHEOSTAT

NOTES:

* NOT ON AIRPLANES WITH MANUAL EMERGENCY LANDING GEAR SYSTEM
** ON EARLY AIRPLANES ONLY

EMERGENCY BRAKE LEVERS
POSITION LIGHT SWITCHES
LANDING LIGHTS
WING FLAP SWITCH
LANDING GEAR SWITCH
PROP SPEED CONTROL
TURBO BOOST SELECTOR
PROP PITCH CIRCUIT BREAKER RESETS
BOMB DOOR WARNING LIGHT
BOMB DOOR SWITCHES AND CIRCUIT BREAKER RESETS
AISLE STAND FUSE PANEL
AISLE STAND PANEL LIGHT

AISLE STAND

LEFT Extract from the B-29 Pilot's Handbook detailing the instruments on the A/C's and co-pilot's control stands (located between them and their respective outer fuselage walls as well as the central aisle stand. *(USAF)*

Flight engineer's station

The flight engineer is primarily responsible for managing the engines and, by varying the cowl flaps, manifold pressures, fuel mixture and fuel distribution, extracting the maximum possible range from the plane.

To complicate his task, the fuel management system fitted to the B-29s changed radically during their production run. Early planes have a fuel transfer system while later planes have a manifold system.

The manifold system allows the flight

BELOW A general view of the flight engineer's station on a B-29 fitted with the fuel transfer system. The large and complex instrument panel and stand is why the two pilots enjoy such an uncluttered view! The window is jettisonable, although this can only be carried out when the aircraft is on the ground as the No 3 engine's propeller is just outside and presents a formidable obstacle if still running! *(Dale Thompson)*

BELOW The central aisle stand. The silver ball to the rear is the vertical flight gyro (pitch and roll) for the autopilot. This mirrors the gyro in the Norden bombsight sighthead, but since this is removable this gyro forms the permanent part of the autopilot system. The red handle with the black end to the right is the hydraulic auxiliary hand pump, while the two red handles partially visible at the top are the emergency brake metering valves. *(Dale Thompson)*

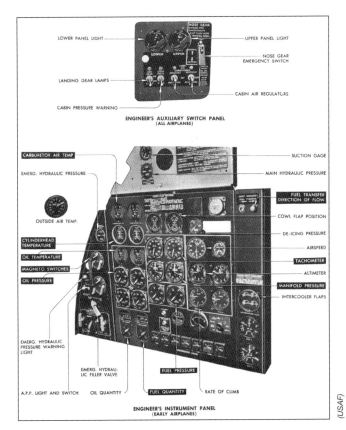

ENGINEER'S AUXILIARY SWITCH PANEL
(ALL AIRPLANES)

LOWER PANEL LIGHT — UPPER PANEL LIGHT

NOSE GEAR
EMERGENCY SWITCH

LANDING GEAR LAMPS

CABIN AIR REGULATORS

CABIN PRESSURE WARNING

CARBURETOR AIR TEMP — SUCTION GAGE

EMERG. HYDRAULIC PRESSURE — MAIN HYDRAULIC PRESSURE

OUTSIDE AIR TEMP.

FUEL TRANSFER
DIRECTION OF FLOW

COWL FLAP POSITION

CYLINDERHEAD
TEMPERATURE — DE-ICING PRESSURE

OIL TEMPERATURE — AIRSPEED

MAGNETO SWITCHES — TACHOMETER

OIL PRESSURE — ALTIMETER

MANIFOLD PRESSURE

INTERCOOLER FLAPS

EMERG. HYDRAULIC
PRESSURE WARNING
LIGHT

EMERG. HYDRAU-
LIC FILLER VALVE — FUEL PRESSURE

A.P.P. LIGHT AND SWITCH — OIL QUANTITY — FUEL QUANTITY — RATE OF CLIMB

ENGINEER'S INSTRUMENT PANEL
(EARLY AIRPLANES)

(USAF)

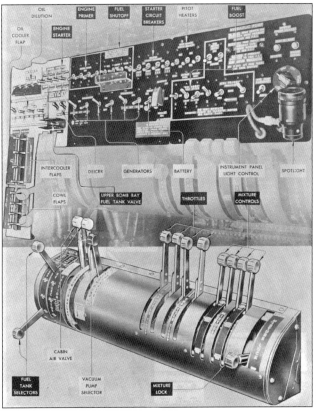

OIL
DILUTION — ENGINE PRIMER — FUEL SHUTOFF — STARTER CIRCUIT BREAKERS — PILOT HEATERS — FUEL BOOST

OIL COOLER FLAP — ENGINE STARTER

INTERCOOLER FLAPS — DEICER — GENERATORS — BATTERY — INSTRUMENT PANEL LIGHT CONTROL — SPOTLIGHT

COWL FLAPS — UPPER BOMB BAY FUEL TANK VALVE — THROTTLES — MIXTURE CONTROLS

CABIN AIR VALVE

FUEL TANK SELECTORS — VACUUM PUMP SELECTOR — MIXTURE LOCK

(USAF)

engineer to direct fuel in any or all tanks, via a single manifold fuel line and a number of electric pumps and shut-off valves, to feed any engine. In the fuel transfer system each engine is fed directly from its own tank and can only be supplied from that tank. The flight engineer can, however, transfer fuel from tank to tank provided it crosses the aircraft centre line (ie fuel from the left wing can be moved to the right wing or vice versa, but fuel cannot

ABOVE AND LEFT
Extracts from the B-29 Pilot's Handbook detailing the instruments on the flight engineer's panel (left) and switch stand for aircraft with the fuel transfer system.

LEFT AND FOLLOWING PAGE TOP The flight engineer's panel in *Enola Gay* and an extract from the B-29 Pilot's Handbook showing the revisions necessary with the manifold system.
(Scott Willey and USAF)

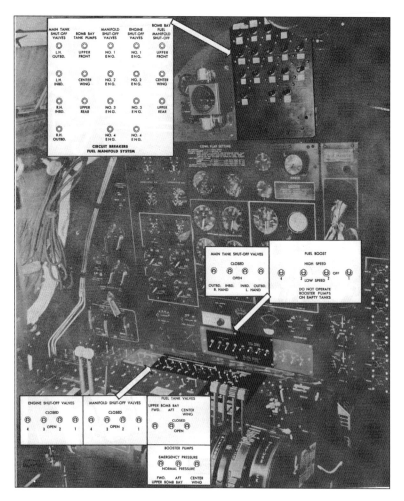

be directly transferred between the tanks in the same wing).

Navigator's station

The navigator sits facing forward behind the A/C, hemmed in by the tub containing the ammunition for the upper forward turret. Behind him is the LORAN receiver that allows accurate fixes up to 1,400 miles from the transmitters. Also available is the AN/APQ-13 radar that can take fixes on distant islands, a drift meter to assess the wind affecting the flight and a radio compass. Each B-29 also has an astro compass and sextant to take star or sun sights should the weather allow.

Radio operator's station

The radio operator occupies a position facing the right-hand wall behind the flight engineer. The standard liaison radio is the AN/ART-13 'Collins' HF transmitter coupled with a BC-348 HF receiver and CU25/ART-13 antenna tuner for the 200–600kHz range. The Liaison radio uses a 72ft wire from the top of the fin to the fuselage beside the astrodome. Some aircraft have a 250ft wire trailing antenna wound on an RL-42B motor-driven reel in the right-hand side of the forward bomb bay. The wire exits the

BELOW The navigator's station. Although T Sq 54 has an upper forward turret, there is no tub inside the fuselage, otherwise this view would have been impossible. Visible are the navigator's table, map case (semicircular tube fixed to the fuselage wall), radio compass dial and control box – under the map case and navigator's instrument panel (beneath the large black box facing the navigator) – containing an altimeter, compass, airspeed indicator and clock. The

large black box above the navigator's instrument panel is the computer for the nose sighting station. Missing from the view is the repeater scope for the AN/APQ-13 radar. This should be hanging from the shelf above the computer. The rounded box below and slightly aft of the window is the navigator's handset – part of the CFC gunnery system. To calculate the ballistic correction the computer needs various inputs. Many of these are derived from the sights but two – true airspeed and density altitude – are calculated using inputs made by the navigator at this panel. The navigator enters barometric pressure (left dial), indicated airspeed (middle dial) and outside air temperature (right dial). These are used to compute true airspeed from the indicated airspeed, while density altitude is computed from the barometric pressure and temperature. The outputs are used by all five CFC computers. True airspeed is also needed by the bombardier as he solves the bombing problem. Note the small green A-4 portable oxygen cylinder. *(Dale Thompson)*

RIGHT Looking rearward at the navigator's cabinet. The AN/APN-4 LORAN indicator occupies the space near the fuselage behind the navigator's handset. Above and to the left of the LORAN indicator is the hydraulic fluid supply tank. *(Dale Thompson)*

RIGHT Looking at station 218, the pressure bulkhead that forms the back of the forward pressurised compartment. The opening to the communication tunnel is top centre with the astrodome and attendant astro-compass just visible at its top front. The rectangular ducts running along each side of the tunnel are for cabin heating. The large hatch with the window below the tunnel leads to the forward bomb bay. To the right of these, on the shelves, is the AM-26/AIC-2 intercom amplifier (silver box) and below this the three carbon pile voltage regulators for the three generators on engines 1 and 2. Note also the release handle for the emergency life raft above the heating duct to the right of the tunnel. The release handle for the second dingy is hidden behind the mass of cable identification tags on the opposite side of the tunnel. Missing from this photo is the drift meter that should occupy a site between the regulators and the hatch. *(Dale Thompson)*

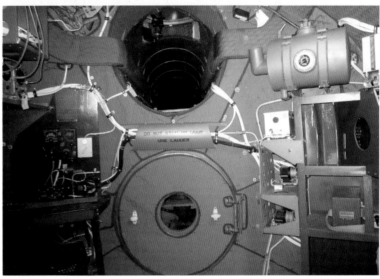

LEFT The Type B-3 drift meter in *Enola Gay*. The drift meter is gyro stabilised and located between the navigator's cabinet and the hatch giving entry to the forward bomb bay. It sights through a small Perspex blister just behind the lower forward gun turret that allows the navigator to view items on the ground and, by rotating the optics so they track along the graticule, determine how much the plane is 'crabbing' into any wind and hence assess the drift. Early planes had a Type B-5 drift recorder. Behind and to the right of the drift meter are the two MG-149 inverters (one primary and one reserve) that converted the 26V DC to 115V AC at 400Hz for those systems that needed AC. *(Scott Willey)*

LEFT A Type B-5 drift recorder as fitted to view through the fuselage side under the navigator's window. Planes with these can be identified by having a streamlined sighting blister on the outside under the window. *(USAF)*

LEFT AND CENTRE A general view of the radio operator's station. The various components are identified in the USAAF photo (centre) apart from the AN/ART-13 'Collins' transmitter. This is the large black item to the left of the photo under the CU-25/ART-13 antenna tuner. Underneath the 'Collins' in the green box with the holes in it are the three carbon pile voltage regulators for the generators on engines 3 and 4. The black box under the desk to the right of the radio operator's seat is the AN/APN-4 LORAN receiver. The green box to the extreme left is the back of the flight engineer's panel, while the green cylinder between it and the CU-25/ART-13 is the emergency hydraulic accumulator. Note also the yellow A-6 portable oxygen cylinder. *(Dale Thompson)*

plane through a retractable fairlead operated by a handle at the radio operator's table. A counter indicates how much cable is out and an amber light warns the radio operator if the landing gear is extended while the trailing antenna is out.

The standard command radio is the SCR-522 four-channel VHF. Although the controls for this are present in the radio operator's station, the radio itself is located under the floorboards just forward of the left scanner in the gunner's compartment. Late in the Second World War the SCR-522 began to be replaced by the more capable AN/ARC-3 eight-channel VHF set.

The radio operator is also responsible for the plane's intercom system. Each crew position has a jack box where microphone and headphones can be plugged in, allowing crew members to talk to each other and selected crewmen (like the pilot) to talk over the various radios.

The system is controlled by an AM-26/AIC-2 amplifier located on the navigator's side to the rear of the forward pressurised compartment.

LEFT The back of the flight engineer's panel showing the 12 tubes that bring fuel pressure and manifold pressure to the dials on the front. Also of note are the two brown shields (one partially hidden by the large green box containing the radio compass relay shield), which surround the exits through the fuselage for the aerials. *(Dale Thompson)*

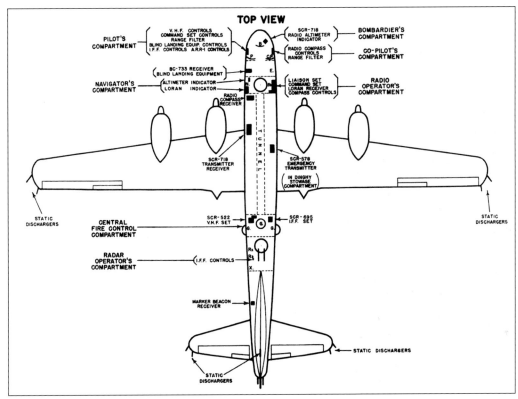

TOP VIEW

ABOVE AND LEFT
Photos and diagram from a report commissioned by the USAAF in 1945 into the 'Operational Suitability of the Radio Equipment in the B-29 Airplanes', showing the locations and use of the various antennas and radio equipment. *(Mike Hanz)*

BELOW The two oval black ports (one just visible at top of photo by the navigator's astrodome) present on *Enola Gay* are 'feed through insulators' an early means of allowing the antennas to penetrate the fuselage, but by mid-1945 were no longer used. Their employment made antenna repairs more time consuming, and the need to solder the wire coming through each of them to a taut antenna wire actually weakened the antenna, so a design change was made to use the short insulated connectors as

shown. The small wire hole in the black oval insulators was simply filled with a sealer. In later planes they were replaced with aluminium patches. The other ends of the HF antennas are fastened to spring-loaded tension units. The one on the horizontal stabilizer is shown below. These tension

units allowed the antenna wires to adjust to temperatures from -60 to +140°F (-51 to +60°C) without breaking.
(Mike Hanz)

ABOVE The pneumatic pump and accumulator for the bomb-bay doors in *Miss America '62*. Both bomb bays had a similar set-up and they were cross connected so should one set fail, the other could operate both doors. *(Eric Nelson)*

Bomb-bay compartment

The bomb-bay compartment contains the forward bomb bay, wing centre section and rear bomb bay. Besides the communication tunnel running along the top of the bay, a catwalk circumvents it with ladders providing access to the top of the wing centre section. Access to the bomb bay is only possible when the plane is unpressurised and is gained through airtight doors in the pressure bulkheads at stations 218 and 646.

The two bomb bays are similar although the rear bomb bay also contains gearboxes for the emergency operation of the landing gear and wing flaps.

On early planes the bomb-bay doors were opened and closed by electrically driven actuating screws at each end of each bomb-bay door. In later aircraft this was replaced by a pneumatic system whereby electric compressors charged accumulators with air at 1,200–1,500psi. Each bomb bay has its own pneumatic system with one pneumatic ram fixed to the forward end of each bomb-bay door, being capable of opening or closing the doors in under a second. To assist with the opening and to help keep the doors in the open position, pneumatically operated bomb-bay doors have air deflectors on the inside of the rear ends.

LEFT Looking rearward in the forward bomb bay. The large box section is the wing centre section, while the large tube at the top is the communication tunnel. The front face of the wing centre section is made up of two removable wing spar webs that give access to the fuel cells inside. Note the yellow Type G-1 oxygen cylinders around the radar antenna. The two boxes on the roof either side of the tunnel above the wing centre section contain the emergency life rafts. The box on the left (the right-hand side of the plane) is larger, as this box also contains the SCR-578 'Gibson Girl' emergency radio. The forward bomb-bay doors and the bomb racks are not fitted in this photo. *(Dale Thompson)*

LEFT The interior of *Doc*'s wing centre section exposed after the wing spar web has been removed. Four fuel cells will occupy this space, two in each cavity with a removable wing rib between them. *(Steve Jantz)*

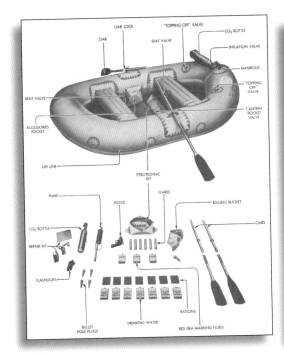

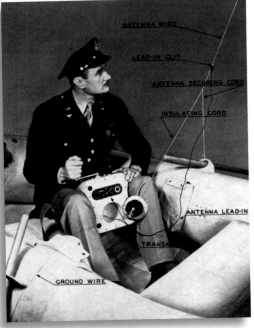

The wing centre section separates the two bomb bays. In the very earliest B-29s this was simply a structural part of the wing, but the space was quickly adapted to carry additional fuel cells. B-29s have four fuel cells whereas B-29As have three with a consequential reduction in fuel capacity. Above the wing centre section and located one either side of the communication tunnel are two externally accessible compartments for emergency life rafts. The compartments each hold either an A-3 four-man life raft or an E-2 six-man life raft with accessories. The space under the wing centre section contains six of the eighteen Type G-1 oxygen bottles and the motor for the AN/APQ-13 radar. The APQ-13 antenna projects below the fuselage covered by a streamlined fairing.

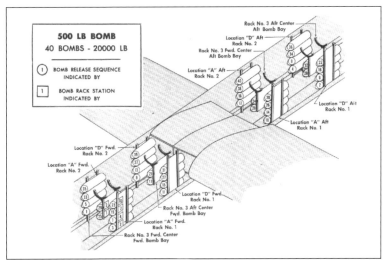

ABOVE AND BELOW Bomb loading and release sequence diagram for 500lb, 1,000lb and 2,000lb bombs. (USAF)

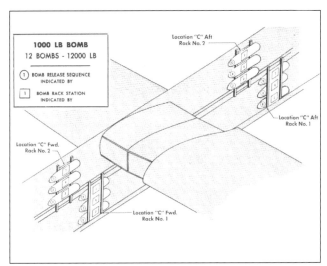

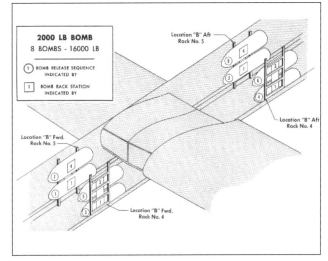

RIGHT The AN/APQ-13 radar scanner ready to be fitted to T Sq 54. The antenna is upside down so the silver dish would project below the fuselage, leaving just the motor and connections to fit between the fuselage lower skin and the wing centre section. *(Dale Thompson)*

LEFT A close-up of a left side 500lb/1,000lb bomb rack. The two small silver cylinders mounted on the front face are A-2 bomb arming controls. The silver hooks attached to the inside edges of the rack are shackle suspension hooks, while a single shackle is clipped to one pair. Visible between the shackle and rack is an A-2 bomb-release mechanism. Note how the levers on the shackle connect to the arms on the release mechanism so that when the electrical impulse from the bombardier's station trips the release mechanism it trips the levers on the shackle. An A-2 bomb arming control and an A-2 bomb-release mechanism is required for every position where a bomb will be loaded. *(Dale Thompson)*

Three types of bomb racks can be accommodated in both bomb bays: 500lb centre racks, left and right 1,000lb racks and left and right 4,000lb racks. Two left and two right 1,000lb racks as well as two centre racks can be installed in each bomb bay for carrying 500lb bombs. When carrying 1,000lb bombs, one left and one right 1,000lb rack can be positioned in each bomb bay while one left and one right 4,000lb rack are located in each bomb bay for 1,600lb, 2,000lb or 4,000lb devices (see images on page 97). Each bomb rack is interchangeable on the same side with others of its own size. The centre racks are completely interchangeable.

The side racks have rails that mate with fittings on the catwalk and with bomb rack support beams above. The entire weight of the rack and its bomb load is carried by the lower fittings on the catwalk. To ensure this, the holes in the upper rail are slotted vertically so this beam only stabilises the rack. The centre racks have semicircular yokes that attach to support beams on either side of the tunnel.

At each point where bombs can be attached the racks have pairs of spring-loaded

LEFT The streamlined fairing containing the AN/APQ-13 radar antenna on *It's Hawg Wild*. The very earliest B-29s had a retractable antenna but this was quickly replaced by the fixed streamlined version as seen here. *(Author)*

shackle suspension hooks bolted to the sides. Depending on the type and number of bombs to be carried, different pairs of hooks will be used. Each used location also needs a type A-2 bomb-release mechanism. The A-2 bomb-release mechanism is an electrically operated mechanical device designed to cause the bomb shackle to release and arm the bomb. The types of shackle vary depending upon the weight of bomb to be carried: the B-7 for bombs of 500lb and 1,000lb; the B-10 for bombs up to 1,600lb and the D-6 for 2,000lb or 4,000lb bombs.

The communication tunnel

To allow crew members to move between the forward and rear pressurised compartments while the B-29 is pressurised, a communication tunnel runs above the two bomb bays. Some 34in in diameter and 33ft long the tunnel has no controls within it although the navigator's astrodome is located near the forward end. Here the navigator can use the astro compass or sextant to take sun or star fixes.

Rear pressurised compartment

This extends between the pressure bulkheads at stations 646 and 834 and accommodates the left, right and CFC gunners as well as the radar navigator. In later planes the electronic countermeasures operator also occupies this area. In addition to the crew positions the compartment houses the computers for the top, left, right and tail sighting stations as well as the tub for the upper rear turret.

Gunners' stations

The two side gunners sit facing rearwards adjacent to large sighting blisters set into the fuselage sides. The top gunner resides between them on a raised chair universally termed the

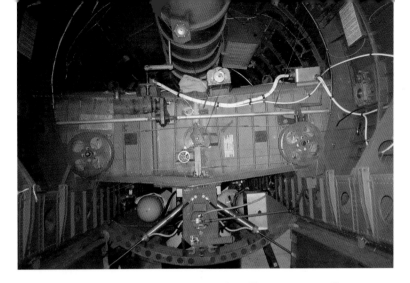

ABOVE Looking forward in the rear bomb bay. The two pneumatic rams indicate that this plane has the pneumatic bomb-bay door opening system. The earlier electrical system had square actuating arms. The silver rectangular box behind the right-hand ram is the cover for the rear bomb-bay pneumatic compressor and accumulator. Of note are the various items attached to the wing centre section; the silver horizontal bar is the wing flap actuating torque bar. The electric motor to drive this is the green cylinder attached to it via the dark rectangular gearbox. The emergency hand crank is inserted into this motor. To the right of the hand crank, the rounded silver box is the elevator servo for the C-1 autopilot. The large green wheels are the aileron drums that redirect the inputs from the control column to the ailerons in the wings. Finally, the silver-grey item on the right fuselage wall is the right main gear emergency gearbox. To raise the gear the hand crank is inserted in the upper socket, 774 clockwise turns being needed. To lower the gear the crank is inserted into the lower socket, with 387 clockwise turns being necessary. A similar gearbox is just visible on the left-hand wall for the left main gear. *(Dale Thompson)*

RIGHT The right gunner's station. The sight is a pedestal type, while to the gunner's front (towards the rear of the plane) is the gunner's oxygen distribution panel and heated flying suit outlet, plus (and probably importantly for some) his ashtray (the small grey-green circle below the oxygen panel). Note the control wires for the elevator and rudder running along the fuselage just above the sighting blister. *(Dale Thompson)*

RIGHT The top gunner's station. The backrest of the 'barber's chair' is at the bottom, while the ring sight, mounted in the top sighting blister, is clearly visible. The ring sight has all the same components and works in the same way as the pedestal sights at the other sighting stations, although it is arranged to fit into the lower rim of the sighting blister. *(Dale Thompson)*

'barber's chair', allowing his head to project into the top sighting blister.

Defensive armament

Most B-29s carried five defensive gun turrets: upper forward, lower forward, upper rear, lower rear and tail. In early planes each turret held two 0.5in Browning M2 machine guns with the tail turret carrying an additional 20mm cannon. All turrets apart from the tail turret are fitted with contour followers, which operate fire interrupters to prevent the guns from hitting their own plane. In later aircraft the 20mm cannon was deleted and the upper forward turret's armament doubled to four 0.5in guns. This doubling was to give greater protection against frontal attack (although this was more imagined than real since trials showed the four-gun turret had a

greater dispersal resulting in only the same number of hits being recorded with the four-gun turret as with the earlier two-gun version). The 20mm cannon was deleted since the ballistic properties of the 20mm shells were so different to those of the 0.5in bullets that it was ineffective. Each 0.5in gun was fed from large cans able to hold 1,000 rounds. The 20mm cannon had 118 rounds.

The B-29's defensive armament is called the remote control turret system (RCT) or the central fire control system (CFC) because the gunner does not occupy the turret. Instead he inhabits a sighting station and controls it remotely. This system allows the gunners to remain in the heated and pressurised crew compartment, keeping them more comfortable and therefore more able to perform their duties well.

The RCT was designed by General Electric and uses one sighting station for each turret although, by using a set of switching boxes, and with the exception of the tail gunner who can only control his own turret, the gunner at each station can take control of other turrets should he have a better sighting angle or should that turret's gunner be incapacitated in any way.

The sight at each sighting station is electrically connected to the turret (or turrets) that it can control. The sight has two attitude sensors called selsyns, one for horizontal and one for vertical. These are essentially rheostats that provide a variable current depending on the position of the sight. The turret has a similar set of selsyns. When a sight is

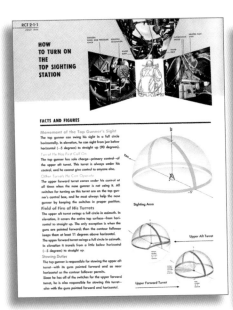

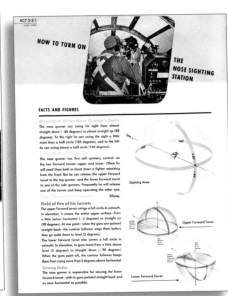

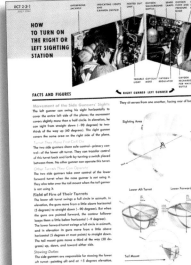

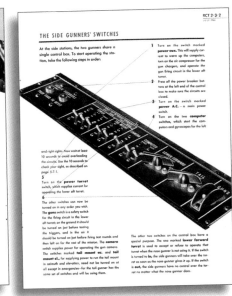

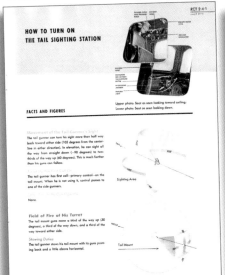

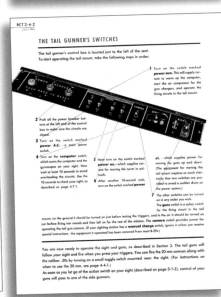

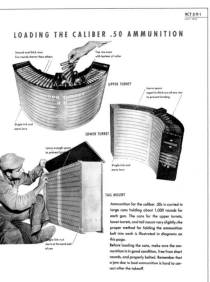

(USAF)

ABOVE Loading the 0.5in ammunition. *(USAF)*

LEFT Schematic showing both the primary and secondary control paths for the gunners. If a gunner has primary control of a turret he can take charge of it at any time by switches at his control box. Gunners with secondary control can only take command of it if the turret is released by that turret's primary gunner. *(USAF)*

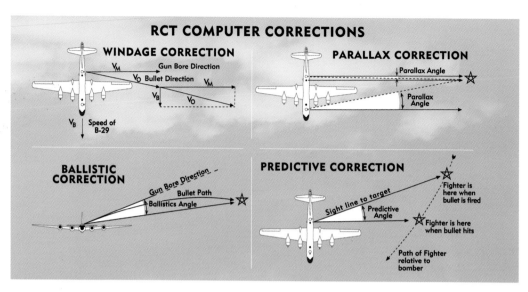

RIGHT Details of the corrections calculated by the computers. *(mark@chidgeyacres.demon.co.uk)*

RCT COMPUTER CORRECTIONS

WINDAGE CORRECTION

Gun Bore Direction
V_M
V_O Bullet Direction V_M
V_B V_O
V_B Speed of B-29

PARALLAX CORRECTION

Parallax Angle
Parallax Angle

BALLISTIC CORRECTION

Gun Bore Direction
Bullet Path
Ballistics Angle

PREDICTIVE CORRECTION

Sight line to target
Predictive Angle
Fighter is here when bullet is fired
Fighter is here when bullet hits
Path of Fighter relative to bomber

connected to a turret, the voltage generated by the sight's selsyns is combined with the voltage engendered by the turret's. If the turret and sight are not aligned a voltage difference exists. This is passed to a servo amplifier that increases it sufficiently to drive the turret servomotors that rotate the turret until it aligns with the sight and the voltage difference drops to zero. This happens almost instantaneously,

allowing the turret to accurately follow the direction of the sight.

Getting the turret to follow the movement of the sight is, however, only half the problem. It also has to compensate for the relative movement of the target so that the bullets will hit. Also, in the B-29 the gunner does not occupy the turret so his line of sight is different to the turret he is controlling. The CFC system handles this by using a mechanical computer between the sight's selsyns and the turret's selsyns that alters the voltages, so that instead of the turret exactly following the movement of the sight it varies such that when the gunner sights directly on to his target the bore axes of the guns in the turret (or turrets) that he is controlling change to a position that will cause the bullets to hit the target.

To do this, the computer calculates three corrections: parallax (to compensate for the distance along the longitudinal axis of the aeroplane between the turret and the sight); ballistics (to compensate for windage and gravity); and lead or prediction angle (to compensate for the distance the target will have travelled from the time the bullet leaves the gun until it strikes the target). The three corrections are combined by the computer and appear as a single total amendment that fools the turret selsyns into thinking they are aligned with the sight's selsyns when in fact they are not. Two kinds of computers are used in the system: type 2CH1C1 single-parallax computers with the nose and tail sighting stations, while type 2CH1D1 double-parallax computers are used

BELOW A diagram showing the locations of the various components for the CFC system. *(Dale Thompson)*

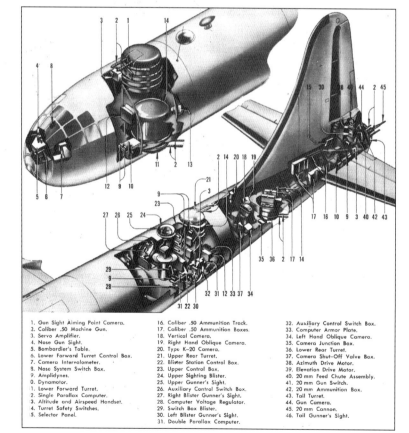

1. Gun Sight Aiming Point Camera.
2. Caliber .50 Machine Gun.
3. Servo Amplifier.
4. Nose Gun Sight.
5. Bombardier's Table.
6. Lower Forward Turret Control Box.
7. Camera Intervalometer.
8. Nose System Switch Box.
9. Amplidynes.
10. Dynamotor.
11. Lower Forward Turret.
12. Single Parallax Computer.
13. Altitude and Airspeed Handset.
14. Turret Safety Switches.
15. Selector Panel.
16. Caliber .50 Ammunition Track.
17. Caliber .50 Ammunition Boxes.
18. Vertical Camera.
19. Right Hand Oblique Camera.
20. Type K-20 Camera.
21. Upper Rear Turret.
22. Blister Station Control Box.
23. Upper Control Box.
24. Upper Sighting Blister.
25. Upper Gunner's Sight.
26. Auxiliary Control Switch Box.
27. Right Blister Gunner's Sight.
28. Computer Voltage Regulator.
29. Switch Box Blister.
30. Left Blister Gunner's Sight.
31. Double Parallax Computer.
32. Auxiliary Control Switch Box.
33. Computer Armor Plate.
34. Left Hand Oblique Camera.
35. Camera Junction Box.
36. Lower Rear Turret.
37. Camera Shut-Off Valve Box.
38. Azimuth Drive Motor.
39. Elevation Drive Motor.
40. 20 mm Feed Chute Assembly.
41. 20 mm Gun Switch.
42. 20 mm Ammunition Box.
43. Tail Turret.
44. Gun Camera.
45. 20 mm Cannon.
46. Tail Gunner's Sight.

RIGHT The computer for the nose sighting station in its rack between the navigator and A/C. The computer is in the large black box behind the green upright at top left. Just visible on the bottom rack under the computer box is an amplidyne (another is hidden behind it) for the lower forward turret, while the black box on the central shelf is the BC-733 blind landing receiver. To the left of this is one of the turbo amplifiers used in the control circuit for the turbosuperchargers. On the top shelf is a BC-645 IFF transponder, part of the SCR-515 IFF set. The SCR-515 was an early design IFF and was almost universally replaced in service with the SCR-595 and SRC-695 IFFs. Indeed, there is some debate as to whether the SCR-515 ever made it into operational service as it was overtaken by the more capable SCR-595s. *(Dale Thompson)*

with the others. The reason for the difference is that the upper and both blister sighting stations can control two or more turrets whose parallax base length is sufficiently dissimilar to require two different parallax corrections. Although the nose station can control either or both of the forward turrets, their azimuth parallax base lengths are approximately the same.

The inputs required by the computers to make these corrections are: azimuth and elevation gun position (obtained from selsyns in the sights); true airspeed and air density

(calculated from indicated airspeed, pressure and outside air temperature as entered by the navigator at the navigator's hand set); range to target (from a range potentiometer in the sight, which varied as the gunner adjusted his range hand wheel to keep the reticule spanning the target); and relative velocity of the target (from two gyros on the sight).

The computer for the nose sighting station is located between the navigator and aeroplane commander just behind the latter's armour, while the computers for the top, left, right and tail sighting stations are all located under the floor in the gunner's compartment.

BELOW LEFT AND BELOW The rear wall of the gunner's compartment showing the bank of amplidynes. Amplidynes are special-purpose motor generators that supply precisely controlled DC current to large-sized DC motors. The CFC system uses ten amplidynes, one for the azimuth motor and one for the elevation motor of each turret. *(Dale Thompson)*

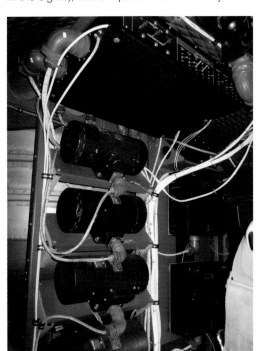

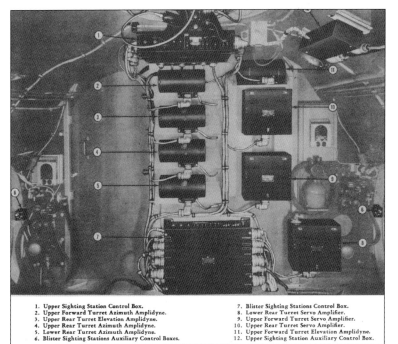

1. Upper Sighting Station Control Box.	7. Blister Sighting Stations Control Box.
2. Upper Forward Turret Azimuth Amplidyne.	8. Lower Rear Turret Servo Amplifier.
3. Upper Rear Turret Elevation Amplidyne.	9. Upper Forward Turret Servo Amplifier.
4. Upper Rear Turret Azimuth Amplidyne.	10. Upper Rear Turret Servo Amplifier.
5. Lower Rear Turret Azimuth Amplidyne.	11. Upper Forward Turret Elevation Amplidyne.
6. Blister Sighting Stations Auxiliary Control Boxes.	12. Upper Sighting Station Auxiliary Control Box.

ABOVE The inside of a CFC mechanical computer showing the complexity of these devices. Although designed by General Electric, the computers were manufactured by IBM. *(Dale Thompson)*

PEDESTAL SIGHT

Front — Rear

RING-MOUNTED SIGHT

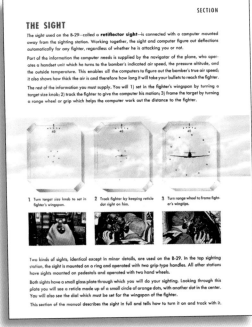

THE SIGHT

The sight used on the B-29—called a **retiflector sight**—is connected with a computer mounted away from the sighting station. Working together, the sight and computer figure out deflections automatically for any fighter, regardless of whether he is attacking you or not.

Part of the information the computer needs is supplied by the navigator of the plane, who operates a handset unit which he turns to the bomber's indicated air speed, the pressure altitude, and the outside temperature. This enables all the computers to figure out the bomber's true air speed; it also shows how thick the air is and therefore how long it will take your bullets to reach the fighter.

The rest of the information you must supply. You will 1) set in the fighter's wingspan by turning a target size knob; 2) track the fighter to give the computer his motion; 3) frame the target by turning a range wheel or grip which helps the computer work out the distance to the fighter.

1 Turn target size knob to set in fighter's wingspan.

2 Track fighter by keeping reticle dot right on him.

3 Turn range wheel to frame fighter's wingtips.

Two kinds of sights, identical except in minor details, are used on the B-29. In the top sighting station, the sight is mounted on a ring and operated with two grip-type handles. All other stations have sights mounted on pedestals and operated with two hand wheels.

Both sights have a small glass plate through which you will do your sighting. Looking through this plate you will see a reticle made up of a small circle of orange dots, with another dot in the center. You will also see the dial which must be set for the wingspan of the fighter.

This section of the manual describes the sight in full and tells how to turn it on and track with it.

ABOVE AND LEFT The B-29 pedestal and ring sights from 'Air Forces Manual No. 27 Gunnery in the B-29': A gyroscope; B rheostat; C filament switch; D computer standby switch; E warning light; F azimuth stowing pin; G azimuth friction adjustment; H elevation stowing pin; I elevation friction adjustment; K sky filters; L hand wheel; L-1 handle; M action switch; N target size knob; O range wheel; O-1 range grip, P trigger; Q push-to-talk button. *(USAF)*

TRAINING ON THE RCT

Apart from the normal flexible gunnery training of shooting at clay pigeons or targets from moving carriages, RCT training used some innovative methods:

B-24s

With B-29s in short supply a number of war-weary B-24s were fitted with the GE RCT system and used to train B-29 gunners.

Pinballs

Perhaps the most bizarre training aid was the RP-63 'Pinball'. Here, gunners used special frangible bullets to live fire at real attacking fighters. The front of the RP-63s was heavily armoured with special aluminium alloy and armoured glass cockpit. Sensors under the alloy registered hits and these were displayed on a sensor in the cockpit. A red light in the spinner flashed for every hit, giving rise to the 'Pinball' nickname. B-17 and B-24 gunners began training in this way during early 1945 and B-29 gunners used them after the Second World War. All Pinballs were retired by 1948, however.

Ground training

Post-Second World War B-29 gunners were trained on CFC turrets and sighting systems set up on ground ranges and used to fire against remotely controlled OQ-19 drones. The drones launched from a circular runway then travelled to the range where they would fly the gauntlet of a line of perhaps six turrets and sighting stations. Despite using live ammunition hits were rare, with gunners being of the opinion that the sights were deliberately set off to save drones!

RIGHT B-29 turrets mounted on ground frames at Stiffkey on the north Norfolk coast for use by RAF B-29 crews and USAF crews while on temporary detached duties. The firing positions have all vanished but the circular runway for the OQ-19 target drones still exists and goes by the local name of the 'Whirlygigg'. (Mike Davies)

ABOVE TB-24D Connells Special, a war-weary 90th BG bomber converted to a B-29 gunnery trainer. (Ray Pritchard)

BELOW Mothballed 'Pinballs' line up at Pyote AAF in 1946. (Pete McLaughlin)

Radar navigator and ECM operator's stations

Behind the gunners, the radar navigator sits facing the left-hand wall of the fuselage in a windowless section, allowing him an easier view of the flickering images on the AN/APQ-13 radarscope. The AN/APQ-13 was a US development of the British H2S and almost all operational B-29s had this fitted as standard. The antenna could rotate through 360° as well as be tilted from -10 to +65° (a negative angle denotes the antenna being pointed upward from the horizontal).

The addition of electronic countermeasures (ECM) equipment, often called Raven, came near

BELOW LEFT Diagram from the ROIF showing the components of the AN APQ-13 radar. The item marked 'computer' mounted on the wall in the centre determines range and altitude accurately for the solution of the bombing problem. Below the computer box are the radar operator's instruments, the four dials being (from left to right) airspeed, flux gate compass, altitude and a voltmeter. *(USAF)*

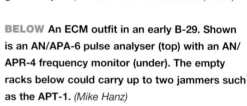

BELOW An ECM outfit in an early B-29. Shown is an AN/APA-6 pulse analyser (top) with an AN/APR-4 frequency monitor (under). The empty racks below could carry up to two jammers such as the APT-1. *(Mike Hanz)*

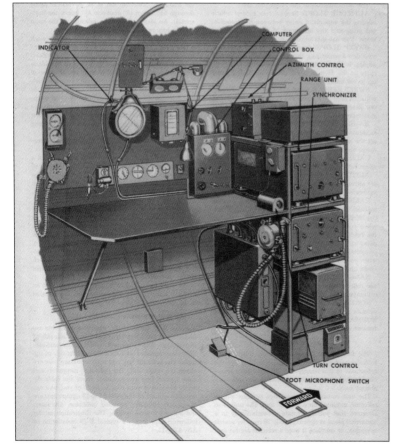

LEFT The underside of the rear fuselage of *It's Hawg Wild* showing the standard, factory-fitted, skin reinforcement to accommodate a teardrop Plexiglas windshield used to protect delicate antenna such as the AT-49 from being buffeted by the slipstream. Other factory-fitted ports and reinforcements can be seen on the fuselage that allowed different antennas to be mounted with relative ease. Also visible is the vertical camera port (top centre with the two rectangular doors). Apart from being the viewing port for the strike camera this opening was also the port through which the radio operator threw the bundles of Rope (chaff). *(Author)*

RIGHT It was not only the rear fuselage that had factory-fitted ports for ECM. Both sides of the forward fuselage also had these, although they were normally unused. However, on this B-29 the port under the 'S' of Sister is fitted with a CW-46/APR-4 fairing protecting an AT-49/APR-4 antenna. The AT-49 was a wide-range general-purpose ECM antenna capable of covering the 300–3,000MHz frequency range. Also note the large antenna above the 't' of 'Sister'. This is the AN-148-B receiver antenna for the SCR-729. The small 'wings' between the two antennas were made of Bakelite and improved the aerodynamics. The SR-729 is often quoted as an IFF set, but in the CBI was more commonly used to trigger the AN/CPN-7 blind approach beacon system (BABS) as part of the SCS-51 instrument landing system. The AN-147 transmit aerial is the small rod antenna just forward of the bomb symbols. The SCR-729 used a twin antenna set-up with the other arrangement being located on the opposite side of the nose. This made the incoming triggered response directional. This antenna set-up was much less common in the Marianas, apart from on planes set up for 'super dumbo' rescue work. The SCR-729 could start a response from standard IFF, the reaction from which when set to the emergency code was very wide, leaving an unmistakable signature on the scope, hopefully allowing for a timely rescue. *(USAF)*

the end of the Second World War and when carried the station comprised a standard rack, capable of holding three ECM units, crammed in between the fuselage wall and the tub for the upper rear turret. The ECM operator, when included, was equally squeezed in, having no seatbelt or even seat, sitting on the lid of the chemical toilet or the floor to operate the equipment. There was no standard Raven fit and different units were swapped in and out on a regular basis as required by the particular mission. Any three of the following units could be put in place, although frequently equipment availability meant only a single APT-1 was installed, pre-tuned to barrage jam the 185–205Mc range:

Type	Function	Antenna
T-28/APT-1 'Dina II'	90–210Mc spot and barrage jammer	Either AT-36/APT, AT-37/APT or AT-38/APT stub masts
T-26/APT-2 'Carpet I'	450–710Mc barrage jammer	Either AS-33/APT-2 or AS-69/APT
T-27/APT-3 'Mandrel'	85–150Mc transmitter	Either AT-37/APT or AT-38/APT
AN/ART-9 'Jackal'	37–43Mc FM transmitter	Three-wire fan, cone or screen antenna
T-9/APQ-2 'Rug'	200–550Mc spot jammer	Uses rectifier PP-4/APQ-2 and antenna AS-65/APQ-2A
T-39/APQ-9 'Carpet III'	475–585Mc barrage jammer	Uses rectifier PP-51/APQ-9 and antenna AS-33/APT-2 or AS-69/APT
R-34/APR-2	400–1,000Mc auto-search receiver	HF cone antenna AS-26/APR-2 or LF stub antenna AS-25/APR-2 and filter F-3/APR-2
R-44/ARR-5	27–143Mc search receiver	Uses rectifier PP-32/AR and antenna AT-38/APT
AN/APR-4	230–3,000Mc radar intercept receiver	Uses tuning unit TN-16/APR-4 and AN-38/APT
AN/ARQ-8 'Dinamate'	25–105Mc receiver/spot jamming transmitter	Either AS-33/ART or AS-97/ART

Essentially, ECM gear has three different functions: barrage jamming, spot jamming and receivers.

Barrage jammers were used to jam a wide range of frequencies. However, due to power limitations, when jamming a wide range it was only possible to emit a small amount of power against each frequency. Consequently it was common for formations of planes to each carry a barrage jammer tuned to the same frequency range so their combined output could swamp the enemy radars. Spot jammers were used to jam a discrete frequency, allowing all the unit's power to be directed against this. Individual aircraft could spot jam but the ECM operator needed to tune the emission to the enemy frequency. Receivers, as the name implies, detected enemy radar emissions and identified their frequencies, letting the ECM operators to tune their spot jammers to counter them.

The prototypes and very earliest B-29s had no radar or countermeasures suite fitted and this compartment contained crew rest bunks. Oddly, many references mention these bunks and imply they were a standard feature on most, if not all,

B-29s. This is not so and bunks played no part in the B-29 story. Indeed, they were only fitted to the 100 B-29s produced in blocks B29-1-BW and B29-5-BW and it is likely that no bunks ever made it in a B-29 to a combat theatre. The Renton-built B-29A and the Martin and Bell B-29s were never configured to have them.

Tail section (unpressurised)

Extending between the pressure bulkhead at station 834 to the diminutive tail gunner's compartment at station 1110, the tail section of the B-29 holds no crew positions. It does, however, contain the rear access door, lower rear gun turret, type G-1, 34-amp per hour, 24-volt battery, auxiliary power unit (APU), camera ports and the hatch allowing access to the upper surfaces.

The APU, universally called the 'Putt-Putt', is a 2-cylinder, 4-stroke, 7hp engine that drives a Type P-2 200-amp, 28.5-volt DC generator. The fuel – AN-F-28 (100 to 130 octane) – is gravity fed from a 4-gallon tank mounted to the rear. The tail gunner has the job of starting this up before engine start. Two makes can be installed, an Andover Model V-32 or a Lawrence Model 20A.

ABOVE The Andover-type 'Putt-Putt' mounted on the left-hand side of the rear fuselage. The Type P-2 200-amp generator is positioned horizontally at the far left of the 'Putt-Putt'. The generator is connected directly to the drive shaft and runs at engine speed. The black pipe with yellow writing brings air to cool the generator. *(Dale Thompson)*

BELOW RIGHT Looking rearward in *Enola Gay* from beside the 'Putt-Putt'. Note the blanked-off lower rear turret space but also the Type G-1 low-pressure oxygen bottles in their correct location. Notice also the rudder autopilot servo to the left of the top oxygen bottle. The servo is covered by its insulating blanket. *(Scott Willey)*

BELOW Looking forward from under the horizontal stabiliser torque box. The silver item at the top left is the C-1 autopilot servo for the elevators. Some planes have a similar servo for the rudder, mounted opposite this on the right-hand side of the fuselage. In others, such as here, the rudder servo is located in the fin. *(Dale Thompson)*

ABOVE Looking rearward from a position beside the 'Putt-Putt' in *Miss America '62*. The fuel tank of the 'Putt-Putt' is on the right (left side of plane). The cylindrical structure in the centre foreground is the lower rear turret surrounded by its two curved ammunition boxes. In the distance, between the two upright rectangular boxes for the tail turret ammunition is the circular hatch leading to the tail gunner's compartment. Missing are the numerous control cables that should line the walls and several oxygen bottles that should also occupy spaces around the walls near the tail gunner's compartment. *(Eric Nelson)*

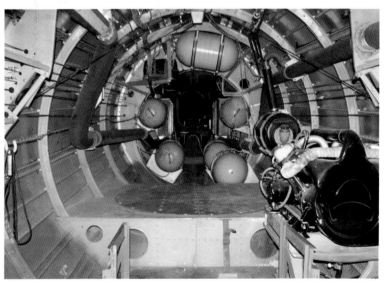

LEFT A view towards the tail gunner's compartment from under the horizontal stabiliser's torque box. The brick-red rectangular boxes contain the ammunition for the tail guns, with the tailskid mechanism on the floor between them. The tailskid is extended, leaving a gap in the lower fuselage. When the plane is in flight it will be retracted and the mechanism will close the gap. The small silver box on the left is the BC-1033 marker-beacon receiver, the 6ft antenna for which is located on the lower left side of the fuselage beside the tailskid and connected to it by a coaxial transmission line. *(Dale Thompson)*

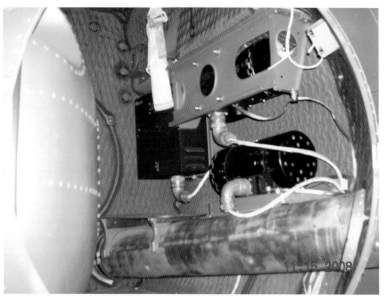

LEFT The left side of the tail gunner's compartment from just outside the entry hatch. The brown tube carries the ammunition tracks from the box in the rear unpressurised section through the compartment to the tail turret. A similar tube is on the other side. The two black cylinders (one covered by a shield) are the amplidynes for the tail turret, while the rectangular black box is the servo amplifier for the tail turret. *(Dale Thompson)*

LEFT The diminutive tail gunner's compartment, taken through the open tail gunner's window. The brown box to the left is the tail gunner's seat in its folded-up position. Below this can just be seen the entry hatch. To enter the compartment the gunner crawls through the hatch before turning round and closing it. He then slides and folds the seat down. The oxygen distribution panel is on the side under the window along with the intercom jack box and an A-4 oxygen bottle. The black box beside this is the tail gunner's control box. The wooden plate under the control box acts as a cover for the tail turret's dynamotor as well as a footrest for the gunner. Finally, the tail sight is just visible to the right, mounted on the armoured back plate to the tail turret. *(Dale Thompson)*

Tail gunner's compartment

This extends between a pressure bulkhead at station 1110 to the armour plate at station 1144. To enter or leave the compartment the tail gunner's seat has to be folded up, allowing access to the airtight door near the compartment's floor. The tail gunner cannot enter or leave his station when the plane is pressurised. Behind the armour plate is the tail turret although this is inaccessible during flight.

Wing

The long slender wing is a defining feature of the B-29. Designated the Boeing 117 aerofoil it has a very high aspect ratio of 11.5. Although this significantly reduces drag, and hence increases speed and range, it gives the B-29 a very high wing loading: 69lb per sq ft at 120,000lb gross weight with flaps retracted. The effect of this on take-off and landing is moderated by the use of large Fowler flaps that extend from the rear of the wing when lowered, enlarging the wing's surface area by 19% and giving the B-29 the same landing speed as the B-17, despite the latter having a wing loading of only 42lb per sq ft at its gross weight of 60,000lb. The flaps run out on five tracks, propelled by two activating screws driven by a torque bar running along the rear of the rear spar and powered by an electric motor mounted on the wing centre section.

The basic wing structure is a long 'box beam' running continuously through the fuselage and formed by the upper and lower skin, the front and rear spars and the centre ribs. The leading and trailing edge structures are attached to this 'box beam' to form the completed wing. To provide sufficient strength in such a slender wing Boeing increased the thickness in the interspar area. Not only did this add to the strength in the primary structure it also provided greater volume for fuel. The ribs are numbered in inches left or right of the fuselage centre line culminating at station 850 at each wingtip. At 850in per wing, this gives the B-29 a span of 141ft 8in, some 5in longer than the advertised span of 141ft 2.76in. The difference is a result of the 4.5° dihedral, meaning the span is slightly shorter than the physical length of the wings.

LEFT The extended wing flap on *Enola Gay*. To extend, the flaps travel down five wing-flap tracks, driven by two screw actuators, powered from a single torque bar that runs along the rear side of the rear spar. Note the landing light just outboard of the flap. A similar unit is also present on the other wing and they are swung down to point forward when in use. *(Author)*

The spars are built-up 'I-beams' constructed from a solid web to which T-shaped extrusions (called chords on the B-29) are riveted to the top and bottom so the end view resembles the letter I. The height of these spars is not uniform along their length as they conform to the tapering and contouring of the wing.

The front spar of the inboard wing is assembled from four sections to meet the sweepback of the wing design. Two centre spar sections are spliced at station 0 and run to station 202. Two additional spar sections extend from stations 202 to 510 where the inboard wing ends. The rear spar of the inboard wing is built from only two sections, as it does not need to follow the sweepback. The two sections are spliced at station 2 and run all the way to station 510.

The ribs joining the two spars and forming the aerofoil are of the solid-web type where a typical interspar rib consists of the metal web, stiffeners (upright bracings across the web) and the skin supports – chord members – to which the skin of the wing is attached. The chords are channels, Zs, Us, angles or other extrusions. Five of the inboard ribs are vapour proof because of their location near the fuel tanks where leakage of fuel vapours would create a fire hazard.

**RIGHT Diagram
showing the elevator
cable runs.** *(USAF)*

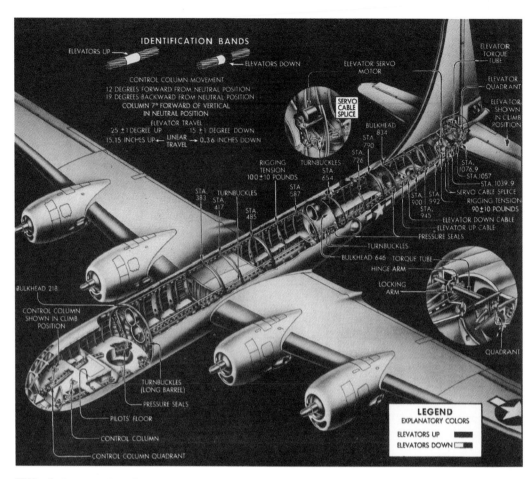

IDENTIFICATION BANDS

ELEVATORS UP

ELEVATORS DOWN

CONTROL COLUMN MOVEMENT
12 DEGREES FORWARD FROM NEUTRAL POSITION
19 DEGREES BACKWARD FROM NEUTRAL POSITION
COLUMN 7° FORWARD OF VERTICAL
IN NEUTRAL POSITION
ELEVATOR TRAVEL
25 ±1 DEGREE UP   15 ±1 DEGREE DOWN
15.15 INCHES UP → LINEAR → 0.36 INCHES DOWN
TRAVEL

ELEVATOR SERVO MOTOR

SERVO CABLE SPLICE

BULKHEAD 834

STA. 790

STA. 726

RIGGING TENSION
100±10 POUNDS

TURNBUCKLES STA. 654

ELEVATOR TORQUE TUBE

ELEVATOR QUADRANT

ELEVATOR SHOWN IN CLIMB POSITION

STA. 1076.9
STA.1057
STA. 1039.9
SERVO CABLE SPLICE
RIGGING TENSION
90±10 POUNDS
ELEVATOR DOWN CABLE
ELEVATOR UP CABLE
PRESSURE SEALS

STA. 383   TURNBUCKLES STA. 417   STA. 485   STA. 587

STA. 900 | STA. 992
STA. 945

TURNBUCKLES

BULKHEAD 646   TORQUE TUBE
HINGE ARM

LOCKING ARM

BULKHEAD 218

CONTROL COLUMN SHOWN IN CLIMB POSITION

QUADRANT

TURNBUCKLES (LONG BARREL)

PRESSURE SEALS

PILOTS' FLOOR

CONTROL COLUMN

CONTROL COLUMN QUADRANT

LEGEND
EXPLANATORY COLORS
ELEVATORS UP
ELEVATORS DOWN

Flight controls

The ailerons, rudder and elevators are operated from conventional pilot's control columns and pedals by means of cables. In spite of their large area no power servo boost is necessary for their operation because of their aerodynamic and static balance characteristics. The cables for the elevators and ailerons are duplicated from the pilot and co-pilot, extending rearwards along opposite sides of the fuselage. Hence, if one set is severed by enemy fire, control is still possible from the other. Also, should both be severed, control may still be possible via the autopilot if this is still operable. No duplicate control is provided for the rudder, as loss of this is not critical.

Cables are flexible preformed carbon steel. Being preformed means they will not unravel if cut. Cable sizes are designated by the diameter, the number of strands and the number of wires per strand. Hence a cable size of $\frac{1}{8}$ – 7 x 19 indicates a diameter of $\frac{1}{8}$in with 7 strands of 19 wires each. Flight cables in B-29s are either $\frac{3}{32}$ – 7 x 19, $\frac{1}{8}$ – 7 x 19 or $\frac{3}{16}$ – 7 x 19. Different-diameter cables are used in different sections of the cable runs and more than one are often present in each run.

Oil system

Engine lubrication is of the dry sump type in which oil is returned from the engine sumps to an external tank by scavenger pumps. All moving parts of the engine are pressure lubricated or have oil sprayed from jets or fed from pressure-supplied wells. Each engine has its own self-sealing oil tank that is filled with 85 gallons of SAE 60, grade 1120, specification AN-VV-O-446, unless the ground temperature is less than 4° when grade 1100 is used. The oil tanks are unique to each engine and are not interchangeable.

Scavenged oil is pumped to the oil temperature regulator. This automatically maintains the oil temperature at approximately 70° by adjusting the airflow through an oil cooler using a movable flap on the underside of each nacelle fairing. An electric actuating motor is thermostatically controlled to open or close the flap to a maximum of 4.5in on the inboard engines and 4.3in on the outboard. Having passed through the oil temperature regulator the oil is returned to the oil tank.

Fuel system

In all B-29s the normal fuel supply is carried in 22 individual self-sealing cells between the interspar ribs of the inboard wings, 11 in each wing. For purposes of identification the cells are numbered 1 through 11 from inboard out with the letter L or R added to indicate left or right wing. The outer seven cells in each wing are interconnected to form the tanks for engines 1 and 4. The inner four cells in each wing are similarly interconnected to form the tanks for engines 2 and 3. Each outboard tank holds 1,320 gallons. Each inboard tank holds 1,415 gallons.

Four additional cells are installed in the wing centre section that can hold 1,333 gallons. Finally, each bomb bay is capable of holding two 640-gallon auxiliary tanks but at the expense of bombs.

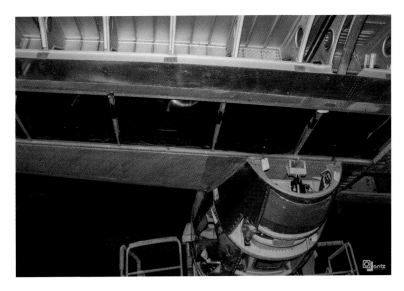

ABOVE The underside of *Doc*'s left wing. The rear fairing of the No 1 engine nacelle is removed, showing the oil cooler flap actuating motor (black cylinder) connected to the oil cooler flap. Note the flap actuating screw and flap track at wing station 374. The activating torque bar is just visible in the cut-out by the track. Also observe the black fuel cells fitted in the interspar area between the ribs. From right to left (inboard to outboard) these are cells 7L, 8L, 9L, 10L and (just visible) 11L, five of the seven interconnected cells that make up the tank assembly for engine 1. *(Steve Jantz)*

BELOW The B-29 oil system. *(USAF)*

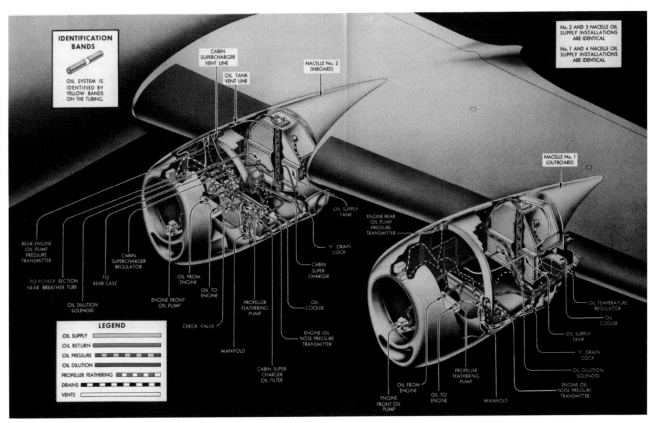

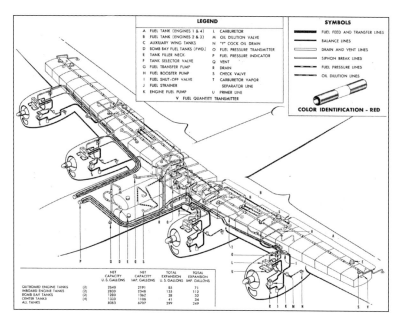

		NET CAPACITY U.S. GALLONS	NET CAPACITY IMP. GALLONS	TOTAL EXPANSION U.S. GALLONS	TOTAL EXPANSION IMP. GALLONS
OUTBOARD ENGINE TANKS	(2)	2640	2191	85	71
INBOARD ENGINE TANKS	(2)	2830	2348	135	112
BOMB BAY TANKS	(2)	1280	1062	38	32
CENTER TANKS	(4)	1333	1106	41	34
ALL TANKS		8083	6707	299	249

ABOVE The fuel transfer system. *(USAF)*

BELOW The operation of the fuel transfer system. *(USAF)*

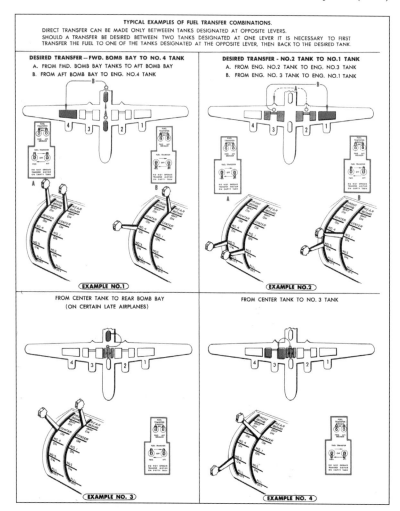

Two types of fuel arrangements are used in B-29s. Early planes have a fuel transfer system while later planes have a manifold system. In the fuel transfer system each engine is fed directly from its own tank and can only be supplied from that tank. Two reversible pumps controlled by circuit breakers, directional control switches and tank selector valves on the flight engineer's control stand can transfer fuel from tank to tank. Fuel can only be passed to tanks on the opposite side of the plane. If it is required to transfer fuel between two tanks in the same wing it must first be relocated to a tank in the opposite wing (or to the wing centre section tanks). In the manifold system the fuel in any or all tanks can be directed, via a single manifold fuel line and a number of electric pumps and shut-off valves, to feed any engine. As with the transfer system, switches at the flight engineer's control stand manage the pumps and shut-off valves.

Automatic pilot

The Honeywell C-1 autopilot comprises nine units: three servo units that drive the control surfaces by means of cables clamped to the regular control cables; a directional stabiliser located in the bombsight assembly that uses a gyro to act as a directional reference; a vertical flight gyro found immediately behind the central aisle stand that directs the attitude of the plane in pitch and roll; the autopilot control panel; an amplifier that manages the operation of the servo units; a rotary inverter that converts the plane's DC into AC as required by the amplifier; and a junction box that provides terminals for interconnecting the various wires of the circuit.

Normally the A/C or co-pilot operates the autopilot. However, it is also connected to the Norden bombsight, allowing the bombardier to fly the plane via the bombsight when on the bombing run.

Landing gear

The B-29 has a tricycle-type landing gear consisting of a dual nose wheel, two dual main wheels and a tailskid. All units are fully retractable and enclosed in flight, with retraction and extension accomplished by electrically driven screw mechanisms.

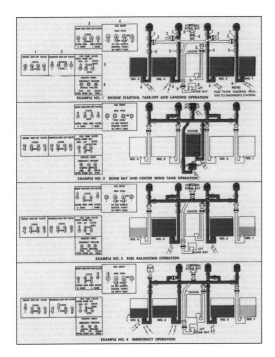

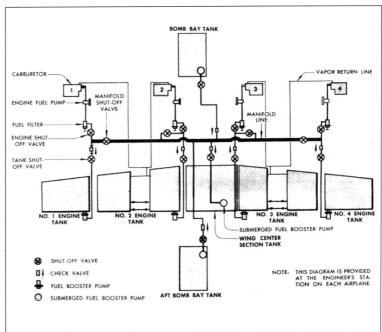

The nose gear has dual 36in ten-ply nylon cord tyres on smooth contour nose wheels. No brakes or steering are provided but the wheels are mounted on an axle connected to a knuckle forging set into a spindle at the base of an air–oil shock strut that allows the gear to swivel 68° either side of neutral. The shock strut is attached to the nose-gear well by a trunnion mounted in bronze bushings. When extended, V drag struts and a yoke hold the shock strut slanted forward so when the wheels contact the ground the force is taken along the axis of the strut. The nut tube of the retracting mechanism is connected to the apex of the drag struts' V and holds the yoke and drag strut joint inline. The nut tube is extended when the gear is down. During retraction the activation screw shortens the nut tube, pulling the yoke and drag struts up, retracting the gear. A safety switch prevents the gear from being retracted when the shock strut is compressed 2in or more from fully extended.

The axle is aft of the spindle giving the wheels 'trail' so they align to the direction of travel. However, to ensure they are neutral, and will therefore fit into the nose-gear well, a roller and cam self-centring mechanism will return them to neutral from within 15° either side once clear of the ground. The 'trail' also reduces the tendency of the wheels to shimmy, but to prevent one from starting, a shimmy dampener is fitted.

ABOVE **The manifold fuel system.** *(USAF)*

ABOVE LEFT **The operation of the manifold fuel system.** *(USAF)*

BELOW **The components of the autopilot.** *(USAF)*

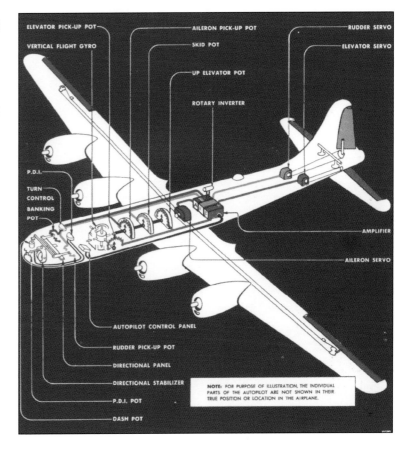

RIGHT The nose gear on *It's Hawg Wild*. The self-centring mechanism is the cylinder mounted to the front of the shock strut. The safety switch (small rectangular box) and its activating arm can be seen attached to the shock strut just above the top torsion link. Note how the rivets on the nose-gear door change from brazier head to flush, halfway along, when sufficiently far from the lower front turret and its potential for muzzle blast. *(Author)*

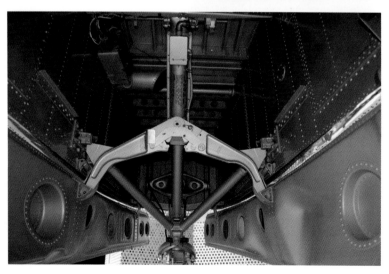

A door-operating spindle mounted on the aft side of the knuckle forging opens and closes the nose-gear doors mechanically as it interacts with an inverted-V brace attached to both doors.

Each main gear has dual 56in 16-ply nylon cord casings and puncture-proof inner tubes mounted on an air–oil shock strut connected by trunnions inserted in bronze bearings on brackets extending down from the rear spar. When the wheels are extended, the nut tube of the retraction mechanism holds the universal drag link and V drag struts in a straight line and these hold the shock strut slanted forward so the resultant force of the vertical landing load and the drag load is along its axis. The retraction mechanism, motor and upper ends of the drag struts are connected to the aft face of the front wing spar and extend below it. During retraction the activation screw lengthens the nut tube, pushing the universal drag link and drag struts up, retracting the gear. As with the nose gear a safety switch prevents the gear from being raised when the shock strut is compressed by more than 2in.

LEFT The right-hand side of the nose gear on *It's Hawg Wild*. The shimmy dampener is the smaller cylinder mounted next to the self-centring mechanism. It is connected to the nose-gear spindle by the lever arm that projects to the front. Below this is the towing lug. To the rear of the shock strut are the torsion links, while below these is the door-opening spindle that interacts with an inverted-V brace to open and close the nose-gear doors as the wheels extend or retract. *(Author)*

LEFT Looking forward in the nose-gear well of *It's Hawg Wild*. The actuation screw is contained within the cylinder extending from the roof to the yoke behind the nose gear. The screw is driven by an electric motor that should be present where the screw meets the roof but is missing here. The rectangular box near the top of the tube is the upper limit switch that stops the motor when the gear is retracted. A similar box that cuts out the motor when extending the gear is hidden behind the inverted-V brace. The inverted-V brace opens and closes the nose-gear doors, pushed by the door-operating spindle fixed to the rear of the shock strut. *(Author)*

RIGHT Without the cowl extension fitted *Doc*'s main gear is fully visible. The massive shock strut at the rear is connected to a universal drag link and drag struts. The retraction screw is the heavier cylinder with the two rectangular boxes mounted on it joining the drag assembly to the forward wing spar. The boxes are limit switches that stop the motor when the gear is fully extended or retracted. Note the red ground lock that prevents the gear being retracted inadvertently. *(Steve Jantz)*

The main wheels are interchangeable with those on later models of the B-17 and B-24. Each of the four main wheels has two brake mechanisms consisting of a brake drum and a brake assembly. The drums are bolted to each side of the cast magnesium alloy wheels. The inner brake assemblies are bolted to flanges on the axle, the outer brake assemblies are splined to the axle so they may be slipped off in order to remove the wheel. Each brake assembly has two expander tubes and a set of brake blocks over each expander tube. When the expander tubes are inflated by the hydraulic fluid they push the composition brake blocks against the cast-iron friction surface of the drum. When the fluid pressure is released, retractor springs push the blocks back on to the expander tube, releasing the blocks from the drum.

LEFT A rear view of *Doc*'s right main-gear shock strut. The wire running down the strut is the electrical connection to the safety switch mounted above the top torsion bar. *(Steve Jantz)*

RIGHT Looking forward at *Doc*'s main landing gear. The two dark cylinders leading to the top are the drag struts, while the silver I-section beam attached to them is the universal drag link. The retraction screw connects to the joint between the two and the forward wing spar where the electric drive motor can be seen connected into the gearbox. Early planes had a second electric motor mounted vertically below the retraction screw, which drove twin retraction screws via a Y gearbox to open and close the nacelle doors. *Doc* has the later mechanical doors that are opened and closed by the gear as it extends or retracts so does not have this second motor. The green tube coming in from the upper right is part of the torque tube/gearbox linkage for the manual emergency retraction system that leads to the gearboxes in the rear bomb bay. *(Steve Jantz)*

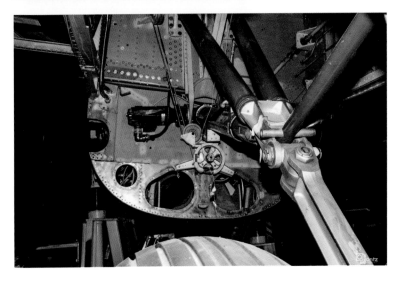

LEFT Looking forward in the main-gear well of *It's Hawg Wild*. The green and silver retraction screws denote this plane as having the electric nacelle doors. The electric drive motor should be hanging vertically below the apex of the V formed by the screws, but is missing in this museum plane. *(Author)*

The tailskid is provided to protect the lower rear turret during take-offs and landings. It is located at the bottom of the fuselage between stations 1039 and 1076. The contact shoe is made of hardened steel and is secured to a steel bracket by six bolts, allowing it to be replaced if worn down. The bracket is connected to a shock strut via a yoke. Two steel drag tubes are welded to the bracket and hinged in plain bronze bearings at their forward end to fittings at station 1039. A sheet metal fairing is secured to the tubes to fair the tailskid to the body contours when retracted. An electrically driven retracting screw connects to the top of the shock strut arranged so the nut tube shortens to retract the skid, swinging the shock strut forward and up between the legs of the yoke.

Hydraulic system

The hydraulic system only provides pressure to activate the expander tube-type brakes on the main landing gear. Hydraulic fluid is provided from a supply tank mounted above the navigator's cabinet and is gravity fed to the hydraulic panel where an electric pump boosts the pressure to 1,000psi then delivers it through a check valve to the accumulator. The floating-piston-type accumulator acts as a pressure reservoir and also absorbs hydraulic shocks. The accumulator requires 250cu in of fluid to provide the 1,000psi for operation. An auxiliary hand pump provides a pressure source in case the electric pump fails although, since the hand pump only delivers 1.5cu in per cycle,

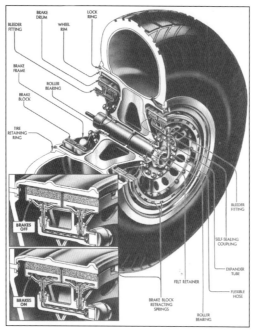

RIGHT A diagram of the wheel and brake assembly. All four main wheels are similar, with the central brake assembly remaining still as the wheel rotates around it. *(USAF)*

LEFT *Doc*'s tailskid showing the reinforced rub strip at the lower edge, the yoke and the shock strut. The jack is inserted in the tail jacking point at station 1039, designed just to stabilise the plane as it is rated for only 2,500lb. *(Steve Jantz)*

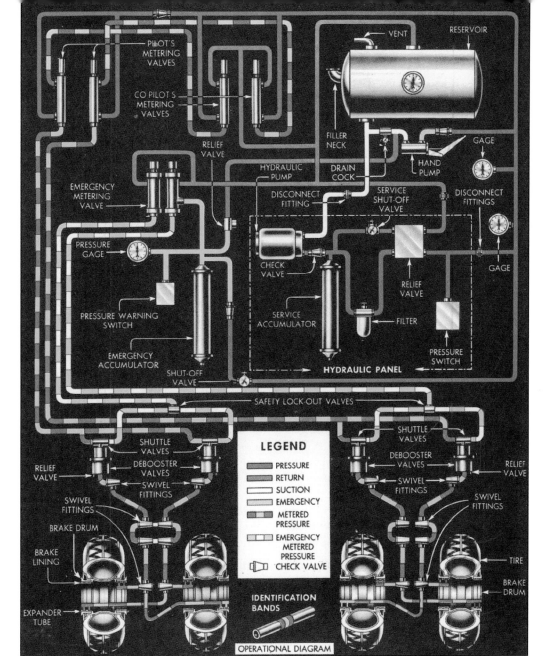

considerable time and effort is required to build the full pressure in the system.

Fluid flows from the accumulator to brake metering valves activated by the pilot's and co-pilot's rudder pedals. The metering valves supply pressures from 0 to 1,000psi, in proportion to applied pedal compression, to the debooster valves of its landing gear. The debooster valves reduce the pressure to a quarter of that supplied and passes this, via flexible couplings, to the brake expander tubes. Both main gears have two debooster valves with each supplying pressure to either the inner expander tube of one wheel or the outer expander tube of the other. In this way, should one valve fail each wheel still retains half of its braking system.

A parking brake, located at the pilot's station, locks the pilot's brake metering valves in a depressed position, sufficient to maintain a pressure of about 185psi in the brake expander tubes.

An emergency hydraulic arrangement duplicates most systems and ensures brake operation should the main structure fail or be damaged. The emergency accumulator receives its charge of fluid from the main system through a manual shut-off valve on the flight engineer's panel. Fluid from the emergency accumulator flows to two emergency metering valves operated by levers on the central aisle stand, and from these to the normal debooster valves and then to the regular wheel brakes.

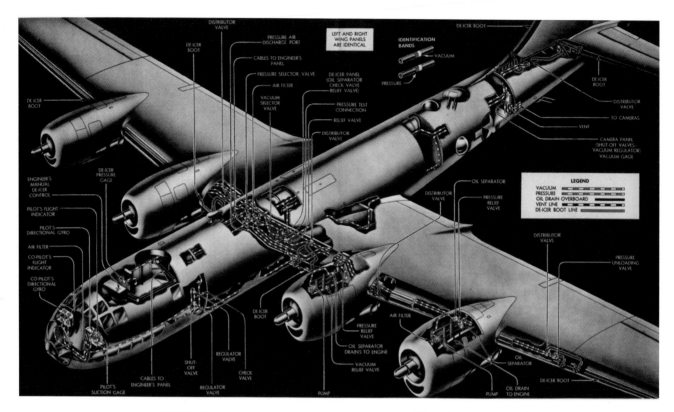

ABOVE The vacuum and de-icer system. (USAF)

De-icer equipment

BELOW The front of *It's Hawg Wild*'s right main gear showing the stainless steel tubes and swivel joints that take the hydraulic lines across the oleo strut. Note the hydraulic lines running down the shock strut and the flexible lines taking the hydraulic fluid to the inner brakes and into the axle for the outer brakes. Also of worth is the jacking point stud at the bottom centre of the axle. The red collar surrounding the shock strut is non-standard, being put on by the museum to avoid having to maintain the pressure in the oleo.
(Author)

BELOW RIGHT A diagram of the propeller de-icer slinger system. (USAF)

The B-29 is fitted with de-icer boots on the leading edges of the wings, horizontal stabiliser and fin. The de-icer boots are fully external in that the leading edges of the wing and tail surfaces have smooth, continuous contours and the de-icer boots fit over them, held in place by screws seated in a continuous hold-down strip along the edges.

The de-icer system provides both air under pressure to inflate the de-icer boots

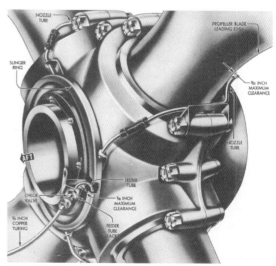

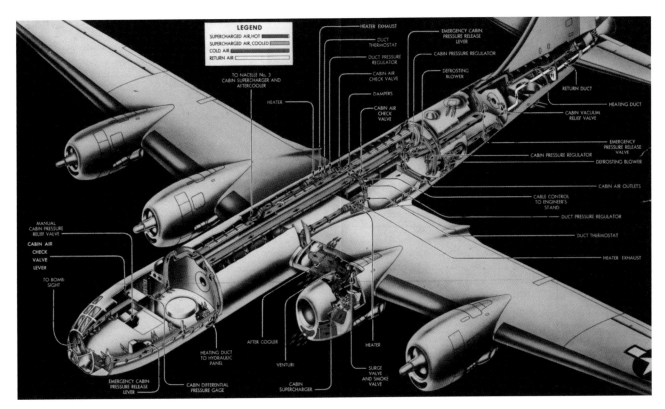

and vacuum to keep them deflated and in place when not in use. Four Type B-8 vacuum pumps are mounted, one each on the inboard accessory pad of each engine. Vacuum is obtained from either inboard pump while pressure is supplied from both outboard pumps and the inboard pump not selected to supply vacuum.

Each de-icer boot is composed of a number of cells: the de-icer boots between the fuselage and the inboard nacelle have nine cells, those between the nacelles have seven cells, while the boots outboard of the nacelles, and on the tail surfaces, have five cells. To operate effectively adjacent cells need to be inflated and deflated in sequence. Hence an electric motor-driven timing switch governs the operation of two solenoids such that one set of alternate cells inflate while the other deflates. The operation takes between 6 and 10 seconds to complete depending on the cell size, while the sequence repeats every 48 to 55 seconds.

Propeller de-icer is a slinger ring mounted to the rear of the propeller hub. The slinger ring is supplied with isopropyl alcohol AN-F-13 fluid from a 24-gallon-capacity tank located under the floor in the forward end of the aft pressurised compartment. Two pumps

pressurise the fluid to 20psi. The left-hand pump supplies fluid to the inboard propellers while the right-hand pump provides fluid to the outboard. Operation is via a switch and two rheostats on the flight engineer's panel. The switch starts the pumps and the rheostats regulate their speed, which varies volume of discharge from two to eight quarts per hour.

Cabin pressurisation and heating

The cabin pressurisation and heating system also performs the functions of ventilating and defrosting. On early planes pressurisation was supplied by two engine-driven superchargers mounted one on each inboard engine, and heating came from two Stewart-Warner petrol-fired heaters, one mounted each side of the fuselage above the wing centre section. On later planes pressurisation air came from the inboard turbosupercharger of each inboard engine with heating drawn from the inboard exhaust shrouds of the inboard engines.

When the plane is at high altitude the heat generated by compression is sufficient to heat the compartments, although at lower altitudes heating is augmented by circulating hot air,

ABOVE The cabin turbosupercharger system. *(USAF)*

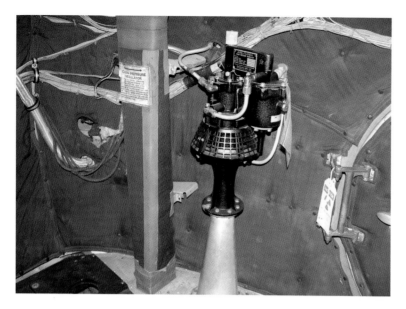

ABOVE The left-hand cabin pressure regulator in *Enola Gay*. A similar device is located on the right side of the compartment. *(Scott Willey)*

BELOW Schematic showing the locations of the regulator panels, oxygen bottles and which regulator would draw from which bottles. *(USAF)*

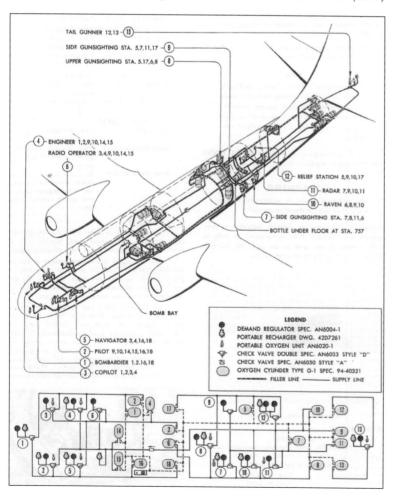

taken from the exhaust shroud, in the aftercooler around the tubes that supply cabin air.

Two cabin pressure regulators located on the floor either side of the communication tunnel entrance in the rear pressurised compartment maintain cabin pressure automatically so that below 8,000ft there is no pressurisation. Above this the internal pressure is maintained equivalent to 8,000ft (22.22in of mercury) until the differential between the inside and outside pressure reaches 13.34in Hg. This occurs at about 30,000ft. Above this the internal pressure will drop so as to sustain the 13.34in differential, resulting in the internal pressure dropping to 10,000ft equivalent when the plane is at 33,000ft and 12,500ft should the plane reach 40,000ft. Cabin air flows through the regulator and is vented to the aft bomb bay from the bottom of the regulators if the internal pressure is more than 13.34in Hg above the external pressure.

To limit air loss when pressurised, all seams, stringer laps and joggled structural connections in the pressurised compartments are sealed with zinc chromate impregnated tape or putty. Control cables passing through pressure bulkheads have seals of synthetic rubber.

Oxygen system

To provide breathing oxygen for the crew when the cabin pressure is less than that corresponding to an altitude of 10,000ft, each crew station has an oxygen regulator panel that supplies oxygen from the plane's main oxygen system of 18 interconnected Type G-1, low-pressure, shatterproof oxygen cylinders. The system is filled from one filler valve located on the outside of the left fuselage just forward of the wing root. When full (400–450psi) and with automix on, it provides more than 10 hours' supply for 11 men flying at 15,000ft. Each crew position is supplied from two separate distribution lines so the loss of a line or its associated cylinders still leaves each station with a reserve of oxygen.

In addition to the main oxygen system three types of rechargeable portable bottles can be found on B-29s: an A-4 cylinder is painted green and will last for 4 to 8 minutes between charges; D-2 or A-6 cylinders are painted yellow and will last for about 40 minutes.

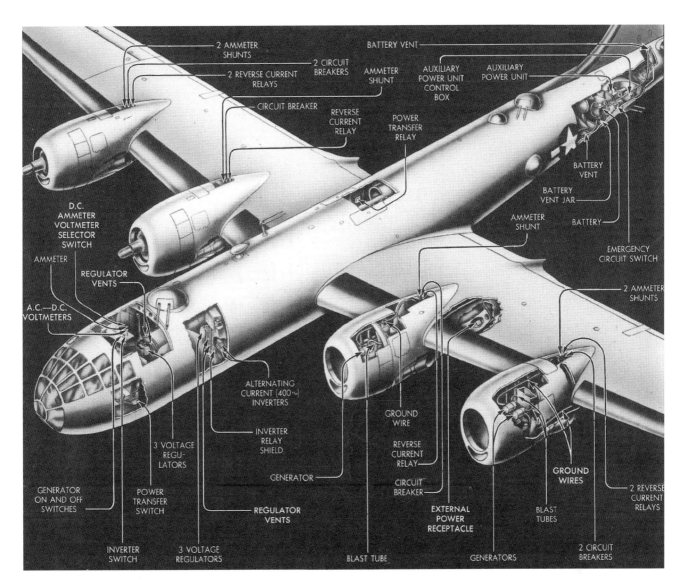

Labels on diagram:

2 AMMETER SHUNTS
2 CIRCUIT BREAKERS
2 REVERSE CURRENT RELAYS
AMMETER SHUNT
BATTERY VENT
AUXILIARY POWER UNIT CONTROL BOX
AUXILIARY POWER UNIT
CIRCUIT BREAKER
REVERSE CURRENT RELAY
POWER TRANSFER RELAY
BATTERY VENT
BATTERY VENT JAR
AMMETER SHUNT
BATTERY
EMERGENCY CIRCUIT SWITCH
2 AMMETER SHUNTS
D.C. AMMETER VOLTMETER SELECTOR SWITCH
AMMETER
REGULATOR VENTS
A.C.—D.C. VOLTMETERS
ALTERNATING CURRENT (400∿) INVERTERS
INVERTER RELAY SHIELD
GENERATOR
GROUND WIRE
REVERSE CURRENT RELAY
CIRCUIT BREAKER
GROUND WIRES
2 REVERSE CURRENT RELAYS
GENERATOR ON AND OFF SWITCHES
POWER TRANSFER SWITCH
3 VOLTAGE REGULATORS
REGULATOR VENTS
EXTERNAL POWER RECEPTACLE
BLAST TUBES
INVERTER SWITCH
3 VOLTAGE REGULATORS
BLAST TUBE
GENERATORS
2 CIRCUIT BREAKERS

ABOVE **Components of the electrical system.** *(USAF)*

Electrical system

A part from the brakes, all systems on the B-29 are electric. A 28-volt DC single wire, ground return system is used for most of the B-29 equipment. Six Type R-1, 300-amp, 30-volt engine-driven generators (two on each outboard and one on each inboard engine), supplemented by a Type G-1, 34-amp per hour, 24-volt battery for voltage stabilisation, supply the normal electrical power (very early planes had six Type P-2, 200-amp generators). An additional Type P-2, 200-amp generator is driven by the auxiliary power unit located in the rear unpressurised section to provide power to start engines and to supplement the main electrical supply during take-offs and landings. A carbon pile voltage regulator controls the field current

of each generator so that a constant voltage is maintained regardless of the load conditions. On early planes a selector switch and voltmeter on the engineer's instrument panel allowed voltage readings to be taken singly for any generator, and seven ammeters, one per generator, let load readings be taken for all generators at the same time. In later planes the seven ammeters were replaced by a single ammeter that operated with the selector switch along with the voltmeter, permitting load and voltage readings to be taken singly for any generator.

The auxiliary power unit (APU), universally called the 'Putt-Putt', is located in the unpressurised tail section. Its 200-amp Type P-2 generator is used to supply electrical power for starting the engines as well as for extra electrical power for the landing gear and

Item	Normal load (amps)	Peak battle load (amps)
Upper forward turret	132.5	275.5
Upper aft turret	132.5	275.5
Lower forward turret	84.0	84.0
Lower aft turret	84.0	84.0
Tail turret	252.0	420.0
Tail ammunition booster motors (2)	40.0	40.0
Flight clothing (for 10)	75.0	150.0
C-1 autopilot	6.0	6.0
Defroster blower motor (RH)	13.4	13.4
Defroster blower motor (LH)	25.0	25.0
Landing gear (2)	460.0	–
Nose gear	155.0	–
Wing flaps	200.0	–
Hydraulic pump	110.0	110.0
Landing lights	52.0	–
Liaison radio	38.0	38.0
Interphone	1.7	1.7
Radar	100.0	100.0
Radio compass and marker beacon	3.3	3.3
IFF radio	5.0	5.0
VHF command radio	11.5	11.5

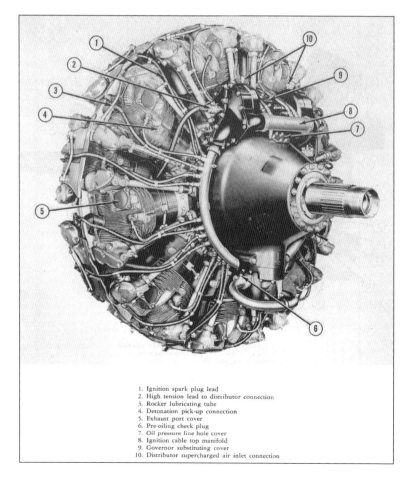

1. Ignition spark plug lead
2. High tension lead to distributor connection
3. Rocker lubricating tube
4. Detonation pick-up connection
5. Exhaust port cover
6. Pre-oiling check plug
7. Oil pressure line hole cover
8. Ignition cable top manifold
9. Governor substituting cover
10. Distributor supercharged air inlet connection

wing flaps. It has its own air-cooling system, fuel, oil supply and controls. Two types of APU may be installed: the Lawrence or the Andover. They are interchangeable. The APU fuel tank holds 4 gallons of 100-octane gasoline, giving approximately four hours of operation. The unit can be started either manually by a rope pull or electrically using the P-2 generator as a motor to crank the engine.

For systems needing AC, two MG-149 inverters (one primary and one reserve) convert the 28-volt DC to 400Hz AC at 26 volts for the fuel flow-meter and 115 volts for the radio compass, turbosupercharger control, gyro flux gate compass and air position indicator.

Engines

The B-29 Superfortress has four 18-cylinder, twin-bank R-3350 Wright radial engines capable of delivering more than 2,200hp each. The four-bladed propellers, reduction geared (.35) to the crankshaft, rotate clockwise when viewed from the rear.

Each engine has two exhaust-driven turbosuperchargers mounted vertically, one each side of the engine nacelle. The turboboost on all four engines is controlled simultaneously by a Minneapolis-Honeywell electronic turbosupercharger control system operated by a single manual rheostat control knob on the central aisle stand. On planes fitted with R-3350-23A engines the carburettors are Chandler-Evans automatic. Other planes have Bendix (R-3350-57) or Bosch (R-3350-59) direct fuel injection systems.

Development

Wright began the development of the R-3350 in 1937, incorporating many established Cyclone Model R-1820 attributes into the new engine. The R-3350 is an air-cooled duplex engine with eighteen cylinders arranged in two radial rings of nine surrounding the crankshaft. The cylinder heads radiate outward where they can be cooled by the airflow from the propellers. The design created an engine with twice the power of the R-1820 as used on the B-17, but

LEFT Annotated view of the R-3350. *(USAF)*

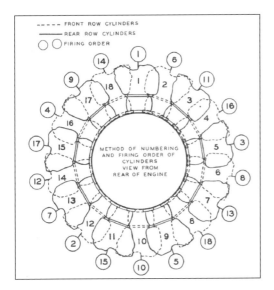

with the same frontal area. Ever concerned with drag, Boeing's designers encased the engine in a snug cowl. Unfortunately, although this was aerodynamically efficient, it limited airflow causing cooling problems. In an attempt to improve the cooling, Wright's engineers did the following: increased the aluminium fins on each cylinder barrel from 40 to 54, enlarging

the cooling area to 325sq ft per cylinder head and giving a total of 5,850sq ft per engine; fitted the top five cylinders (Nos 1, 2, 3, 17 and 18) with rocker box crossover oil lines, allowing the circulation of oil from the intake to exhaust valve rocker arms; and introduced a ring of aluminium plates mounted above the front row of cylinders. Termed 'orange peel' these made the

ABOVE A general view of an R-3350 Wright duplex cyclone engine. *(USAF)*

ABOVE LEFT Cylinder numbering system and firing sequence. *(USAF)*

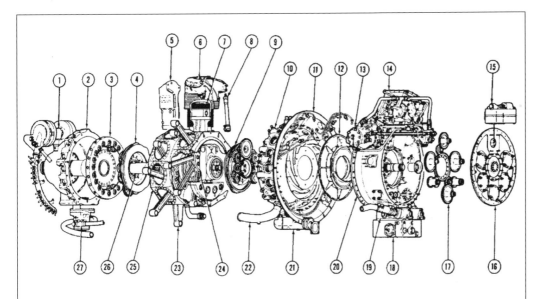

1. Distributor and governor drive
2. Crankcase front section
3. Propeller shaft reduction gearing
4. Front cam and second order balancer assemblies
5. Rear cylinder air deflector
6. Rear cylinder No. 1
7. Rear piston No. 1
8. Push rod and push rod housing
9. Rear cam and second order balancer assemblies
10. Supercharger front housing
11. Fire seal adapter
12. Impeller shroud plate
13. Fuel injection pump
14. Master control unit
15. Magneto
16. Supercharger rear housing cover
17. Accessory drive gear train
18. Rear oil sump
19. Rear oil pump
20. Supercharger rear housing
21. Rear oil sump elbow
22. Intake pipe
23. Front master rod assembly
24. Rear master rod assembly
25. Crankcase main section
26. Crankshaft
27. Front oil pump and sump

LEFT Exploded view of the R-3350. *(USAF)*

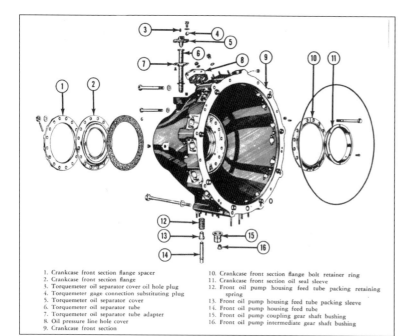

1. Crankcase front section flange spacer
2. Crankcase front section flange
3. Torquemeter oil separator cover oil hole plug
4. Torquemeter gage connection substituting plug
5. Torquemeter oil separator cover
6. Torquemeter oil separator tube
7. Torquemeter oil separator tube adapter
8. Oil pressure line hole cover
9. Crankcase front section
10. Crankcase front section flange bolt retainer ring
11. Crankcase front section oil seal sleeve
12. Front oil pump housing feed tube packing retaining spring
13. Front oil pump housing feed tube packing sleeve
14. Front oil pump housing feed tube
15. Front oil pump coupling gear shaft bushing
16. Front oil pump intermediate gear shaft bushing

air circulating around the front cylinders divert to circulate around the rear cylinders rather than taking the path of least resistance and rising over the tops of the rear cylinders and out from the cowl flap area.

However, cooling problems were never fully overcome, with the rear cylinders being most susceptible, as the tight-fitting cowl did not give enough clearance with the cylinder baffles. When a cylinder overheated it could burn the lubricating oil off the valves, which then stuck, resulting in the engine 'eating' its valve and causing fires. Another problem was the tendency of the engine to backfire through the carburettor causing a gasoline fire. This was only solved with the introduction of fuel injection in the -57 and -59 models. The constant design changes required to correct problems as they arose or to improve performance produced

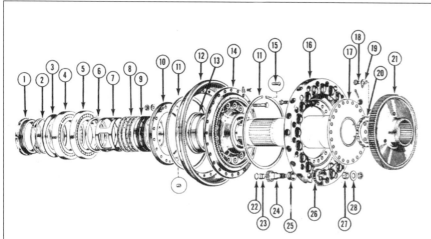

1. Propeller shaft thrust bearing nut
2. Propeller shaft thrust bearing nut oil seal ring
3. Propeller shaft thrust bearing oil slinger
4. Propeller shaft thrust ball bearing
5. Propeller shaft roller bearing
6. Propeller shaft thrust bearing spacer
7. Propeller shaft oil seal spacer
8. Propeller shaft oil seal sleeve rings
9. Propeller shaft oil seal sleeve
10. Stationary reduction gear support spacer
11. Stationary reduction gear adapter lock rings
12. Stationary reduction gear
13. Stationary reduction gear support bearing
14. Stationary reduction gear adapter
15. Stationary reduction gear adapter lock ring rivet
16. Stationary reduction gear pinion carrier
17. Propeller shaft
18. Reduction driving gear nut lock bolt
19. Reduction driving gear nut lock
20. Reduction driving gear nut
21. Reduction driving gear
22. Reduction gear front pinion plug retaining circlet
23. Reduction gear front pinion plug
24. Reduction gear front pinion
25. Reduction gear pinion front bushing
26. Reduction gear rear pinion
27. Reduction gear rear pinion spacer
28. Reduction gear pinion nut lock washer

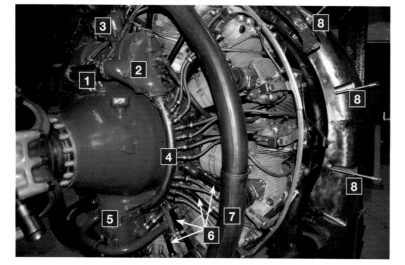

ABOVE Exploded view of the nose section (top) with the reduction gears (above). *(USAF)*

LEFT Front view of the nose section.
(Dale Thompson)

1 Ignition cable top manifold
2 Left distributor
3 Governor
4 Ignition cable side manifold with ignition cable spark plug leads
5 Front oil pump
6 Valve push-rod housings
7 Front exhaust collector ring
8 Cowl flap actuating screws

an amazing 6,427 design changes, each usually involving groups of parts and these in turn needed 48,500 engineering releases and change notices.

The engine has four main sections:

Nose section

This contains the planetary-type reduction gears that reduce the speed of the propeller shaft to .35 that of the crankshaft. It also contains an oil sump at the bottom with a combination scavenger and pressure pump. The propeller governor is mounted at the top.

Power section

This contains the eighteen cylinders staggered in two rows of nine. Valve actuating rods extend externally, activated by four-lobe cams rotating at ⅛ crankshaft speed at the nose

RIGHT The crankshaft. *(USAF)*

BELOW Each row of cylinders connected to the crankshaft via a master con rod and eight articulated rods. The master rod attached to the No 1 cylinder on the rear row and the No 10 cylinder on the front row. Changing the No 1 master cylinder was rare and required special care. As the cylinder was lifted off the piston, it was necessary to rig a holder to keep the master rod centred in the open port. All articulating rods, those to the other cylinders, connected to it. If it tilted beyond certain bounds, attached articulating rods would pull pistons too far into the crankcase and the piston rings would pop to full expansion, making it impossible to put them back. The entire engine would need to be removed to correct the problem. *(USAF)*

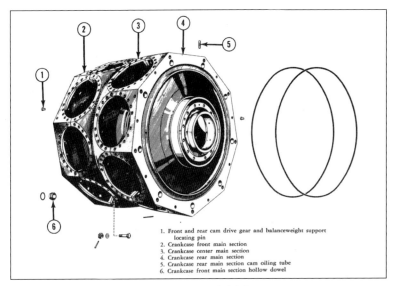

1. Front and rear cam drive gear and balanceweight support locating pin
2. Crankcase front main section
3. Crankcase center main section
4. Crankcase rear main section
5. Crankcase rear main section cam oiling tube
6. Crankcase front main section hollow dowel

ABOVE The power-section engine block. *(USAF)*

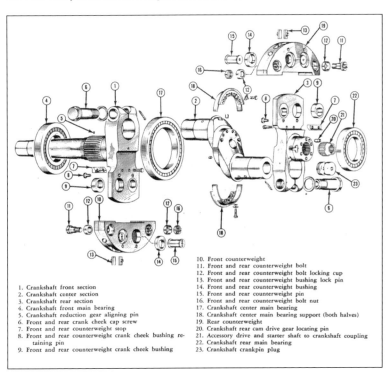

1. Crankshaft front section
2. Crankshaft center section
3. Crankshaft rear section
4. Crankshaft front main bearing
5. Crankshaft reduction gear aligning pin
6. Front and rear crank cheek cap screw
7. Front and rear counterweight stop
8. Front and rear counterweight crank cheek bushing retaining pin
9. Front and rear counterweight crank cheek bushing
10. Front counterweight
11. Front and rear counterweight bolt
12. Front and rear counterweight bolt locking cup
13. Front and rear counterweight bushing lock pin
14. Front and rear counterweight bushing
15. Front and rear counterweight pin
16. Front and rear counterweight bolt nut
17. Crankshaft center main bearing
18. Crankshaft center main bearing support (both halves)
19. Rear counterweight
20. Crankshaft rear cam drive gear locating pin
21. Accessory drive and starter shaft to crankshaft coupling
22. Crankshaft rear main bearing
23. Crankshaft crankpin plug

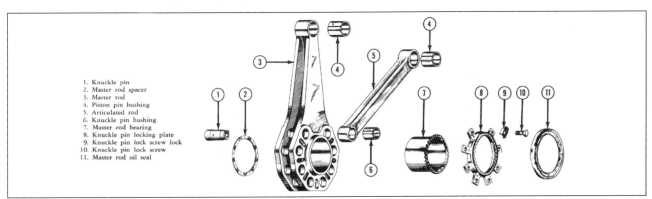

1. Knuckle pin
2. Master rod spacer
3. Master rod
4. Piston pin bushing
5. Articulated rod
6. Knuckle pin bushing
7. Master rod bearing
8. Knuckle pin locking plate
9. Knuckle pin lock screw lock
10. Knuckle pin lock screw
11. Master rod oil seal

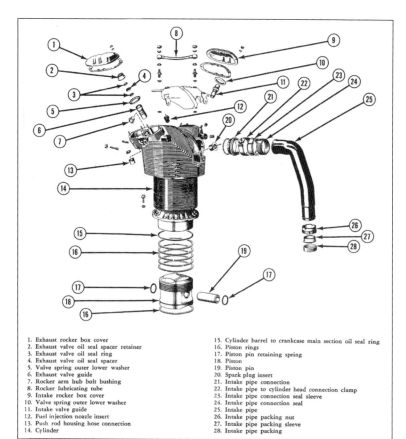

1. Exhaust rocker box cover
2. Exhaust valve oil seal spacer retainer
3. Exhaust valve oil seal ring
4. Exhaust valve oil seal spacer
5. Valve spring outer lower washer
6. Exhaust valve guide
7. Rocker arm hub bolt bushing
8. Rocker lubricating tube
9. Intake rocker box cover
10. Valve spring outer lower washer
11. Intake valve guide
12. Fuel injection nozzle insert
13. Push rod housing hose connection
14. Cylinder

15. Cylinder barrel to crankcase main section oil seal ring
16. Piston rings
17. Piston pin retaining spring
18. Piston
19. Piston pin
20. Spark plug insert
21. Intake pipe connection
22. Intake pipe to cylinder head connection clamp
23. Intake pipe connection seal sleeve
24. Intake pipe connection seal
25. Intake pipe
26. Intake pipe packing nut
27. Intake pipe packing sleeve
28. Intake pipe packing

LEFT The cylinders and pistons. *(USAF)*

and supercharger sections to valve rocker boxes on the front and rear row cylinder heads respectively. The front row of cylinders exhaust forward into the front collector while the rear row exhaust aft into the rear collector. The front collector connects to the rear collector via flexible couplings from where it is directed to the exhaust transition ducts on the left and right side of the nacelle.

Two ignition distributors, driven by a single drive shaft are located at the top of the nose section. The right-hand distributor receives high-tension current from the right-hand magneto and dispenses it using an 18-lobe cam to the front spark plugs of all cylinders. The left-hand distributor receives high tension from the left-hand magneto and administers it using an 18-lobe cam to the rear spark plugs of all cylinders.

Supercharger section
The R-3350 has a single-speed centrifugal distribution, impeller-type supercharger with

LEFT Supercharger-section rear housing. *(USAF)*

BELOW Supercharger-section front housing. *(USAF)*

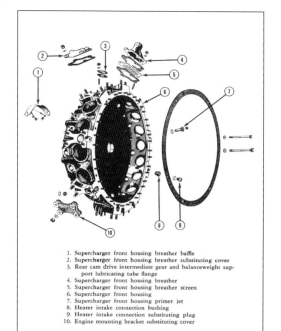

1. Diffuser plate
2. Impeller shroud plate
3. Supercharger front to rear housing vent tube
4. Fuel injection drive housing or substituting cover to supercharger rear housing screw, screw bushing
5. Supercharger rear housing heater exhaust connection substituting plug
6. Supercharger rear housing heater exhaust connection bushing
7. Supercharger rear housing thermometer bulb connection substituting plug
8. Supercharger rear housing thermometer bulb connection bushing
9. Master control or carburetor to supercharger rear housing screw, screw bushing
10. Supercharger rear housing priming connection bushing
11. Supercharger rear housing

12. Supercharger rear housing oil tank vent connection plug
13. Gun synchronizer drive substituting cover
14. Impeller shaft thrust ring retainer and plate to supercharger rear housing screw, screw bushing
15. Tachometer and fuel pump drive housing to supercharger rear housing stud screw bushing
16. Supercharger drain valve return tube
17. Supercharger drain valve
18. Tachometer and fuel pump drive shafts support
19. Supercharger rear housing cover to oil pump oil connection tube
20. Oil pump drive shaft gear bushing
21. Tachometer and fuel pump driven gear bushing
22. Fuel injection tube clamp—outer half
23. Fuel injection tube clamp—inner half
24. Fire seal adapter

1. Supercharger front housing breather baffle
2. Supercharger front housing breather substituting cover
3. Rear cam drive intermediate gear and balanceweight support lubricating tube flange
4. Supercharger front housing breather
5. Supercharger front housing breather screen
6. Supercharger front housing
7. Supercharger front housing primer jet
8. Heater intake connection bushing
9. Heater intake connection substituting plug
10. Engine mounting bracket substituting cover

a vane-type diffuser plate geared to run at 6.06 crankshaft speed. The impeller is 13in in diameter and located forward of the supercharger rear housing. Fuel and air is directed to the impeller where it is centrifugally compressed and distributed to the individual cylinder intake pipes. The impeller boosts the pressure of the fuel–air mixture by approximately 17in Hg at 2,400rpm.

Engine accessory section

This contains a series of gear trains for the starter and accessory drives such as the generators and the fuel, oil and vacuum pumps. The starter is either a Jack and Heintz JH4E (Army Type G-20) or JH5E (Army Type G-10); both are a combination of inertia and direct cranking.

Turbosuperchargers and intercoolers

Two General Electric B-11 turbosuperchargers are mounted one each side of each engine. The superchargers take low-density and low-pressure air, compress it and deliver it to the engine intake at the required pressure and

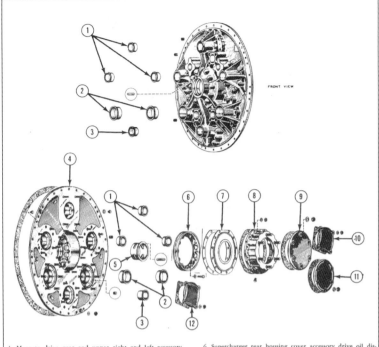

FRONT VIEW

1. Magneto drive gear and upper right and left accessory drive gear bushing
2. Right and left generator drive gear bushing
3. Oil pump and lower center accessory drive gear bushing
4. Supercharger rear housing cover
5. Accessory drive gear and impeller drive pinion carrier support bushing
6. Supercharger rear housing cover accessory drive oil distributing ring
7. Starter coupling thrust ring support
8. Starter adapter
9. Starter substituting cover
10. Upper right and left accessory substituting covers
11. Right and left generator substituting covers
12. Lower center accessory substituting cover

ABOVE The accessory section. *(USAF)*

LEFT Rear view of the engine. *(Dale Thompson)*

1 Magneto
2 Generator
3 Starter
4 Right fuel injection pump
5 Master control unit
6 Cowl flap actuating screws with flexible drive between
7 Right high-tension lead (wire)
8 Electrical tachometer

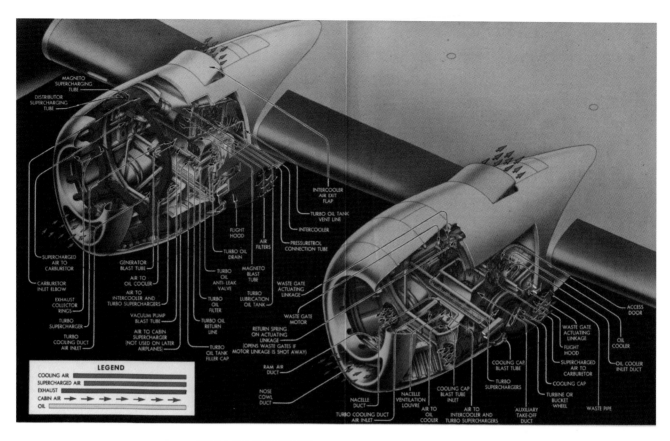

ABOVE The air
induction system.
(USAF)

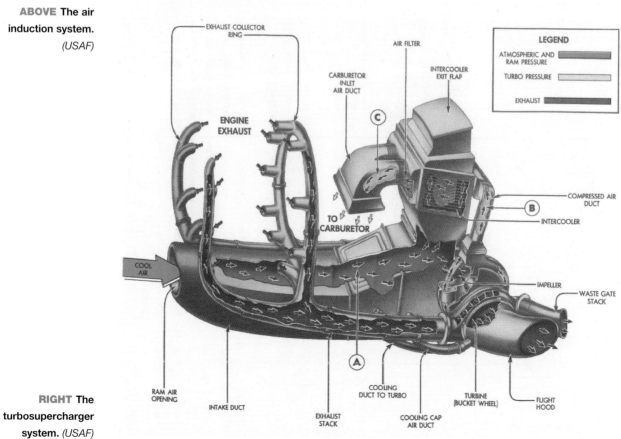

RIGHT The
turbosupercharger
system. *(USAF)*

RIGHT A turbosupercharger. The exhaust stack is the pipe leading to the unit from the upper right. The green ring contains the turbo wheel through which the exhaust gases pass before exiting via the flight hood. The hole in the top of the flight hood is to allow the turbine bucket wheel to be seen in this museum exhibit. The waste gate stack is to the left of the flight hood. The amount of exhaust that passes through this is controlled by the waste gate, a swivel valve moved by the arm in its top. The rotation of this is controlled electrically by a motor connected to the turboboost dial on the central aisle stand. The large silver ring contains the impeller wheel that compresses the air entering on its far side and directs this up the silver pipe to the compressed air duct and then to the intercooler.
(Dale Thompson)

density. Compressing the air heats it so it is passed through an intercooler, before moving to the carburettor or the master control unit on fuel injection engines.

A single dial mounted on the central aisle console controls the output pressure of all turbosuperchargers simultaneously. The pressure is varied by opening a waste valve adjacent to the turbosupercharger that diverts varying amounts of exhaust gases to a waste gate rather than through the turbine wheel of the supercharger.

The controls for the intercoolers are on the engineer's switch panel with intercooler flap position indicators and carburettor air temperature gauges on his instrument panel.

Cowl flaps

There are six cowl flaps on each side of each engine. Numbered 1 through 6 from top to bottom on both sides, flaps 2 to 5 are movable.

RIGHT The No 2 engine nacelle on *It's Hawg Wild* showing the partially open cowl flaps and their actuating screw jacks. Note how the flaps overlap each other. Observe also the exhaust stack with the turbo waste gate stack between it and the nacelle. *(Author)*

LEFT *It's Hawg Wild*'s **No 1 engine and Hamilton Standard propeller. Note the de-icer nozzles near the hub on each blade. The large chin air intake is also very evident. This provides air to the cylinders via the turbosuperchargers.** (Author)

The flaps are worked by an electric motor in each nacelle connected to jack screws on the flaps by a flexible drive shaft. The motors are controlled by four spring-loaded toggle switches on the engineer's switch panel. Opening or closing these flaps alters the amount of cooling air advancing through the engine. Open cowl flaps mean more air but higher drag so cowl flaps need to be closed as much as engine heat will allow. Maximum opening is 6.47in or 27°. On most planes flap 1 is fixed open at 2½in but on some this is spring loaded or movable. On early planes the cowl flaps were 16in long but these were shortened to 13in on later planes, allowing greater opening (and hence cooling) for the same drag.

Propeller – Hamilton Standard

Most B-29s are fitted with 16ft 7in-diameter Hamilton Standard four-bladed, hydromatic, full feathering, constant-speed propellers. A governor, mounted on the top centre of the nose section of each engine controls blade pitch hydraulically using pumped engine oil. Switches located on the central aisle stand control the governor rpm setting electrically. Each propeller also has a feathering switch under a spring-loaded transparent plastic cover on the central aisle stand. These control propeller feathering pumps that, when activated, supply oil at a pressure sufficient to depress the governor transfer valve and rotate the blades under all conditions of rpm and

LEFT **The Curtiss electric reversible propeller on** *Enola Gay*'s **No 2 engine. Note the cuffs near the root designed to increase the cooling air passing into the engine. Just visible are the green square electrically powered actuating screws for the main gear nacelle doors, confirming that** *Enola Gay* **has the electric doors rather than the mechanically actuated type.** (Author)

power expected in flight. Adjustable stops in the propeller dome limit the propeller blade pitch angles between 21.25° at low pitch and 83.25° when fully feathered.

Propeller – Curtiss-Wright electric

Some B-29s are equipped with 16ft 8in-diameter Curtiss-Wright electric constant-speed, feathering and reversing propellers. An electric reversible motor mounted on the front of the speed reducer changes the blade angle. The electric power for this is transmitted through brushes and slip rings in the hub. Blade angles are 17° at low pitch, 57° at high pitch, 85.7° when feathered and 15.7° for reverse. The automatic propeller control system synchronises the four engines at the desired speed by a synchroniser and alternator. The synchroniser incorporates one master motor that drives four contactor units,

each of which is electrically connected to an alternator mounted on the governor drive pad for each engine. Four voltage boosters are incorporated within the system to boost the normal 24V to 72V to speed up the blade angle change for feathering and reversing.

Crew protection

Despite the zealous desire to limit weight, the B-29 did carry some armour protection for the crew and vital equipment in the form of 'deflecting plates' and shrapnel curtains.

BELOW B-29s carried a reasonable amount of armour (red in diagram) to protect not only the crew members but also some of the vital electronic equipment. Note the 'deflecting plates' under the floor in the radar compartment that protected the CFC computers for the top, left, right and tail sighting stations. The nose sighting station computer was located immediately behind the A/C's armour plate and protected by this. (USAF)

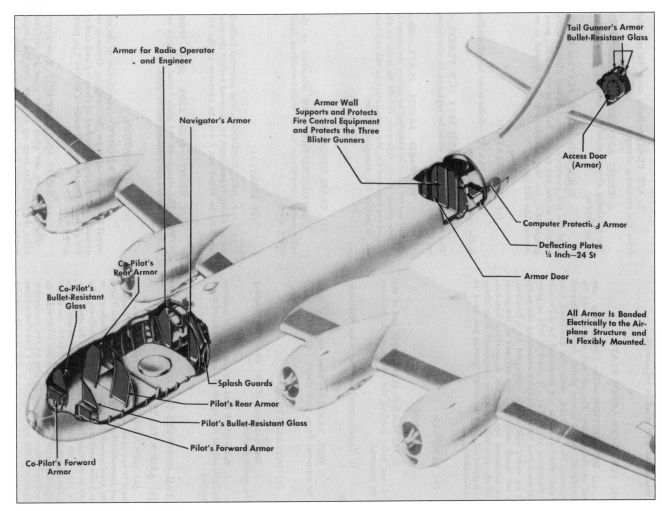

Chapter Four

Flying the B-29

Although big, the B-29 was generally regarded as being easy to fly, which was just as well since the missions were long and often required tight formations. Planning for these was complex, involving not only the air and ground crews but also a host of other personnel to ensure that all necessary supplies were ready to allow the great armadas of bombers to take to the air.

OPPOSITE B-29s of the 499th BG taxi out in the early afternoon for a night mission. *(USAF)*

135

ALTITUDES OUT AND OVER TARGET — RAILING 15 April 1945

7800 Tobin 1 KB24	7800 Schofield 6 KB34	7800 White 11 KB36	7800 Carroll 16 KB10	7800 Parker 21 KB12	7800 Rutherford 26 KB53	7800 McDonald 31 KB40
7600 Malloy 2 KB29	7600 Murphy 7 KB23	7600 Simmons 12 KB7	7600 O'Leary 17 KB23	7600 Floyd 22 KB15	7600 Beck 27 KB49	7600 Miller, JC 32 KB44
7400 Blakeley 3 KB21	7400 Savage 8 KB32	7400 Chandler 13 KB2	7400 Readhimer 18 KB6	7400 Hammond 23 KB8	7400 Neill 28 KB55	7400 Morris 33 KB52
7200 Reither 4 KB25	7200 Bates 9 KB33	7200 Wells 14 KB5	7200 O'Neill 19 KB1	7200 Maupin 24 KB11	7200 Jagatich 29 KB54	
7000 Crandall 5 KB30	7000 Williams 10 KB35	7000 Robinson 15 KB14	7000 Saitz 20 KB3	7000 Lucas 25 KB42	7000 Brewer 30 KB56	

Strike Photo Camera Planes -- 52, 44, 48, 56, 54, 55, 49, 53, 42, 11, 8, 15, 13, 3, 1.
Air-Sea Rescue Channel "C" (Queen) -- 5, 29, 55.
Strike Reports -- 7, 24, 44.
Planes carrying "rope" -- 24, 34, 36, 12, 10, 29 (alternate).
IFF off 150 miles before reaching coast of Japan and back on 100 miles after leaving coast.
All aircraft will monitor Channel "A" 30 minutes from target until bombs away for direction from XXI BC "Master of Ceremonies" who will identify himself as "Dragon". His altitude will be 22,000 feet.

Mission planning

During the Second World War operations began at XXI BC headquarters on Guam where planners selected the next targets from a list provided by the Joint Chiefs. Targets were decided based on several factors: priority, previous damage, expected weather and expected plane availability as reported upwards by the various bombardment wings. With the target chosen the planners set about defining a framework for the mission. Items defined by XXI BC headquarters were:

■ The enemy situation.
■ The target and location.
■ For each bombardment wing:
■ Take-off time.
■ Aiming point, altitude band and axis of attack.
■ Bomb load, fusing, intervalometer setting and ammunition to be carried.
■ Route and altitude band out, assembly point, initial point (IP) and route back.
■ Special instructions.
■ Communications.

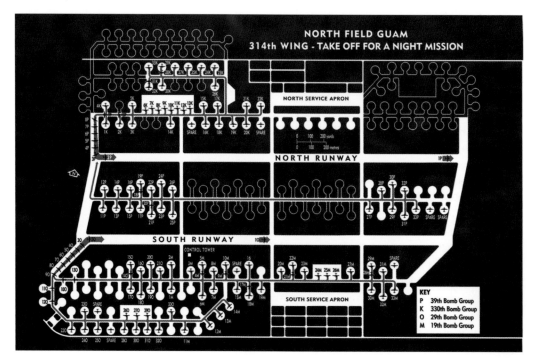

NORTH FIELD GUAM
314th WING - TAKE OFF FOR A NIGHT MISSION

NORTH SERVICE APRON

NORTH RUNWAY

SOUTH RUNWAY

CONTROL TOWER

SOUTH SERVICE APRON

KEY
P 39th Bomb Group
K 330th Bomb Group
O 29th Bomb Group
M 19th Bomb Group

RIGHT A 'Mission Flimsy' for the 19th BG day formation mission to the naval arsenal at Toyokawa. The top section identifies the planes and their place in the formation along with the A/C, outbound altitude and take-off order. The assembly altitude and location are given in the next section, followed by the bombing altitude and axis of attack. As with the night mission, the take-off order assigns different outbound altitudes to successive planes, since the first part of the flight will be in darkness. *(mark@ chidgeyacres.demon.co.uk)*

The XXI BC also coordinated air-sea rescue with the US Navy, providing surface vessels and submarines for 'lifeguard' cover at agreed locations along the flight path. To help the ships find ditched planes the USAAF provided airborne 'dumbo' or 'super dumbo' planes to act as spotters, drop emergency equipment and direct the US Navy vessels as required.

The route out, axis of attack and route back were chosen to avoid known concentrations of enemy flak, fighters or other operations and to give the navigators easily recognised features from which they could gain fixes by radar or visually. Similarly, the IP was chosen to be uniquely identifiable. The altitude bands prevented planes from different wings interfering with each other.

Bomb loads, intervalometer settings and fuse types were defined based on the target type and density of bombs required to destroy it.

RIGHT A typical take-off pattern for a daylight mission. Here, only the 32 planes of the 29th BG are shown lifting off. The aircraft are divided into north and south. As soon as the first plane has been given the green light, 8N taxis over behind 7N while 2S slides down the south runway into its take-off position. This continues until all the N planes are lined up. Then the backlog of seven S planes take their positions. For clarity all B-29s are shown on the taxiway. In reality the last 16 would still be dispersed on their hardstands when the group leader takes off. Using both runways keeps the group bunched together, hopefully, making the assembly in six hours' time easier to achieve. *(mark@chidgeyacres.demon.co.uk)*

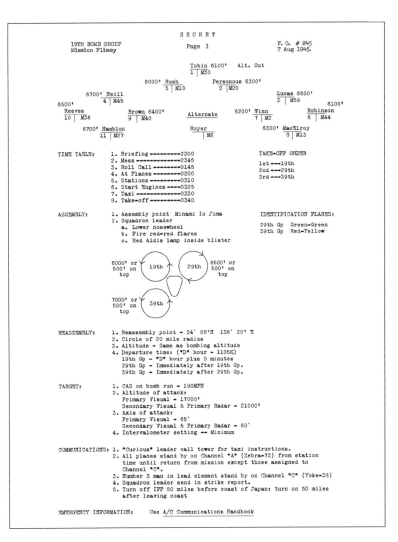

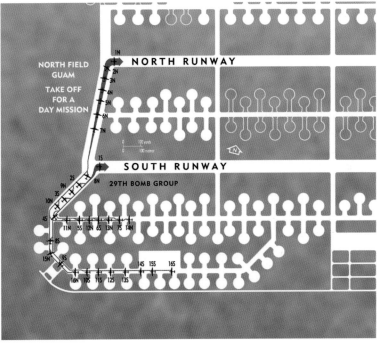

All the above was set down in a standard format within a XXI BC 'Field Order' and transmitted to the affected bombardment wings about two days prior to the planned mission date. The bombardment wings converted it into a bomb wing Field Order by adding details specific to their bombardment groups:

- Summary of mission and other wings involved.
- Take-off instructions.
- Assembly point instructions.
- Formation.
- Altitude band out (each group may have a subset of the altitude band allocated by XXI BC to the wing).
- Bombing altitude and point of climb (again may be a subset of the bombing altitude band allocated by XXI BC).
- Bomb load, fusing, intervalometer setting and ammunition to be carried (if different groups have different tasks).

This bomb wing Field Order was then transmitted to the individual bomb groups who refined it even more into a 'Mission Flimsy' by adding in information based on the aircraft availability estimates provided by each squadron's engineering section. For individual aircraft this was:

- Crew.
- Altitude out.
- Bombing altitude.
- Bomb loading.
- Fuel load.
- Ammunition load.
- Cameras to be carried.
- Aircraft carrying 'Rope'.

This information was then provided to the crews at the mission briefing.

Air crew briefings and pre-flight procedures

On the day of the mission the aircrews gathered for the briefing, learning for the first time the target, routes and altitudes to be used. After the general briefing the different specialisations split for their own instructions – bombardiers getting the bombing settings,

ABOVE General briefing for the 500th BG's daylight mission to Osaka arsenal on 26 June 1945. The route in enters at the lower left with the IP selected as a distinctive peninsula. If the primary target is obscured the route deviates to the left and circles back to the secondary target of Wakayama with the secondary IP at an equally identifiable headland. If the primary could be bombed the planes would turn right and go home. Note the formation diagram to the right. *(USAF)*

BELOW A specialised briefing for navigators and radar navigators. Note the radarscope photos taken on previous missions to help the radar navigator identify the relevant points. *(USAF)*

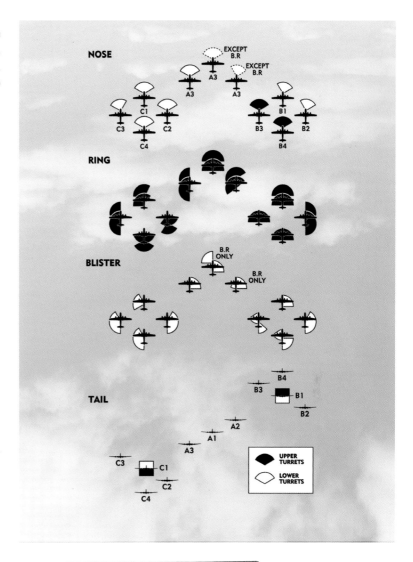

RIGHT The scan pattern for gunners in a standard 11-ship stacked-high, right formation. Other scan patterns apply for other formations. *(mark@chidgeyacres.demon.co.uk)*

gunners the sectors to scan in their formation, radio operators the relevant frequencies and call signs, and the flight engineers the loading lists, weights and centres of gravity (CofG).

Flight engineer

Before each flight the flight engineer (FE) completes Forms F and F-1 with the weights that allow him to compute the balance of the plane, ensuring the CofG is, and will remain, within limits as the flight progresses and fuel is burned, bombs dropped etc. Another responsibility of the flight engineer is to create the 'Flight Plan', a document that indicates expected fuel usage for each stage of the flight based on all-up weight and flight conditions (take-off, climb, cruise etc). The usage figures are entered using graphs and tables computed by Boeing during test flights and cover all expected operating speeds and weights. Similar curves for three- and two-engined operation are also provided, allowing the FE to calculate ranges should an engine fail etc. These forms are presented to the aeroplane commander for signing off before take-off.

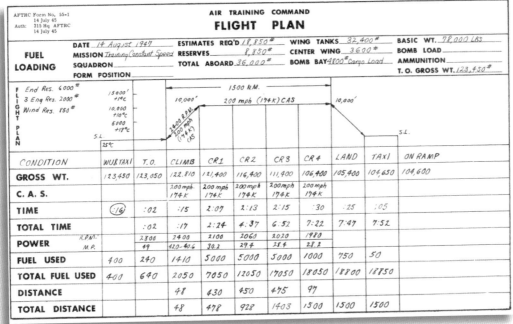

LEFT Example 'Flight Plan' indicating how the gross weight and fuel diminish as the flight progresses. The FE has to calculate this based on the gross weight and mission profile for the coming flight to confirm that there will be sufficient fuel to complete it. On the reverse side of the Flight Plan is space for the FE to record actual fuel consumption and so check the accuracy of his pre-flight predictions. *(USAF)*

WEIGHT and BALANCE CLEARANCE — FORM F

DATE *November 27, 1943* MISSION *Combat (Bomb)*
AIRPLANE *B-29* FROM *Denver (Lowry F.) Colo.*
SERIAL NO. *430862* TO *Lowry Field, Colo. Via Uvalde, Tex.*

COMPARTMENT	ITEM	WEIGHT	INDEX OR MOMENT
	Basic Airplane	74,550	58.7
A (STRUCTURAL CAPACITY)	Crew 1-200 / Cargo / TOTAL 200	200	56.4
B (STRUCTURAL CAPACITY)	Crew 3-200 / Cargo / TOTAL 600	600	48.4
C (STRUCTURAL CAPACITY)	Crew 2-200 / Cargo / TOTAL 400	400	44.2
D (STRUCTURAL CAPACITY)	Crew / Cargo / TOTAL		
E (STRUCTURAL CAPACITY)	Crew / Cargo / TOTAL		
F (STRUCTURAL CAPACITY)	Crew / Cargo / TOTAL		
G (STRUCTURAL CAPACITY)	Crew 2-200 / Cargo / TOTAL 400	400	48.2
H (STRUCTURAL CAPACITY)	Crew / Cargo / TOTAL		
I (STRUCTURAL CAPACITY)	Crew 1-200 / Cargo / TOTAL 200	200	51.7
J (STRUCTURAL CAPACITY)	Crew 1-200 / Cargo / TOTAL 200	200	55.8
K (STRUCTURAL CAPACITY)	Crew / Cargo / TOTAL		
L (STRUCTURAL CAPACITY)	Crew 1-200 / Cargo / TOTAL 200	200	61.2
M (STRUCTURAL CAPACITY)	Crew / Cargo / TOTAL		
N (STRUCTURAL CAPACITY)	Crew / Cargo / TOTAL		
O (STRUCTURAL CAPACITY)	Crew / Cargo / TOTAL		
P (STRUCTURAL CAPACITY)	Crew / Cargo / TOTAL		
TOTALS TO BE CARRIED FORWARD		76,750	61.2

COMPARTMENT	ITEM	WEIGHT	INDEX OR MOMENT
	Totals Brought Forward	76,750	61.2
Q	Crew / Cargo / TOTAL		
R	Crew / Cargo / TOTAL		
S	Crew / Cargo / TOTAL		
T	Crew / Cargo / TOTAL		
Minimum Landing Gross Weight		76,750	61.2

AMMUNITION BY COMPARTMENT

	Rd.	Cal.		
C (2000)	(50)		610	54.0
G (1000)	(50)		305	
J (1000)	(50)		305	54.0
K (5000)	(50)		1525	100.5

BOMBS

Forward 20-500#	10,000	43.1
Aft 20-500#	10,000	82.9
External		

OIL (U.S. 7.5 & Imp. 9 lb./gal.)
Inboard 170 Gal. — 1275 — 79.5
Outboard 170 Gal. — 1275 — 77.2

FUEL (U.S. 6 & Imp. 7.2 lb./gal.)
Inboard 1533 Gal. — 9198 — 73.5
Outboard 1533 Gal. — 9198 — 73.0

Bomb Bay:

TOTAL WT. & INDEX (Uncorrected) 120,441 — 73.6
Corrections (if required) — 73.6
TAKE-OFF WEIGHT & INDEX 120,441 — 73.4
T.O. Wt. & Index Wheels & Limits 120,441 — 60.4
Recommended Max. Take-off Gross Weight ___ LB.
Recommended Max. Landing Gross Weight ___ LB.

COMPUTED BY *E. G. Bartlett, 2nd Lt. A.C.*
APPROVED BY
PILOT *Joe Blow, Col. A.C.*

CARGO LOADING SUPPLEMENT — FORM F-1

DATE *November 27, 1943* MISSION *Combat (Bomb)*
AIRPLANE *B-29* FROM *Lowry Field, Colo.*
SERIAL NO. *430862* TO *Lowry Field, Colo. Via Uvalde, Tex.*

ITEM	QUAN.	UNIT WEIGHT	Nose	A Pilots	B Nav Radio	C Fwd Bomb Bay	D Rear Bomb Bay	F Rear Upper Turret	Camera	I Rear Lower Turret	Rear Amm	Tail Turret	Inboard Oil	Outboard Oil	Inboard Fuel	Outboard Fuel
Crew Member	1	200	200													
	3	200		600												
	2	200			400											
								400								
	1	200							200							
	1	200								200						
	1	200										200				
Ammunition	2000	30/1000					610									
	1000							305								
	1000									305						
	5000										1525					
Bombs	20,500					10,000										
	20,500						10,000									
Oil	170	7½ gal												1275		
	170	7½ gal													1275	
Fuel	1533	6 gal														9198
	1533															9198
TOTAL (OR SUB-TOTAL)			200	600	1010	10,000	10,000	705	200	505	1525	200	1275	1275	9198	9198

ABOVE AND LEFT Forms F and F-1 filled in for a B-29 training flight. *(USAF)*

BELOW The weights and balance chart for the B-29 showing the moments exerted by different loads in different parts of the plane and used to help the FE complete the forms F and F1. *(USAF)*

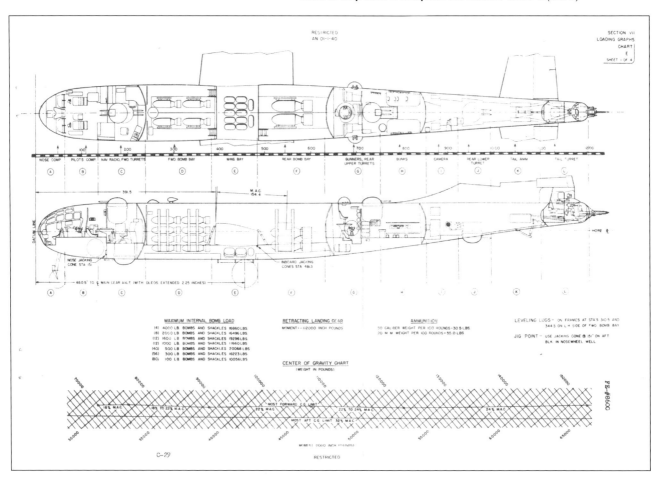

TAKE-OFF, CLIMB & LANDING CHART

AIRCRAFT MODELS B-29, B-29A, B-29B[1], B-29 RECEIVER

ENGINE MODELS R3350-23A, -57AM and -57M

TAKE-OFF DISTANCE FEET

GROSS WEIGHT LB.	HEAD WIND		HARD SURFACE RUNWAY						SOD-TURF RUNWAY						SOFT SURFACE RUNWAY					
			AT SEA LEVEL		AT 3000 FEET		AT 6000 FEET		AT SEA LEVEL		AT 3000 FEET		AT 6000 FEET		AT SEA LEVEL		AT 3000 FEET		AT 6000 FEET
	M.P.H.	KTS.	GROUND RUN	TO CLEAR 50' OBJ.	GROUND RUN	TO CLEAR 50' OBJ.	GROUND RUN	TO CLEAR 50' OBJ.	GROUND RUN	TO CLEAR 50' OBJ.	GROUND RUN	TO CLEAR 50' OBJ.	GROUND RUN	TO CLEAR 50' OBJ.	GROUND RUN	TO CLEAR 50' OBJ.	GROUND RUN	TO CLEAR 50' OBJ.	GROUND RUN	TO CLEAR 50' OBJ.
HEAVY WEIGHT 130,000 LBS.	0		4250	6250	4775	7100	5400	8000	5200	7200	5775	8100	6750	9350	7750	9750	8400	11000	11400	14000
	20		3125	4925	3525	5600	3800	6250	3800	5600	4325	6400	5200	7400	5800	7600	6300	8500	9000	11200
	40		2275	3750	2575	4325	2900	4750	2825	4300	3050	4800	3850	5700	4275	5750	4550	6400	6750	8600
AVERAGE WEIGHT 110,000 LBS.	0		2725	4000	3075	4525	3500	5100	3200	4475	3600	5050	4300	5650	4375	5650	4900	6500	6200	7800
	20		2100	3125	2350	3575	2600	4050	2475	3500	2775	4000	3300	4600	3400	4425	3750	5050	4850	6150
	40		1525	2350	1775	2750	1950	3000	1775	2600	2050	3000	2450	3500	2525	3350	2800	3850	3550	4600
LIGHT WEIGHT 90,000 LBS.	0		1750	2575	1975	2900	2225	3300	1975	2800	2200	3200	2525	3600	2500	3325	2725	3800	3325	4400
	20		1400	2000	1550	2300	1675	2500	1560	2150	1700	2450	1975	2800	1950	2550	2125	2950	2575	3400
	40		1075	1550	1200	1750	1325	1950	1175	1650	1350	1900	1475	4100	1425	1900	1575	2200	1925	2550

NOTE: INCREASE CHART DISTANCES AS FOLLOWS: 75°F + 10%; 100°F + 20%; 125°F + 30%; 150°F + 40%.
OPTIMUM TAKE-OFF WITH 2800 RPM, 49 IN. HG. A 25 DEG. FLAP IS 80% OF CHART VALUES.

DATA AS OF 7-20-46   BASED ON: FLIGHT TEST

CLIMB DATA

GROSS WEIGHT LB.	AT SEA LEVEL				AT 5000 FEET					AT 10,000 FEET					AT 15,000 FEET					AT 25,000 FEET					AT 30,000 FEET			
	BEST C.A.S.		RATE OF CLIMB F.P.M.	BAL. OF FUEL USED	BEST C.A.S.		RATE OF CLIMB F.P.M.	FROM SEA LEVEL TIME MIN.	FUEL USED	BEST C.A.S.		RATE OF CLIMB F.P.M.	FROM SEA LEVEL TIME MIN.	FUEL USED	BEST C.A.S.		RATE OF CLIMB F.P.M.	FROM SEA LEVEL TIME MIN.	FUEL USED	BEST C.A.S.		RATE OF TIME MIN.			BEST C.A.S.		RATE OF TIME MIN.	
	MPH	KTS			MPH	KTS				MPH	KTS				MPH	KTS				MPH	KTS				MPH	KTS		
HEAVY WEIGHT 130,000 LBS.	190		670	90	190		610	8	210	190		520	16.5	340	190		410	27	500	190					190			
AVERAGE WEIGHT 110,000 LBS.	190		1030	90	190		960	5	165	190		860	10.5	250	190		740	16.5	340	190					190			
LIGHT WEIGHT 90,000 LBS.	190		1430	90	190		1360	3.5	145	190		1260	7.5	205	190		1140	11.5	265	190					190			

POWER PLANT SETTINGS (DETAILS IN FIG. 3-2 SECTION III): 2000 BHP & 2400 RPM

DATA AS OF 9-15-45   BASED ON: FLIGHT TEST

LANDING DISTANCE FEET

GROSS WEIGHT LB.	BEST C.A.S. APPROACH				HARD DRY SURFACE						FIRM DRY SOD					
	POWER OFF		POWER ON		AT SEA LEVEL		AT 3000 FEET		AT 6000 FEET		AT SEA LEVEL		AT 3000 FEET		AT 6000	
	MPH	KTS	MPH	KTS	GROUND ROLL	TO CLEAR 50' OBJ.	GROUND ROLL	TO CLEAR 50' OBJ.	GROUND ROLL	TO CLEAR 50' OBJ.	GROUND ROLL	TO CLEAR 50' OBJ.	GROUND ROLL	TO CLEAR 50' OBJ.	GROUND ROLL	
LIGHT WEIGHT 90,000 LBS.	125		125		2370	3150	2580	3480	2820	3750	2640	3420	2880	3750	3150	

DATA AS OF 2-20-45   BASED ON: FLIGHT TEST

REMARKS:

[1] TAKE-OFF AND LANDING DATA ARE APPLICABLE TO B-29B HOWEVER DRAG CORRECTION IN FIGURE 1A-40 MUST BE MADE TO CLIMB DATA FOR B-29B USE.

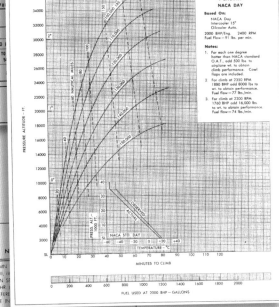

190 CAS

TYPE A6   CLIMB CURVE
4 ENGINES
NACA DAY

Based On:
NACA Day
Intercooler 15°
Oilcooler Auto.
2000 BHP/Eng.   2400 RPM
Fuel flow = 91 lbs. per min.

Notes:
1. For each one degree hotter than NACA standard O.A.T. add 500 lbs. to airplane wt. to obtain climb performance. Cowl flaps are included.
2. For climb at 2330 RPM 1880 BHP add 8000 lbs to wt. to obtain climb performance. Fuel flow = 77 lbs./min.
3. For climb at 2300 RPM 1760 BHP add 16,000 lbs. to wt. to obtain climb performance. Fuel flow = 74 lbs./min.

FLIGHT OPERATION INSTRUCTION CHART

HOT DAY — NO WIND
CHART WEIGHT LIMITS: 130,000 TO 120,000 POUNDS

AIRCRAFT MODEL(S) B-29, B-29A, B-29B[4] AND B-29 RECEIVER
ENGINE(S): R3350-23A, -57AM and -57M

INSTRUCTIONS FOR USING CHART: SELECT FIGURE IN FUEL COLUMN EQUAL TO OR LESS THAN AMOUNT OF FUEL TO BE USED FOR CRUISING. MOVE HORIZONTALLY TO RIGHT OR LEFT AND SELECT RANGE VALUE EQUAL TO OR GREATER THAN THE STATUTE OR NAUTICAL AIR MILES TO BE FLOWN. VERTICALLY BELOW AND OPPOSITE VALUE NEAREST DESIRED CRUISING ALTITUDE (ALT.) READ RPM, MANIFOLD PRESSURE (M.P.) AND MIXTURE SETTING REQUIRED.

LIMITS	R.P.M.	M.P. IN HG	BLOWER POSITION	MIXTURE POSITION	TIME LIMIT	CYL. TEMP.	TOTAL G.P.H.	
WAR EMERG. DRY	2800	52.5	- -	A.R.	5	260	1400	FOR DETAILS SEE POWER PLANT CHART (FIG. 3-2 SECT. III)
MILITARY POWER	2600	47.5	- -	A.R.	5	260	1200	

COLUMN I [2]		FUEL U.S. GAL.	COLUMN II		COLUMN III		COLUMN IV		FUEL U.S. GAL.	COLUMN V [3]	
RANGE IN AIRMILES			RANGE IN AIRMILES		RANGE IN AIRMILES		RANGE IN AIRMILES			RANGE IN AIRMILES	
STATUTE	NAUTICAL		STATUTE	NAUTICAL	STATUTE	NAUTICAL	STATUTE	NAUTICAL		STATUTE	NAUTICAL
		8268			SUBTRACT FUEL ALLOWANCES NOT AVAILABLE FOR CRUISING [1]				8268		
2230	1940	7200	2870	2500	3470	3020	3560		7200	4640	4030
2110	1830	6800	2690	2340	3240	2820	3820	3320	6800	4320	3750
1980	1720	6400	2510	2180	3020	2620	3540	3080	6400	4000	3480
1850	1610	6000	2330	2030	2800	2430	3290	2860	6000	3720	3230
1730	1500	5600	2160	1880	2580	2240	3040	2640	5600	3430	2980
1600	1390	5200	1990	1730	2360	2050	2780	2420	5200	3140	2730
1470	1280	4800	1820	1580	2140	1860	2530	2200	4800	2850	2480
1350	1170	4400	1660	1440	1940	1690	2300	2000	4400	2590	2250
1220	1060	4000	1480	1290	1740	1510	2070	1800	4000	2320	2020
1090	950	3600	1320	1150	1530	1330	1840	1600	3600	2070	1800
965	840	3200	1160	1010	1340	1160	1600	1400	3200	1810	1570
MAXIMUM CONTINUOUS			(.36 STAT. (.31 NAUT.) MI./GAL.)		(.40 STAT. (.35 NAUT.) MI./GAL.)		(.49 STAT. (.425 NAUT.) MI./GAL.)			MAXIMUM AIR RANGE	

M.P.		MIX- TURE	APPROX.		PRESS. ALT. FEET	M.P.		MIX- TURE	APPROX.		M.P.		MIX- TURE	APPROX.		M.P.		MIX- TURE	APPROX.		PRESS. ALT. FEET	M.P.		MIX- TURE	APPROX.		
R.P.M.	INCHES		TOT. G.P.H.	T.A.S. M.P.H.		R.P.M.	INCHES		TOT. G.P.H.	T.A.S. M.P.H. KTS.	R.P.M.	INCHES		TOT. G.P.H.	T.A.S. M.P.H. KTS.	R.P.M.	INCHES		TOT. G.P.H.	T.A.S. M.P.H. KTS.		R.P.M.	INCHES		TOT. G.P.H.	T.A.S. M.P.H. KTS.
					40000 35000 30000																40000 35000 30000					
2400	41.0	A.R.	910	320 279	25000 20000 15000	2400	40.8	A.R.	910	325 283											25000 20000 15000					
2400	41.3	A.R.	915	308 268		2380 2360	40.0 39.5	A.R. A.R.	875 845	315 274 301 262	2260	35.8	A.R.	691	278 242							2080 2050	33.1 34.0	A.L. A.L.	400 382	216 188 209 182
2400	42.2	A.R.	920	296 257	10000 5000 S.L.	2340	39.8	A.R.	800	285 248	2250	36.1	A.R.	666	267 232	2200	35.5	A.L.	505	246 214	10000 5000 S.L.					
2400	43.0	A.R.	910	284 247		2320	39.8	A.R.	758	270 235	2220	36.7	A.R.	632	254 221	2190	36.0	A.L.	497	243 211						
2400	44.0	A.R.	900	273 237		2300	39.8	A.R.	734	261 227	2200	37.5	A.R.	598	242 210	2180	37.0	A.L.	487	238 207						

SPECIAL NOTES

[1] MAKE ALLOWANCE FOR WARM UP, TAKE-OFF & CLIMB (SEE FIG A-1) PLUS ALLOWANCE FOR WIND, RESERVE AND COMBAT AS REQUIRED.
[2] RANGE VALUES LISTED IN COLUMN 1 ARE FOR 1000 FT. FLIGHT ALTITUDE.
[3] FOR DETAIL LONG RANGE CRUISE CONTROL SEE APPENDIX 1A.
[4] THESE CHARTS ARE SLIGHTLY CONSERVATIVE FOR B-29B

EXAMPLE

AT 130,000 LB. GROSS WEIGHT WITH 6000 GAL OF FUEL (AFTER DEDUCTING TOTAL ALLOWANCES OF 1200 GAL) TO FLY 2800 STAT AIRMILES AT 10,000 FT. ALTITUDE MAINTAIN 2250 RPM AND 36.1 IN MANIFOLD PRESSURE WITH MIXTURE SET, AUTO-RICH UNTIL GR. WT. IS REDUCED TO 120,000 LBS. THEN USE SETTINGS IN COL III, SHEET 3 OF 7.

LEGEND

ALT   PRESSURE ALTITUDE
M.P.   MANIFOLD PRESSURE
GPH   U.S. GAL PER HOUR
TAS   TRUE AIRSPEED
KTS   KNOTS
S.L.   SEA LEVEL TO 1000'
A.R.   AUTO RICH
A.L.   AUTO-LEAN

DATA AS OF 15 SEPT. 1945 BASED ON: FLIGHT TEST

RIGHT Somewhat staged but showing the quantity of fuel needed to keep the B-29s in the air. *(USAF)*

Ordnance and fuel sections

For a maximum effort mission there could be 120-plus B-29s operating from each airfield, needing a stupendous 1,080,000 gallons of fuel, 36,000 gallons of oil, 1,008,000 rounds of 0.5in ammunition made into 1,440 belts of 700 rounds each and a staggering number of bombs: M-47A2 100lb incendiary bombs were installed multiply suspended, allowing 144 to be conveyed by each plane, making 17,280 per airfield. Larger bombs were carried in fewer, but still large, numbers: 12 x 1,000lb, 8 x 2,000lb or 20 x 500lb per aircraft. All of these had to be prepared in the two days before the mission, then delivered to the correct hardstands, while coordinating with the ground crews so aeroplanes requiring an air test could do this before being loaded with the heavy fuel and ammunition loads needed for the mission.

Bomb loading

The bombs are dropped off at the edges of each hardstand until the armament team can come and prepare them and then load them into the bomb bays. Preparation varies depending on the bomb. In most cases it involves readying and inserting the correct fuses; however, where small incendiary bombs are multiply suspended

LEFT Inserting a tail fuse into an AN-M64 500lb general-purpose bomb. The bombs are delivered to the hardstands without fuses and both nose and tail fuses are inserted, along with the shackles, before hoisting the bombs into the aeroplane. The AN-M64 was the standard general-purpose (GP) bomb carried by the B-29. Between 50% and 55% of the bombs' total weight was high explosives with four main fillers being used: Amatol (the most common), TNT, Comp B or Tritonal. Because of the different densities of these explosives, although called a 500lb GP bomb, the actual weight as dropped varied from 510lb to 544lb. *(USAF)*

RIGHT Ordnance workers chalk messages on AN-M66 2,000lb GP bombs in what is almost certainly a posed shot for the camera. Although writing messages looked impressive, the frantic rush to prepare and load all the bombs seldom left time for such activities. The AN-M66 was used against reinforced structures. Note the long belt of 50-calibre bullets being loaded into the forward upper turret. Loading bullets in this way was discouraged as 50-calibre bullets weighed 30.5lb per 100 rounds, and allowing a long belt to hang could distort the links, possibly leading to a jam when the guns were fired. The technical orders (TOs) state that bullets should be carried in boxes to the upper surfaces or supported as they are pulled up. *(USAF)*

RIGHT Working in the bomb bays was heavy, tiring and hot work. Here an armourer checks the arming wires on 500lb bombs in the forward bomb bay. With the planes sitting in the tropical sun, temperatures in the bomb bay were frequently well over 100°F, making for unpleasant work. *(USAF)*

RIGHT An E-28 aimable incendiary bomb cluster being loaded on to a trolley before being pulled under the bomb bay and winched into the B-29. The E-28 weighs approximately 435lb and contains 38 AN-M69 incendiary bombs. Once loaded, two mechanical time-delay fuses are set for the desired delay and installed in the tail fin so that once the cluster is released they will detonate a burster, splitting the cluster and releasing the incendiary bomblets to fall individually to the target. The delay is set individually per plane, as it depends on the bombing altitude to ensure the canister will burst at the desired height. The AN-M69 bomblets each weigh 6.1lb and contain approximately 2.2lb of jellied gasoline (eg napalm) with a white phosphorous igniting charge. Just visible behind the E-28 are two fragmentation bomb clusters, with AN-M41 20lb fragmentation bombs. The B-29s carried clusters of 20 AN-M41s weighing approximately 430lb and suspended from a 500lb rack. These were often mixed in with the incendiary bomb clusters to deter firefighters from attempting to extinguish the incendiaries before their individual fires could combine into a large conflagration. *(USAF)*

LEFT A busy and cluttered hardstand as armourers ready AN-M47A2 incendiaries. The AN-M47A2 weighed approximately 69.8lb of which 40lb was the napalm filling. B-29s carried up to 180 multiply suspended, 6 per 500lb station – the number limited by space rather than weight. The bombs were delivered individually to the hardstand where armourers made clusters using a single shackle and a T-19 cluster adapter. Here armourers connect the T-19 to three M47s; other M47s lie scattered around awaiting their turn to be added in. *(USAF)*

BELOW Instructional photographs showing how the M47 bombs are connected to the single shackle by the T-19 cluster adapter – the wires are clipped to the suspension lugs of the outer bombs and the multiple arming wires. *(USAF)*

LEFT Hoisting a 1,600lb Mk 1 Mod 12 mine into the rear bomb bay. Note the sling supporting the mine; a similar arrangement is used for bombs. *(USAF)*

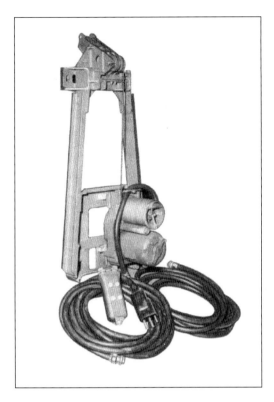

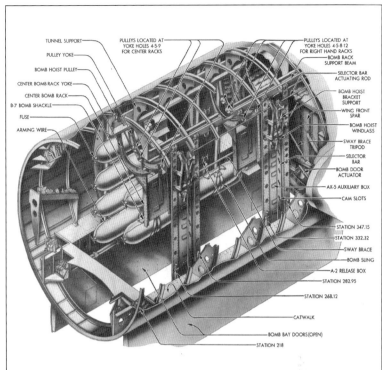

ABOVE A diagram showing the method used to hoist 500lb bombs. *(USAF)*

ABOVE RIGHT A Type C-6 bomb hoist and support frame. The C-6 is electric and operates on 110 volts, but can be manually operated by inserting two hand cranks. *(USAF)*

the cluster has to be made up as well. To load, the correct bomb racks are installed at the required locations and Type A-2 release boxes provided at only the stations where bombs are carried. Where needed pulley yokes are supplied along with the necessary pulleys. The bomb hoist and support frame are fastened to the outboard side of the bomb rack.

When loading, the front bomb bay is loaded first to ensure the plane's CofG remains forward of the main gear.

The guns are loaded 'hot' (ie a round is in

RIGHT Loading 50-calibre bullets into a four-gun forward upper turret. The bullets are loaded into the gun and lowered down to the ammunition drums. Note the contour follower on the arm between the two middle guns. *(USAF)*

the breech), so after loading the turrets are
stowed safe:

Turret	Azimuth	Elevation
Upper forward	0°	+45°
Upper rear	180°	+45°
Lower forward	180°	-90°
Lower rear	180°	-90°
Tail	180°	+30°

Aeroplane commander

When the crew arrive the FE confers with the
ground crew and finalises the Form 1A while
the aeroplane commander (A/C) and co-pilot
perform the external inspection:

- Condition of tyres – examine carefully for
cuts and slippage.

- Wheel chocks – 2in in front of inboard tyres
and 2in behind outboard.
- Oleo struts – 13.25in between pin centres on
main gear, 10in on nose gear.
- Hydraulic lines – check for leaks.
- Shimmy dampener – check oil level. Top of
pin should be even with groove.
- Engine fire extinguishers – check red disc at
end of line running down from each
CO_2 bottle in nose-wheel well. If bottle has
been accidentally discharged the red disc will
be missing.
- Gear and door motor cannon plugs – check
each plug for looseness. If the rotating collar
is not screwed tight, engine vibration can
shake the plug out.
- Cables on main-wheel well doors –
cables should be on pulleys and free of
obstructions.
- Pitot tube covers off.
- All fastenings on inspection plates should
be tight.
- See that engines and nacelles are free of oil
and grease.
- Inspect control surfaces and trim tabs for
dents or damage.
- Inspect all windows and blisters for cracks
and dirt.
- Check all seams and connections for
fluid leaks.

To ensure no liquid locks exist in the cylinders,
with the ignition switches off the propellers
are each pulled through a minimum of twelve

blades with no more than two men per blade. If a propeller sticks the spark plugs are removed from the lower cylinders to drain any oil, then clean spark plugs are installed and the engine pulled through again.

With the engines pulled through the A/C checks the Form 1A, loading list, weight and CofG and Flight Plan that the FE has prepared, confirming the CofG is within limits, any defective items are acceptable and the fuel is sufficient for the intended mission. The A/C performs a crew inspection, confirming all have the correct personal equipment (eg parachute, headphones etc) and the crew board to perform their individual checklists, reporting to the A/C when complete. When these are done, the crew can relax until the appointed engine start time.

Engine start

Just before the appointed engine start time the tail gunner starts the APU to provide electrical power for starting the engines.

The FE sets the cowl flaps to fully open (15°).

Engines are started in the order 1, 2, 3, 4. At the appointed time the A/C tells the flight engineer to start No 1 and signals to the ground crew by holding up one finger. The FE then starts the engine:

- Turn the fire extinguisher to the engine being started.
- Turn the master ignition switch on.
- Turn the boost pump on.
- Energise the starter for 12 to 16 seconds.
- Move starter switch to START.
- After the propeller has made one revolution, turn the ignition switch on and hold the primer down as needed to start and smooth out the engine at 800–1,000rpm.
- Move the mixture control to AUTO-RICH.

The FE handles the throttles throughout the starting process, keeping the rpm between 1,000 and 1,200. When the engine is running the throttle is reduced to 700rpm after which the FE hopefully reports: 'Engine operating normally.' The other engines are started in turn, with the co-pilot signalling the ground crew for engines 3 and 4.

With all four engines running the vacuum is confirmed to be between 3.8in and 4.2in Hg, the gyros are uncaged and all instruments checked

for normal readings. The bomb-bay doors are closed and the plane is then ready to taxi.

Taxiing

The B-29 engines can quickly overheat when running on the ground so planes do not linger on their hardstands. The A/C signals the ground crew to remove the chocks and then waits to join their place in the take-off queue. Like all tricycle-gear aircraft the B-29 taxis easily. The brakes are effective but the B-29 is a heavy machine and can gain momentum quickly. For maximum cooling of the engines it is recommended that both speed and direction are controlled with brakes alone while the engines remain at 700rpm. If the plane gains too much speed the brakes should be used to bring it to a near stop before starting off again,

ABOVE Pulling the props through, two men per blade for twelve blades confirms there is no liquid lock in the lower cylinders. Note the hand fire extinguisher, not of use here but needed during engine start. *(Steve Smisek)*

BELOW B-29s taxi out in the early hours for a daylight mission, illuminating their way with their landing lights. *(USAF)*

staying off the brakes as long as possible to allow them to cool.

When their place in the take-off queue appears, the A/C advances the throttles to get the aeroplane moving. As it starts the A/C tests the emergency brakes then taxis out to join the queue and the throttles are returned to 700rpm. The FE recharges the emergency brake accumulator.

Engine run-up

As they near the end of the queue they turn into the wind, stop, the A/C sets the brakes and performs the engine run-up:

■ All throttles are increased to 1,500rpm while the co-pilot extends the flaps. While the flaps are extending the FE checks that the generators are working. The flaps are run to full down and then back up to the 25° used at take-off in order to have an electrical load on the normal bus so the FE can properly check the generators. Since the flaps cannot be seen by the crew in the forward compartment, the left and right gunners report their operation: 'Left flap coming down sir', 'Right flap coming down sir', 'Left flap full down sir', 'Left flap about 25° sir' etc.

■ The A/C operates all four propeller switches to full decrease then full increase (from limit warning light to limit warning light) to test the governors. At full decrease rpm the engine tachometers should be stable between 1,200

and 1,300rpm. At full increase tachometer readings should be 1,500 as before. Any propeller that overshoots the original setting is not being properly governed and must be corrected before take-off.

■ All throttles are reset to 700rpm and the FE checks the magnetos one engine at a time by increasing the engine's throttle to 2,000rpm. When settled the FE turns off the left magneto and registers the rpm drop. He then turns both on before turning off the right magneto and observing that rpm drop, then turns both on again. The allowable drop at 2,000rpm is 100. With both magnetos on and the engine at 2,000rpm the manifold pressure is noted. At sea level this should be around 30in, decreasing by 1in for every 1,000ft altitude. Changes in temperature will also influence the readings, but affect all engines the same.

■ Once the magnetos are checked the A/C sets turboboost to 8 and advances the throttles one at a time to fully open to check manifold pressure and rpm. For this ground check gauges should read between 2,500rpm and 2,600rpm and 46.5in and 47.5in of manifold pressure.

With the engine run-up complete the A/C confirms the autopilot is off and is ready for take-off.

Take-off

This is a critical time in any flight, more so in wartime when filled to overload with bombs, bullets and fuel. To gain a slight advantage the aircraft can be moved on to the runway from the engine run-up point using the throttles to line up. This can give a very beneficial extra 10–15mph, easing the strain on engines and aircrew.

As the plane rolls forward the A/C walks the throttles forward slowly until the rudder becomes effective at about 60–65mph. In this way directional control can be maintained, first with the throttles and then with the rudder, eliminating the need to use brakes that will slow the acceleration. Once the rudder becomes effective the throttles can be fully opened providing 2,600rpm with 47.5in of manifold pressure, confirmed by the co-pilot who continually checks the power during the take-off run. As the power is increased and the aeroplane accelerates, the FE carefully monitors the cylinder head

BELOW Take-off distance chart. *(USAF)*

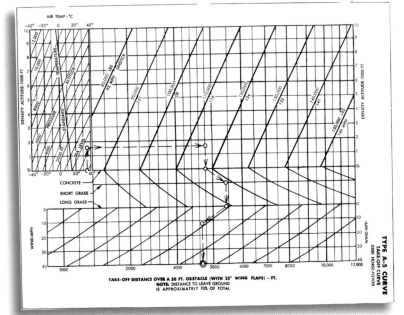

Bud Farrell, gunner, 19th BG

Nearly every day was a mission day on Kadena Air Force Base, Okinawa, but some mission days were special … very different … with an atmosphere of high tension and excitement, something more urgent … MAXIMUM EFFORT! It started early with very early wakeup of the Combat Crews scheduled for that night's mission … with none of the usual quiet rustling around since EVERYBODY was awakened and everyone was GOING! And the buzz started and was apparent from wakeup through the day until late afternoon briefing, with a lot of pre-flight work and inspections to be done in between … before Briefing … without knowing where you were going … or when or IF you'd be back!

By late afternoon the crackling atmosphere of electricity had spread over the whole base … among all personnel, air and ground crew, American military dependants and civilians, even the Native Okinawans … the Gooks … old and young, Mamasans and Papasans, some simply labourers of all kinds who invariably found some means to find their way down to the flight line around evening take-off times at dusk. It was a grand scene, with a profusion of costumes, uniforms, colours and characters … with much raucous noise and bluish smoke of starting engines, squealing of brakes and tires groaning under extreme weight loading of bombs, fuel, equipment, ammunition … and crewmembers! This was 'kick-off time'… and ya' had to be there!

The cacophony of noise … a DIN … is the only way to describe the massive roar of the fifty some B-29s cranking up their collective total of 200 [x] 2,200 horsepower engines … 444,000 horsepower, plus the spares, both Airborne and ground, with all APUs adding their whining power lawn-mower-like sounds … and trucks and Weapons carriers scurrying to and fro, dropping off last minute crew additions, equipment etc. Interphone connections and check-in … '3 clear, fire guard posted'. Hands circling in the air to 'turn 3', 4, then 2 … and 1 … the smoky metallic rattling of cold pistons into a warm purr … signals directing taxiing instructions … thumbs up from the Crew Chief, release of the brakes and you're on your way … a long taxi from the hardstand to the runways with other ungraceful looking ships loaded and bottoming out on their gear struts leaving their hardstands and falling into a line of black bottomed battle wagons, a mile long string of ominous looking bombers like the great circus elephants, nose to tail, that would soon be as graceful in the air as they were now ugly on the tarmac!

Final engine run-ups were done at the end of the runway, with each engine wound out with throttles to the firewall, checking RPM, mag drop etc., a miracle to me that they just didn't fly apart … and then a slow jockeying to position

closely behind the ship ahead with only a slight alternating offset staggering the long column of ships … with 60 seconds separation between take-offs … to allow the slow lumbering and accelerating B-29s ahead to break ground OR get out of the way and off the runway in the event of a take-off roll abort, due to engine failure or other malfunction. Sometimes the little cyclones of moisture drawn off even a DRY tarmac at the lowest point of the 16 foot diameter propeller rotation fascinated me, dancing like a little tornado, and I always wondered what would happen to a hand passed through that whirlwind? Now it's your turn … safety belts tightened again … reach for a metal blister frame or some other solid reassurance … 'Crew Standby for take-off' … all engines wound out, brakes released … a deep breath and 'Crew … we're rollin!'

On the take-off roll there was just enough time to say the usual prayers … twice … always twice … once was not enough. … The Lord's Prayer … twice … and then the only other prayer I ever really knew and know today … and say today … before every flight I have ever taken in the past fifty years … 'Now I lay me down to sleep …' TWICE!

You knew every eye on that flight line was watching … from every hardstand position, every ramp level up the terraced side of Kadena … from every maintenance engine dock … from the tower … every viewpoint … all watching … probably holding their collective breath as much as the crew within the rolling ship! And the next ship in line was already cranking up their full power before yours broke ground. But now you were past the point of thumps and bumps on the gear … starting to float a little on the struts … and the A/C holds it down, forward on the yoke a little … gaining more speed … air speed … precious air speed for a margin of safety if an engine fails now … and at this point some comedian always said on interphone 'EVERYBODY STAND UP … and JUMP', like that was gonna lighten the load and help us get off. … Bombardier calling out '115 … point of no-return … 120 … 125 … 26 … 27 … 28 … 30 … 35' … two miles and a minute later … a lifting of the gear more than a 'take-off' and we were airborne … a very slow gradual slogging climb out over the beach just feet above The East China Sea, usually a setting sun low over the water … and you were on your way. The Gunner/Scanner's reports, with various grinding and thunking noises in between … 'Left flap and Gear comin' up, 1 & 2 lookin' OK'! 'Right flap and gear comin' up, 3 & 4 lookin' OK.' 'Left flap and Gear full up, nacelle doors closed, 1 & 2 lookin' Ok'! 'Right flap and gear full up, nacelle doors closed, 3 & 4 lookin' OK'! The Engineer's report … 'The Panel is green, lookin' good … we're clean A/C.' … Navigator's directions … 'A/C, take a heading of 350 degrees'… almost due North … to Korea!

temperatures, making sure they remain below the 260° maximum while slowly closing the cowl flaps. Open cowl flaps allow more cooling but offer a lot of drag so as more cooling air passes through the engine the FE gradually shuts them so they will be closed to 7.5° by the time the plane leaves the ground. This setting allows rapid acceleration while ensuring the maximum cylinder head temperature is not exceeded. At 90mph the A/C eases back on the control column, allowing the machine to fly itself off the ground at about 130mph. As soon as the aircraft is safely off, the A/C brakes the wheels and calls for gear up. At 150mph the A/C calls for 'flaps up easy'. The co-pilot raises the flaps 5° at a time, waiting for the plane to fly out of the tendency to settle before raising them another 5°. Gear and flaps pull a total of 965 amps and may be safely raised together provided the switches are not tripped simultaneously.

When the gear and flaps are full up the A/C calls for 'climb power' (43.5in Hg and 2,400rpm) reducing the strain on the engines and allowing the plane to climb to the designated altitude for the long northerly flight to Japan.

Cruise control

To gain the cruising altitude and speed, the plane is first flown above the desired altitude by about 500ft. The A/C then holds the climb power settings at a zero rate of climb until the B-29 reaches 210mph, an airspeed that puts the B-29 'on the step'. Once here the predetermined cruising power indicated in the cruise control chart is set, cowl flaps are opened to 10° and the plane is nosed down slightly, allowing it to descend to the desired altitude at 210mph. Upon reaching the required altitude close the cowl flaps to 3° and use the elevators to hold this height. Depending on the plane's all-up weight, the B-29 will use about 435 gallons of fuel per hour at cruising power.

The cruise continues until a predetermined point either near the rendezvous point for daytime missions or a set distance off the enemy coast for night operations. In either case, at this point the A/C increases power and climbs to the new altitude before once more settling into cruise power.

Assembly

For daytime missions the B-29s need to form into their self-defensive formation as briefed beforehand. However, flying in formation is tiring and uses more fuel so the aircraft fly individually to a designated rendezvous. These are selected so as to be easily identifiable on radar and visually – usually being an island off the coast of Japan – and far enough off mainland Japan to limit the chance of Japanese fighters

RIGHT In the apparent empty Pacific sky, three parachute flares drift down. Lead planes dropped flares of designated colours to mark the assembly point and show how finding planes in the vast Pacific could be difficult. Lead planes also lowered their nose wheel to make themselves more identifiable.
(Steve Smisek)

interfering with the assembly. The arrival at the assembly point is frequently timed for just after dawn, allowing the planes to see each other while also permitting the attack to take place in the morning, before the storm clouds that sometimes build over Japan in the afternoon.

The aeroplanes orbit the rendezvous point at the indicated altitude searching for their correct formation. The leader identifies his machine by lowering his nose gear and/or dropping predetermined coloured flares. It is here that the unit markings become important, resulting in the unit identifier being painted as large as possible on the fin (see Appendix II).

At the appointed time the formation heads towards the target regardless of whether it has been completed or not. Late planes may latch on to other formations or may head off for targets of opportunity.

Entering enemy airspace

During the flight out and at assembly, if the altitude warrants it, the B-29s fly pressurised, affording their crews greater comfort and allowing them to wear their standard flight gear. However, as they approach enemy airspace, with the potential for battle damage, the crews don their protective equipment and oxygen masks and the plane is depressurised.

Landing

No mission can be considered successful unless the plane lands safely back at base afterwards. For the B-29 the landing sequence begins about 10 minutes away from base when the pilot makes the before-landing checks and the tail gunner starts the APU.

After calling the tower for landing clearance the A/C sets the altimeters to the setting given by the tower. If one is fitted, the trailing antenna is confirmed as being in, the autopilot is off, all turrets stowed, hydraulic pressure checked OK, propellers to 2,400rpm then, providing the airspeed is less than 180mph, the landing gear is lowered, its operation visually inspected by the left and right gunners. The visual check is considered essential since the indicator lights are only connected to the limit switches on the landing gear retraction screws. If these have become unset it is possible for the indicator lights on the co-pilot's instrument panel to show three greens

LEFT Crew members had personal armour in the form of flak suits, aprons made of overlapping metal plates and a steel helmet. Concerned that the extra weight would restrict movement, many crewmen chose not to wear these but sat on them instead to 'protect their vitals'. Whether this was a sensible precaution or not has been lost to history! *(USAF)*

when in fact the gears have not all fully extended. The co-pilot examines the nose gear through the viewing port in the cockpit floor. Flashlights are used during night operations.

The FE reports the plane's weight and CofG, allowing the co-pilot to look up the stall speed on a chart attached to his control column. The co-pilot extends the wing flaps to 25° just before turning on base leg, increasing this to full down on final approach while maintaining speed at 30mph above the stall speed as read from the chart.

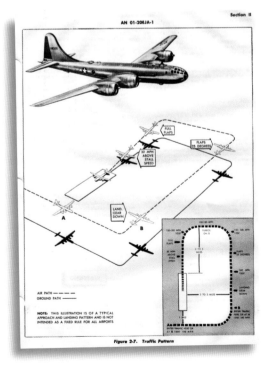

LEFT Traffic-pattern diagram for B-29s landing. *(USAF)*

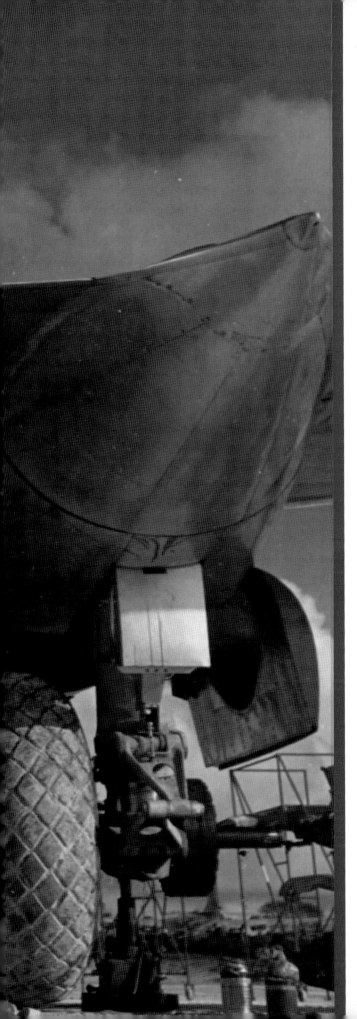

Chapter Five

Maintaining the B-29

Much has been written about the maintenance problems associated with the B-29's mighty Wright Cyclone R-3350 engines. However, although engine changes were all too frequent, the vast majority of maintenance effort was expended against the seemingly never-ending lists of inspections, lubrications and replacements of smaller parts.

OPPOSITE Wheel change in progress. Note the jack located on the axle between the two wheels and the inner brake assembly still attached to the axle. The outer brake assembly will fit into the brake drum seen on the wheel. If only one wheel is being replaced it may be done without jacking but by pulling (not pushing) the remaining wheel on to a 9in high inclined block. If jacking other than at point E (as here), a torsion link spacer bar should be used to prevent the oleo extending as the jack takes the weight. *(USAF)*

The B-29 was a large and complex machine and came with an equally large and complex need for maintenance. This began as soon as a plane returned to its hardstand. The aircrew recorded their aircraft status on Form 1A; the ground crew used Form 41B. After each flight, information was exchanged and the ground crew added the defects to the list of items needing inspection or maintenance before the next flight. Engines were checked first since replacement was a long-lead item and orders were placed with the depot immediately. On average ground crews had two days to work on a plane, with take-off near the end of the second day, providing the benefit of daylight for final preparation. Engine changes were frequent, causing crews to work all day and into the night, so that the engine could be slow timed (flight tested) before the aircraft was loaded with bombs and fuel for a mission.

Maintenance periods

The 'Technical Orders' (TOs) defined the inspection and maintenance periods as: daily, pre-flight, post-flight and then every 25, 50 and 100 flight hours. Longer-period maintenance was also specified but specialist engineers normally carried these out away from the flight line. Much of the maintenance involved replenishment and lubrication but any item that showed signs of cracking, leaking or excessive wear needed to be adjusted and/or replaced.

Daily

The daily inspection is to determine the general condition of the complete aeroplane. It is designed to detect aggravated conditions, maladjustments, structural breaks etc, but is not meant to detect slight wear or early stages of deterioration. Essentially it is a thorough visual inspection of the aircraft both inside and out as well as examination of the various filters and drains for evidence of contamination.

25 hours

The 25-hour inspection can be performed at any time between the 20th and 30th flight hour. If any of the required work cannot be made before the 25th flight hour it is recorded on Form 41B with a red dash. Should it not have been made by the 30th hour it is recorded with a red diagonal.

The numerous trunnions, torsion links and hinges for the landing gear, flight surfaces, flight

RIGHT A diagram showing the many items needing replenishing between missions. This diagram is from an early document and does not show the wing centre section tanks nor the later distribution of oxygen bottles around the rear fuselage. All items shown here had to be filled to the specified levels before a flight. *(USAF)*

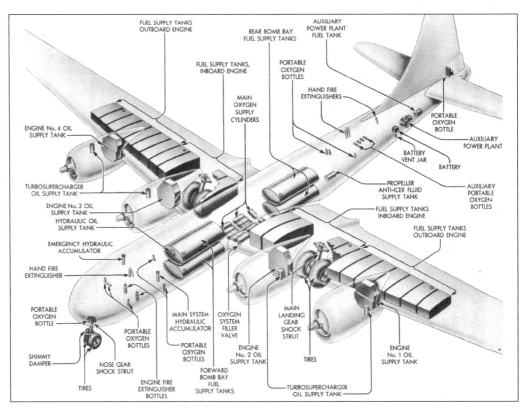

controls and doors are lubricated. This is simplified by the prodigious use of Zerk fittings (see box on page 88), allowing the easy application of AN-G-3 Low Temp – Grease via a grease gun.

All cables for flight and engine controls are checked for frayed cables, worn linkages or any other misalignments. When inspecting for fraying, a cloth pad is rubbed along the cable to snag on any broken strands. All 7 x 9 and 7 x 19 cables are considered serviceable unless more than six broken strands are found in any single inch of cable; 7 x 7 cables remain serviceable if there are less than three broken strands in any single inch.

All 144 spark plugs are removed, examined for condition and have the gap reset to 0.012in (+0.002/-0.001) then replaced and tightened to 300–360 inch-pounds torque. Damaged spark plugs are to be replaced with Types AC-LS88 or RC358.

Other checks involve confirming the operation of the cowl and intercooler flaps, ensuring that they operate at the prescribed speed.

RIGHT Lubrication chart. *(USAF)*

BELOW Lubrication diagram. *(USAF)*

LUBRICATION CHART

FIG.	TITLE	DAILY & PRE-FLIGHT	25 Hrs.	50 Hrs.	100 Hrs.	200 Hrs.	500 Hrs.	1000 Hrs.	SPECIFIED LUBRICANT AN SPEC. NO.
3-10	MAIN LANDING GEAR								
3-10	ZERK FITTINGS	X							AN-G-3
3-10	RETRACTING MECHANISM			X					AN-G-10
3-10	SCREW GEAR BOX					*X	*X		AN-G-10
3-10	WHEEL BEARINGS				X				AN-G-15
3-10	WHEEL WELL DOORS								AN-0-6A
3-10	EXPOSED UNIVERSALS		X						AN-0-6A
3-10	RETRACTING SCREW			X					AN-G-10
3-10	SCREW GEAR BOX					*X	*X		AN-G-10
3-10	ZERK FITTING	X							AN-G-3
3-10	DOOR HINGES	X							AN-0-6A
3-11	NOSE LANDING GEAR								AN-G-3
3-11	ZERK FITTINGS	X							AN-G-3
3-11	RETRACTING SCREW			X					AN-G-10
3-11	SCREW GEAR BOX					*X	*X		AN-G-10
3-11	WHEEL BEARINGS				X				AN-G-15
3-11	CENTERING MECHANISM								
3-11	UPPER BEARING				X				AN-G-3
3-11	ROCKER ARM BEARINGS		X						AN-G-3
3-11	MANUAL RETRACTION SYSTEM					*X	*X		AN-G-10
3-12	MANUAL RETRACTION SYSTEMS								
3-12	GEAR BOXES					*X	*X		AN-G-10
3-12	UNIVERSALS				X				AN-G-3
3-13	TAIL SKID								AN-G-3
3-13	ZERK FITTINGS	X							AN-G-3
3-13	RETRACTING SCREW			X					AN-G-10
3-13	GEAR BOX					*X	*X		AN-G-10
3-14	NACELLES								
3-14	INTERCOOLER DOOR MECHANISM								
3-14	ACTUATING MECHANISM					*X	*X		AN-G-10
3-14	DOOR HINGE			X					AN-0-6A
3-14	TURBOSUPERCHARGER								
3-14	ANGLE DRIVE				X				AN-G-3
3-14	FLEXIBLE DRIVE SHAFT				X				AN-G-3
3-14	OIL COOLER FLAP								
3-14	ACTUATING MECHANISM					*X	*X		AN-G-10
3-14	DOOR HINGE			X					AN-0-6A
3-14	COWL FLAP ZERK FITTINGS			X					AN-G-3
3-15	MAGNETO			X					AN-VV-0-446 GRADE 1120
3-15	DYNAFOCAL ENGINE MOUNTS							X	AN-VV-0-446 GRADE 1080

FIG.	TITLE	DAILY & PRE-FLIGHT	25 Hrs.	50 Hrs.	100 Hrs.	200 Hrs.	500 Hrs.	1000 Hrs.	SPECIFIED LUBRICANT AN SPEC. NO.
3-15	CARBURETOR CONTROL ARM LINKAGES		X						AN-0-6A
3-16	WING FLAP MECHANISM								
3-16	ZERK FITTINGS		X						AN-G-1
3-16	FLAP ACTUATING SCREW	X							AN-G-10
3-16	GEAR BOXES						*X	*X	AN-G-10
3-16	UNIVERSAL JOINTS					X			AN-G-3
3-17	AUTOMATIC FLIGHT CONTROLS			X					SEE TEXT
3-17	LIFE RAFT DOOR MECH. & AILER-ON ACTUATING ARM & LINKAGE					*X	*X		AN-0-6A
3-17	UNIVERSAL JOINTS					X			AN-G-3
3-18	BOMB CONTROL UNIT						*X	*X	AN-G-3
3-18	BOMB HOIST				X				AN-0-6A
3-18	BOMB DOOR MECHANISM								
3-18	RETRACTING SCREWS			*X			*X		AN-G-10
3-18	GEAR BOXES						*X	*X	AN-G-10
3-19	PNEUMATIC BOMB DOOR ACTUATOR			X					AN-0-6A
3-19	PNEUMATIC BOMB DOOR LATCH ACTUATOR			X					AN-0-6A
3-19	PNEUMATIC BOMB DOOR COMPRESSOR					*X	*X		AN-0-6A
3-20	LIMIT SWITCH GEAR BOXES						X		AN-0-6A
3-20	TRAILING ANTENNA								AN-0-6A
3-20	CABLE GUIDE				X				AN-0-6A
3-20	WORM GEAR						X		AN-G-10
3-20	CAMERA WELL DOORS				X				AN-0-6A
3-21	TRIM TABS								
3-21	ZERK FITTINGS				X				AN-G-3
3-21	HINGES				X				AN-0-6A
3-21	ACTUATING SCREWS					X			AN-G-10
3-21	PRINCIPAL UNIVERSAL					X			AN-G-3
3-21	RUDDER EXPOSED UNIVERSAL				X				AN-0-6A
3-21	CONTROL LOCKS				X				AN-0-6A
3-22	FORWARD PRESSURIZED COMPARTMENT								
3-22	RUDDER PEDALS				X				AN-G-3
3-22	ZERK FITTINGS				X				AN-G-3
3-22	HAND BRAKE LINKAGES						X		AN-0-6A
3-22	CONTROL COLUMNS						X		AN-G-3
3-22	DOOR, WINDOWS			X					AN-0-6A
3-22	SLIDING SURFACES				X				AN-G-3

*REFER TO THE REFERENCE FIGURE NOTED FOR AN EXPLANATION WHEN MORE THAN ONE LUBRICATION PERIOD IS CHECKED FOR A SINGLE ITEM.

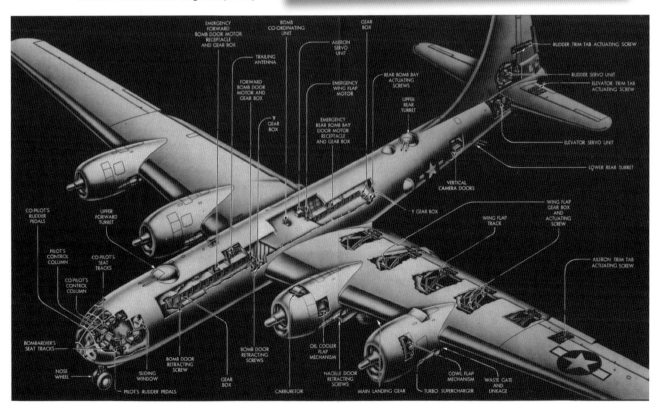

ABOVE A tiny portion of the cables that need checking for frays each 25 hours: $\frac{3}{32}$ 7 x 7 cables for the elevator trim tabs (upper two); $\frac{3}{16}$ 7 x 19 cable for the rudder; and $\frac{3}{16}$ 7 x 7 cables for the elevators (lower two). *(USAF)*

50 hours

The 50-hour inspection can be performed at any time between the 40th and 60th flying hours. Inspections not made by the 50th hour are recorded on Form 41B with a red dash;

RIGHT Wheel-changing without jacking. *(USAF)*

BELOW Diagram of jacking points. *(USAF)*

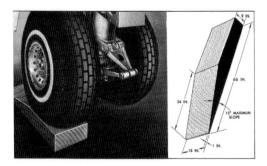

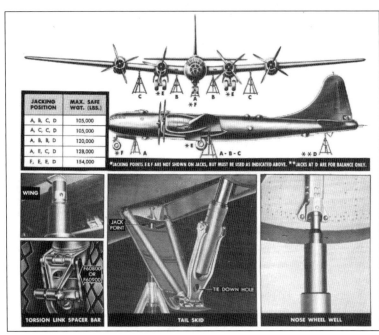

inspections not made by the 60th hour are recorded with a red diagonal.

The brushes in the normal and emergency motors for the wing flap, nose gear, main gear and, if fitted, nacelle doors are checked for wear. These need replacing if less than $\frac{5}{16}$in (ie have worn more than $\frac{3}{16}$in).

100 hours

The 100-hour inspection can be performed at any time between the 90th and 100th flying hours. Checks not made by the 100th hour are recorded on Form 41B with a red dash; examinations not made by the 110th hour are recorded with a red diagonal.

The wheel brakes and wheel bearings are checked for wear by jacking the plane and removing each main wheel. Brake pads are looked at for wear by removing two or more blocks and measuring their thickness. Blocks must not wear to less than $\frac{1}{2}$in (thickness when new is $\frac{5}{8}$in). Brake drums need to be replaced if they are scored, are not within 0.015in of being concentric with the axle, have cracks more than $\frac{1}{8}$in long or the cracks show on the outer rim.

Control cable tension is also inspected. If out of specification tension can be adjusted at the turnbuckles installed in each cable run or the cable replaced.

BELOW Despite the vast industrial backup for the B-29 programme, spares were always in short supply, so should a plane be assessed as unrepairable it was quickly reduced to parts as maintainers stripped it of any useful items. *(USAF)*

R.A. Mann, mechanic, 54th WRS, Guam, 1950

When you talk about working on airplanes, you have to start with the weather you were working in. We were lucky(?) being on Guam where we did not have to put up with frostbitten fingers. But Anderson AFB, at the northern end of the island, gets close to 200 inches of rain a year (usually in twenty minute showers), the temperature seldom gets below 80 degrees, and the humidity is so high that you had to keep a 100 watt light bulb burning in your clothes locker to keep the fungi from eating your clothes. We worked in fatigue pants and tee shirts, the standard USAF-issue coveralls being just too hot to put up with. A few of the hardier souls with very high pain thresholds stripped down to PT shorts and GI shoes, but this was generally considered extreme. I tried it once and burned both legs and my ribs on sun-heated aluminium within an hour.

To all of us who worked on it, the Wright R-3350 radial engine was an object of consuming hatred. Basically, it was two nine-cylinder engines mounted on a double throw crankshaft. Voila! Instant eighteen-cylinder engine – and a mechanic's nightmare. The aircraft itself was bad enough to maintain, but those engines! The two banks of cylinders created by the double mounting were so close together that the mounting bolt flanges on the cylinder bases had to have the edges planed down in order to fit next to each other on the engine housing. This engine had a reputation of being a voracious eater of valves and rings, as well as a prodigious swallower of oil, and cylinder changes were almost as common as engine changes. There was seemingly a Rule that allowed only those cylinders on the bottom of the engine to fail. This is so that the oil can run out of the engine housing and drip ceaselessly into the mechanic's hair, ears, nose and down the back of his neck.

So, you have pulled the cylinder, gotten your oil bath for the day, and held the cylinder in place while your fumble-fingered partner got the mounting bolts started. You've run the bolts, all twenty of them, in tight and torqued them down to Tech Order requirements. Are we done yet? Hell, no! You still have to safety wire those twenty bolts. Picture the rough-cast, quarter inch thick aluminium cooling fins projecting from the bodies of each cylinder. Picture the cylinder mounting bolt heads three quarters of an inch away from each other and only an inch and a half away from the mounting bolts of the cylinders in the other bank. Picture the safety wire that had to be strung and pulled tight through each bolt head. Picture the bloody mess where your hands used to be after you finished safety wiring twenty bolts and repeatedly dragging your knuckles across those cooling fins on each and every one of them.

Another innovation was what we called the 'orange peel'. These were aluminium plates, my memory says 12 inches by 6 inches, mounted in a ring around the engine in the area between the front and rear banks. The intent was to keep the air flowing around the front cylinders diverted to the bodies of the rear cylinders, rather than it taking the path of least resistance, rising and flowing over the tops of the rear cylinders and out in the cowl flap area.

From an engine performance point of view I go along with the design. The rear bank needed all the cooling air it could get. From a mechanic's point of view different story. The individual pieces were held in place by, I think, a couple of Dzus fasteners and by a cable running around the engine in a channel on the upper side of each piece of orange peel. Being located essentially between the two banks of cylinders, the peel did not interfere with all

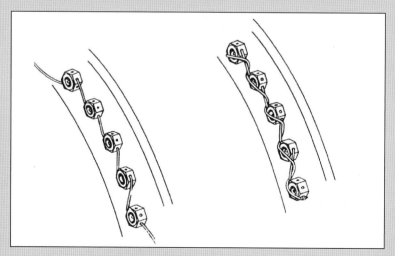

BELOW Safety wire as required for the cylinder hold-down bolts. (USAF)

maintenance in that area, but when it did, the securing mechanism on the cable had to be loosened and the necessary pieces of peel removed. There was the problem. The cable had to be loosened just enough to allow it to slip out of the channel on the pieces of peel being removed, but not so loose as to allow it to drop out of the channel on the pieces on the bottom of the engine. If it did it meant that The Tub had to be dropped (two man job) and the cable replaced in the channel and held there (by two men) while the guy up on top clamped it down to secure it. This was enough to secure the orange peel a place of honor on the mechanic's Oogablah List.

I have always maintained that I can look at a man's right wrist and tell you if he had been a B-29 mechanic. The secret mark of the fraternity is found there: a scar an inch or so long on the inside of the wrist directly below the thumb. A new mechanic collected his scar the first time he was assigned to drain the front oil sump. The front sump was located at the bottom rear of the nose section of the engine housing, a few inches lower than the

lip of the ring cowl on the front of the engine. To supposedly make access easier, Boeing engineers, none of whom had obviously ever worked as mechanics, placed an eight inch square door in the upper surface of the air inlet. Theoretically, this allowed the mechanic to reach upward through the hole, put his ¾ inch box end wrench on the sump plug, and by pulling forward, loosen the plug. Well, first of all, that plug NEVER just gradually loosened. It came loose with a snap, at the precise moment you were applying even more pressure to make it come loose at all. Secondly, Boeing did not believe in wasting production time or coddling mechanics by rounding edges on access doors and hatches. The edge of the hole you were putting your arm through was sharp, very, very SHARP. Plug snaps loose, arm jerks towards you, wrist hits edge of hole, and another cursing mechanic is seen carrying his bloody box end wrench in his equally bloody hand down to the welding shop, where he will have the wrench shaped so that he can get to the plug from above, through the ring cowl opening in front of the engine, where there are no sharp edges.

BELOW A close-up of the twin rows of cylinders showing the closeness of fit that made for such a compact design but such a mechanic's nightmare. The 'orange peel' has been removed from this engine but would fit over the aluminium supports and be secured by the wire running in the groove to their rear.
(Dale Thompson)

After you got the plug out, the sump drained, the magnet on the sump plug checked for metal chips (hoping you wouldn't find any and have an engine change on top of everything else), the plug back in, tightened and safety wired, your fun and games with engine oil were far from over. There was still the rear sump to be drained and checked. That was usually a real adventure. First you scrounged up a short work stand and placed it under the nacelle. Stepping up on the stand, the first step was to remove an access door approximately eighteen inches square. This allowed you to reach a similar door above it that formed part of the lower surface of the air intake. Removal of that door brought you to still another same-sized door on the upper surface of the air intake. Removal of that door finally got you into the bottom of the engine accessory compartment. CORRECTION: It allowed *access* to the accessory compartment.

You got there by putting your right arm, clutching the inevitable ¾ inch box end wrench and a pair of dykes for cutting the plug safety wire, above your head and into the hole you had just opened. The work stand was climbed step by step until your hips were level with the bottom of the nacelle and your head and arm were in the accessory compartment. Putting the wrench down somewhere handy, the safety wire was removed and the dykes dropped in your breast pocket, it being the only one reachable. The wrench was retrieved and placed on the sump plug. One-handed pressure was applied until the plug (eventually) loosened. It was then backed off until held in by only a couple of threads. The wrench was again stashed somewhere, and you yelled down to your buddy through the inch or so of space between your body and the edge of the hole to pass up the oil drain hose. He, of course, is not there, having been dragged off ten seconds earlier by the crew chief to empty ash trays, fluff the pilot's seat cushion, and to perform other similar critical maintenance tasks.

So you climb down off the stand, carefully avoiding the sharp edges, put the drain line up in the hole and follow it with yourself. The drain line was a piece of two-inch hose about eight feet long. The lower end was in a five-gallon can and the upper end slipped over the outlet in the bottom of a rectangular metal box. The theory was that when you pulled the sump plug the oil drained into the metal box and ran down the hose into the waste bucket on the ground. That was the theory. In the real world, ruled by Murphy and his Law, no matter what the size and shape of the collector box, one of two things ALWAYS happened: the box overflowed or the line came off the outlet. Either way you got drenched from the middle of your chest to your toes with black, slimy, yucky engine oil. If you were very, very lucky, and the airplane had come back at midnight instead of half an hour ago, the oil had had a chance to cool. One usually was not lucky. It goes without saying that when hot oil is sloshed on you, you tend to jerk in a reflex action. Remember that little door by the front oil sump that you put your wrist through? Well, now you have your entire body through THREE doors. The swirling patterns to be seen in a mixture of black oil and fresh red blood are truly fascinating.

Difficult as the job of safety wiring the cylinder mounting bolts was, it did not even come close to the sheer frustration and muscle cramps that were the lot of any mechanic who had to change a fuel injection pump. On later models of the R-3350 engine, the old carburettor system was replaced with direct fuel injection. The required gasoline was sprayed directly into each cylinder through a nozzle mounted above the rear spark plug. The flow of fuel to these nozzles came from two pumps, each about fifteen inches long and eight inches in diameter, mounted on opposite sides of the upper accessory section of the engine. The forward edge of the pump mounting flange was no more than three inches from the firewall separating the power section from the accessory section of the engine. When a pump was replaced it was not the bolts on the rearward half of the flange that were a problem. It was the bolts on the forward side that were bad news. Because of the spacing involved, to reach the forward-side bolts you had to reach around both sides of the pump, rather like putting your arms around a horizontal log.

In order to do this, the mechanic had to lean in through the main access hatch on the side of the nacelle and feel for the holes on the forward side of the pump. With no more than three inches of total clearance back there, you were reduced to the use of fingertips just to start the threads on several of the bolts. Once the bolts were started by finger (and you were reasonably sure they weren't cross-threaded), it was juuuuust possible to get a socket with a universal joint drive on the bolt heads. Forget the torque wrench; no way. Unfortunately, there was barely enough room to move the ratchet one click. Turn one click, fingertip it back one click, forward one click, back one click ad nauseum.

Finally, with cramps in every finger, the bolts were tightened down with what you hoped was sufficient torque to prevent any gasoline leakage. With the easy part of the job finished, those rotten bolts that couldn't be seen and could barely be touched had to be safety wired. This was strictly a feel job, and the accepted practice on my crew was to cut off a piece of wire about three feet longer than you really needed. The wire had to be run through each bolt head from the upper left quadrant to the lower right quadrant to prevent the bolts from vibrating loose. The technique generally used was to feel for the appropriate wire hole with the tip of the wire. When you found it, you pushed a minimum of twelve inches of wire through the hole. This brought the end of the wire below the pump, where it could be grabbed with a pair of pliers and carefully drawn tight without kinking the wire. If it kinked, you ripped everything out and started again. All this was going on while the mechanic was bending sideways and the edge of the hatch was digging into his ribs. Just to add a little more joy to the mechanic's day, there was usually an Airplane Driver down on the ground yelling up something encouraging, like, 'Sergeant! What the hell's the holdup? We would like to get off the ground sometime soon so that we can get back in time for Happy Hour at the Club tonight. Speed it up, will you?' Exactly what was needed for motivation. It usually motivated me into dropping a bolt and spending an additional twenty minutes trying to find it.

My personal all-time favourite for raising the blood pressure was the reinstallation of the heat shield shrouding following a turbosupercharger change. Each nacelle on the B-29 held two turbosuperchargers, driven by engine exhaust gas diverted from the exhaust manifold, with a heat shield shrouding between the exhaust manifold and the engine accessory compartment. You had to pull the shrouding off when you changed a turbo, and reinstall it after the turbo was mounted and the hold-down bolts safetied.

There were several pieces of shrouding, and they fit together like a three-dimensional jigsaw puzzle. In addition, they were usually badly distorted from the extreme temperatures that they were subjected to. Four pieces, the center, the upper center, upper forward and forward, had multiple planes, and all four overlapped forward and above the turbine bucket wheel. At the point of overlap, there was a bolthole that ran through all four pieces. I defy anyone to get that hole lined up on the initial installation. The only way to handle it was to loosely install the shroud mounting bolts on all four pieces and then, starting with the bolts farthest away from the overlap, tighten here, loosen there, back and forth, back and forth, until eventually the holes in all four pieces lined up and you could run a bolt through them. Attacking the problem from the other direction, putting in the bolt and then trying to install the shroud mounting bolts never seemed to work, although I think every mechanic has wasted a half a day on it.

We mechanics were really pressed to prove the adage that where there's a will there's a way during the first six months of the Korean War/Conflict/Police Action/Whatever. The 19th Bomb Group was stationed down at the other end of the field, and on the 27th of June, 1950, they moved out for Okinawa and four years of combat missions. The maintenance people of the 19th stripped the base shops of every engine and spare part they could put their sticky little fingers on. In fact, they snuck up into our area in the dead of night and stole all four engines off 44-86267, one of our shiny new airplanes. When the crew of 267 got out to the flight line the morning of the 27th, the Bomb Group was gone, there was a jack under the tail and four gaping holes in the wings where the engines used to be. With the Bomb Group taking everything loose, and some things that weren't, the only parts we had available to us were those we had on hand in the Squadron Tech Supply hut. It wasn't much to keep twelve airplanes flying.

Whenever we had to replace an engine, we had to send a wire to Japan, and then wait for them to pull an engine out of the pipeline and divert it to Guam. As for getting replacement parts, forget it. So, to paraphrase a current expression, we went into creative maintenance. One of our band of Rock Happy Fools spent all of his spare time boondocking (wandering through the jungle looking for Japanese souvenirs). Most of the time his finds were highly useful items such as 155mm cannon barrels without breechblocks, rusted out jeeps and weapons carriers, fifty-five gallon drums filled with unidentifiable liquids, and similar goodies. In our hour of travail he came through. In a small overgrown WWII dump between Anderson and Northwest Fields he came across a dozen large crates containing brand new R-3350 engines. They had been sitting there since 1945, but the cosmoline was still thick and, when we got the crates open, found that the desiccant bags were still active. We had our engine parts. A veritable plethora of magnetos, distributors, fuel and oil pumps, cylinders, injection valves, prop governors, all those good things.

To keep the paper shufflers (and the Inspector General) off our necks, whenever we replaced a bad unit, say a magneto, with a dump part, we also swapped the manufacturer's data plates. This apparently kept the same model and serial number on the engine that the paperwork said was supposed to be there. If we hadn't covered our tracks on this, half the brass at FEAMA (Far East Air Material Area) would be swarming all over us, grounding everything in sight, while they tried to determine what to do about a problem that was not covered by The Book. It should be pointed out that the 'dump parts' were used for interim replacement only; they were carefully checked for interchangeability and performance, and were immediately replaced when legitimate parts became available. Needless to say, we didn't tell the Operations people what we were doing, either. The flight crews were insecure enough without knowing that some very essential parts of their engines had come out of a dump.

All I've talked about to this point is the problems B-29 mechanics had with the engines. Don't get the idea that the airframe maintenance was any easier; it wasn't. In fact, I am convinced that Boeing had a crew of people that went over all prototypes, saying things like, 'This fitting is too easy to get at for maintenance, weld a panel in front of it.'

Have you ever changed a rudder in a fifteen to twenty mile an hour crosswind and have a hinge bolt hang up? Gotten drunk on, and suffered the world's worst hangover from, gas fumes flowing into your face while changing a center wing tank fuel booster pump? Had a main gear wheel dropped on your foot when pulling it for a brake change? Had to dump the relief can after a flight because the flight crew 'forgot'? Spent two weeks scrubbing exhaust stains on the flaps and nacelles because the CO thought they looked 'messy'? Tried to talk reason to a know-it-all Second Lieutenant, without getting court-martialled, who insisted that the clutch was slipping on a direct-drive electric flap motor? Passed out from the 120-degree heat in the tail section while installing the cables on a new elevator? Spent seven hours on a Saturday 'looking busy' on the engines of an in-commission airplane because the CO thought a visiting VIP might want to inspect the flight line? And then have him drive past without stopping anywhere but the Officers' Club?

[Or] had a brand new junior assistant deputy OJT engineering officer order you to spend ten hours changing a cylinder because of low compression when experience told you it was probably only carbon on the valve seat that could be popped off in a few seconds by rapping the rocker arm with a mallet? Risked losing a hand every time you reached across the edge of the bomb bay doors to put a down lock on the door actuator? Got second-degree burns from putting your hands on the aircraft skin in the middle of the day? Worked through the night to have the plane ready for a 08:00 takeoff, only to be told at 07:30 that the flight was cancelled?

I don't regret my years as a B-29 mechanic; in fact, I loved them. But it would have been so much nicer, if even just once, someone from the clean khakis crowd in Engineering, Operations and the CO's office had come out to oil and grease land and said, 'Nice job, guys.'

Chapter Six

Story of a survivor

T Square 54 led a charmed life, serving in the Second World War, with SAC and as a target tow before being left to languish as a target on a weapons range. Rescued by a dedicated team of volunteers she has slowly re-emerged to return to the condition she was in during the Second World War.

OPPOSITE No 729's nose while having new glazing installed. Note the cabin pressurisation intercooler mounted on the wing leading edge between the No 2 engine and fuselage.
(Dale Thompson)

ABOVE T Square 54 unloading a full load of 12 x 1,000lb bombs in 1945. *(USAF)*

ABOVE No 729 while configured as a KB-29M. Note the large cut-out for the refuelling hose in the lower rear fuselage where the rear lower turret would have been. *(USAF)*

Built by Boeing at their Wichita plant, No 729 was accepted by the USAAF on 4 January 1945. Allocated to the 20th Air Force she deployed to the Pacific theatre of operations as a replacement plane. Assigned to the 875th Bombardment Squadron (BS), 498th Bombardment Group (BG), 73rd Bombardment Wing (BW) with the identification T Square 54 she completed an impressive 39 combat missions and an unknown number of POW supply drops before returning to the USA in October 1945. Here she was stored along with some 742 other B-29s at Pyote AAF in Texas.

In 1949 No 729 was selected to become a KB-29M so was flown to Boeing's Wichita factory for conversion. The conversion saw all defensive armament and systems removed, and revised fuel system plumbing and a large winch, hose and associated hydraulics installed in the rear unpressurised compartment. Emerging on 9 January 1950 she was assigned to the 55th Air Refuelling Squadron (ARS), 55th Strategic Reconnaissance Group (SRG), 2nd Air Force based at Ramey AFB, Puerto Rico.

In October 1952 the 55th SRG returned to the USA, taking up residence at Forbes AFB, Kansas, and being redesignated the 55th Strategic Reconnaissance Wing (SRW). The change of location also meant a change of parent air force, with the 55th SRW being taken on by the 15th Air Force.

During the next 16 months the 55th ARS supported the RB-50s of the 55th SRW out of

Parked outside in a protective white cocoon at Boeing's Museum of Flight in Seattle, WA, is one of the few surviving B-29s. Having been rescued from the China Lake weapons test range, B-29-60-BW 44-69729 is a true Second World War and SAC veteran and over the last 40 years has been faithfully restored to the condition she was in while flying bombing missions during 1945.

RIGHT No 729 in China Lake. She is the plane at the front of the vic of three and the only one with a fin still standing. The plane behind and to the right of 729 is 44-69972 *Doc*, currently being restored to flying status at the Boeing plant in Wichita. *(Dale Thompson)*

Forbes AFB as well as RAF Sculthorpe and RAF Upper Heyford on temporary detached duties (TDY).

In February 1954 the 55th ARS moved to Lincoln AFB, Nebraska, to be inactivated. Following this deactivation 729 was struck from the inventory, being assigned, as a target, to the China Lake Naval Air Weapon Station (NAWS) in California where, parked in the desert alongside many other redundant B-29s, she awaited her fate.

Although many B-29s did perish at China Lake (it was after all a firing range), 729 survived and, in 1986, was found by the Lowry AFB Heritage Museum who intended to return her to her original Second World War bomber trim.

To rescue the derelict airframe the museum contracted with Mel Blanscette from Ogden, Utah. Mel had B-29 engineering knowledge as well as a significant amount of battle-damage repair experience (gained in the Vietnam conflict), while the remainder of the recovery and restoration crew was made up of volunteers, mainly Second World War veterans who had either flown or maintained B-29s during the war. Soon the team became a tight-knit bunch who took on the name of 'Mel's Misfits'.

Mel's Misfits dismantled No 729 and transported her to Lowry AFB on seven large flatbed trucks, where the items were unloaded and, with the help of winches, hoists, ropes and lots of manpower, were pieced back together. The resident 3415 Consolidated Maintenance Squadron provided support, including machine-shop work, cranes and tow personnel. Missing

pieces (and there were many) were bought, obtained by trading with other museums, made from scratch or ingeniously constructed from substitute parts (the prop hub covers were old fire extinguishers!) and, over a period of several months 729 re-emerged.

The effort culminated on 2 October 1986 (the 50th anniversary of the opening of Lowry AFB) with a ceremony to dedicate T Square 54.

TOP No 729 at rest in China Lake.
(Dale Thompson)

ABOVE No 729 arrives at Lowry AFB.
(Dale Thompson)

LEFT No 729's dedication ceremony.
(Dale Thompson)

Present were many B-29 veterans but, significantly, nine of these had flown in 729 during the Second World War.

No 729 remained on display outdoors at Lowry for five years until the closure of the base necessitated a new home and, in 1992, she was moved to Boeing's Museum of Flight in Seattle.

The Museum of Flight had the ambitious intention of restoring 729 to as near flying condition as possible and, even if there was never a serious thought given to actually putting her back in the air, it was hoped that all her systems would be operable and she would be able to taxi under her own power. Unfortunately, there was insufficient space to house 729 indoors so the restoration continued outside, at the constant mercy of the elements, although covered work and storage areas with utilities helped the 25 or so volunteers who worked on the plane each week.

The 1950 conversion to KB-29M left some surprises for the restorers. When the lower rear turret was removed for refurbishment it was discovered that two body frames had been cut and partially taken away to provide space for the refuelling gear. To return the plane to bomber configuration and safely support the turret, longerons, frames, skin and the floor above, the turret and turret support structure had to be built from scratch.

Throughout this time corrosion control had to be ongoing as the Seattle weather threatened to undo the good work done so far. Fortunately, in 2003 space was found in the disused Boeing Plant II and No 729 was finally moved indoors, allowing the restoration to continue at a greater rate. Unfortunately, in late 2011 729 was once more cast outside when Plant II closed prior to its demolition in 2013. To protect the nearly finished restoration from the Seattle weather she was encased in a white protective cover until a new building can be completed to house her. While she waits, cocooned, restoration work is carrying on where possible to ensure her slow return to her Second World War trim and to be one of the most complete examples of a B-29 anywhere.

The following pages contain pictures from No 729's various restoration works. Given the extraordinary state of restoration it is sincerely hoped that space can soon be found to display her indoors for people to enjoy; after all she is one of the most famous Boeing creations.

RIGHT The restoration team at the Museum of Flight, Seattle.

1 Mac Van Wyk
2 Dale Nicholson
3 Terrence McCosh
4 Sherrie Van Berg
5 Paula Schmitz
6 R.W. Johnson
7 Rich Heasty
8 Roger Caldwell
9 Donald Goehler
10 Herb Phelan
11 Syd Baker
12 Neale Huggins
13 David Bales
14 Howard Holder
15 Sam Lehtinen
16 Larry Tietze
17 Ted Schumaker
18 Dean Paul
19 Dale Thompson
20 Bill Weisner
21 Dick Peterson.

(Dale Thompson)

ABOVE Dale Thompson (left) and Dick Peterson with the restored AN/APQ-13 radar antenna. *(Dale Thompson)*

ABOVE RIGHT Donald England with a partially restored engine. Note the missing No 4 cylinder exposing the piston. *(Dale Thompson)*

BELOW Roy Foote. *(Dale Thompson)*

LEFT Syd Baker making the radome for the AN/APQ-13. *(Dale Thompson)*

LEFT Ted Schumaker working on the engine accessory door. *(Dale Thompson)*

LEFT Terry, the Boeing forklift and crane operator, with the No 2 engine just before lifting it into place. *(Dale Thompson)*

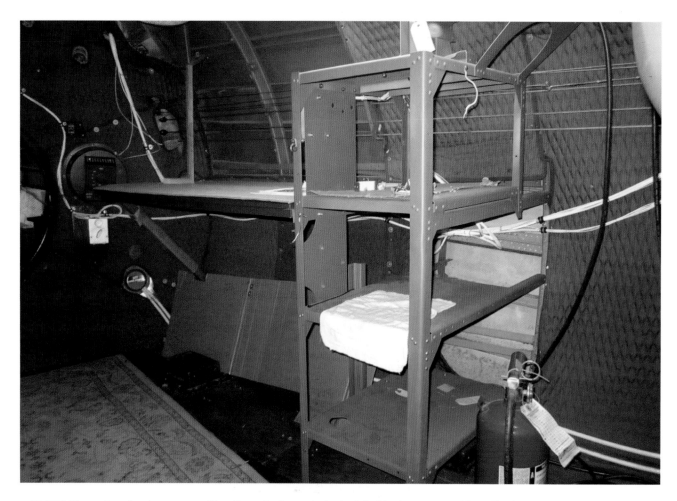

ABOVE The restored radar area awaiting the radar boxes to be installed in the empty cabinet. The boxes are being recreated but will not be ready for several months. Note the control cables running along the wall and the quilted insulation blankets that were reproduced from original templates. *(Dale Thompson)*

RIGHT The 'barber's chair', communication tunnel and entrance to the rear bomb bay during restoration. *(Dale Thompson)*

FAR RIGHT The partially restored gunner's compartment looking rearward towards the tub for the upper rear gun turret. The shelves on the wall now hold the amplidynes. *(Dale Thompson)*

ABOVE The fully fitted out and restored tail gunner's compartment awaiting installation. The silver tubes bring pressurisation from the main compartment to the tail gunner's. The red-brown wheels to the right of the hatch take the control cables to the elevator quadrants. Note also the red handle on the pressure bulkhead. This is the emergency release for the entry hatch.
(Dale Thompson)

RIGHT The communication tunnel having the insulation blankets fitted. Note the wire hoops used to hold the blankets against the tunnel walls. Also observe the brackets running down the tunnel. These will hold the ducts for the cabin heating once fitted. The bare-metal sections leading up to the astrodome are the brackets where the astro-compass can be installed.
(Dale Thompson)

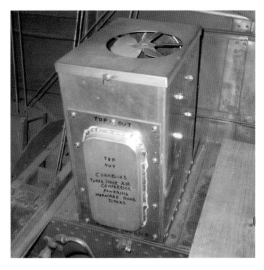

ABOVE The partially finished newly created compressor for the forward bomb-bay doors. *(Dale Thompson)*

ABOVE RIGHT All turrets function and can be controlled from either the aeroplane-mounted sights or an external one. Here the rear lower turret is positioned on a test stand and connected to an external sight. The turret is mounted upside down in the test stand, so note how the sight is pointing down while the turret points up. On the table behind the sight are all the components of the CFC system apart from the computers: control box, two amplidynes, a dynamotor and a servo amplifier. The computer is not included to make the already complex system less complex and because the small refinements made by the computer are not needed in the demonstration system. The external sight can operate any of the turrets in the aircraft as well, and by means of high-quality speakers mounted under the turret domes, when the trigger is depressed the sound of the 0.50-calibre machine guns firing gives visitors an idea of what it would have been like in reality. *(Dale Thompson)*

RIGHT CENTRE The rear lower turret installed in its housing within the rear fuselage. *(Dale Thompson)*

RIGHT A four-gun forward upper turret and ammunition cans. This turret was donated by the Imperial War Museum and, with the help of Boeing and the USAF, was transported to Seattle. It is mounted externally to allow visitors to see it working (it operates from the external sight) and to make room in the forward pressurised compartment. If it was installed in its correct place it would seriously inhibit movement in this area. *(Dale Thompson)*

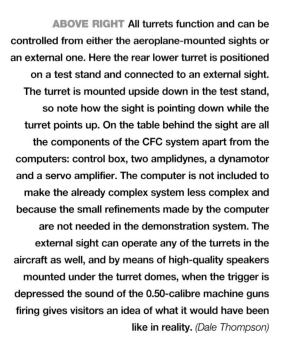

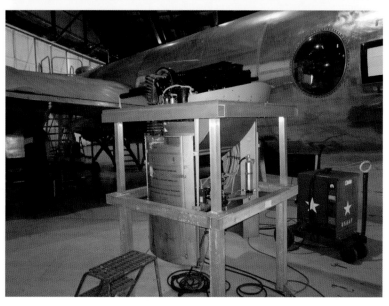

LEFT A close-up of the workings of the upper forward turret. The guns are wooden replicas. *(Dale Thompson)*

BELOW A general view of 729 nearing completion. *(Dale Thompson)*

BOTTOM No 729 cocooned and with the outer wings removed after being forced to leave the old Boeing factory at Seattle. As the photo was taken near Christmas some of the restoration crew had applied gift-wrap ribbons. *(Dale Thompson)*

Appendix 1

B-29 survivors

Some 26 complete B-29s are known to survive, either on display or storage in museums. In addition a number of partial airframes also remain.

COMPLETE B-29S	
42-65281	Travis, AFB, Fairfield, California.
44-27297	USAF Museum, Wright-Patterson AFB, Dayton, Ohio.
44-27343	Tinker AFB, Oklahoma City, Oklahoma.
44-70064	Castle AFB, Merced, California (parts of 44-61535 and 44-84084).
44-61669	March AFB, Riverside, California.
44-61671	Whiteman AFB, Knob Noster, Missouri.
44-62220	USAF History & Traditions Museum, Lackland AFB, San Antonio, Texas.
44-69729	Museum of Flight, Seattle, Washington.
44-70016	Pima Air Museum, Tucson, Arizona.
44-70113	Dobbins AFRB, Marietta, Georgia.
44-84053	Robins AFB, Warner Robins (Macon), Georgia.
44-84076	Strategic Air Command Museum, Omaha, Nebraska.
44-86408	Hill AFB, Ogden, Utah.
44-87627	Barksdale AFB, Shreveport, Louisiana.
44-87779	Ellsworth AFB, Rapid City, South Dakota.
45-21748	National Atomic Museum, Kirtland AFB, Albuquerque, New Mexico.
44-62022	Pueblo Weisbrod Aircraft Museum, Pueblo, Colorado.
42-93967	Georgia Veterans State Park, Cordele, Georgia.
44-61975	New England Air Museum, Windsor Locks, Connecticut.
44-61748	Imperial War Museum, Duxford, England.
44-62070	Commemorative Air Force, Midland, Texas – *FiFi* is currently the only B-29 that is airworthy. The black square 'A' tail marking is unique to *FiFi* and is worn to honour Vic Agather, who rescued the B-29 from China Lake in 1971. She is named *FiFi* after Vic's wife.
44-69972	*Doc's Friends*, Kansas Aviation Museum, Wichita, Kansas.
44-86292	NASM, Washington DC.
45-21739	KAI Aerospace Museum, Sacheon, South Korea.
45-21787	Weeks Fantasy of Flight Museum, Polk City, Florida.
44-70049	In storage at Borrego Springs, California, for Kermit Weeks.

PARTIAL AIRFRAMES	
42-65401	Stockton Field Aviation Museum, Stockton, California (nose section).
44-61739	Museum of Aviation, Robins AFB, Warner Robins (Macon), Georgia (nose section).
44-62139	USAF Museum, Wright-Patterson AFB, Dayton, Ohio (forward fuselage painted to represent 44-87657).
42-24791	In storage in Maryland for QuestMasters Online Museum (nose section).
44-70102	In storage at the Naval Museum of Armament and Technology, China Lake, Ridgecrest, California.
44-84084	In storage at Borrego Springs, California, for Kermit Weeks.
42-94052	On the range at Dugway Proving Ground (forward fuselage).
44-62112	Pima Air Museum, Tucson, Arizona.

Appendix 2

Second World War markings and colours

The YB-29s and very earliest B-29s were camouflaged in standard olive drab upper surfaces and medium grey undersides. This was quickly discontinued and B-29s were then delivered in natural metal. Later in the war, with night missions becoming more common, B-29s began to arrive with their undersides painted in a glossy black lacquer, shade 622, Specification No AN-L-29, or enamel, Specification No AN-E-3. Aircraft in service were also painted as time allowed but, although the intent was for all B-29s to have black undersides, only a few had them before the war ended and the painting programme was terminated.

Unit markings were vital for the planes to find their correct place in the formations. The 58th BW in the CBI had no standardised scheme, with each bomb group adopting their own markings. In the Marianas a standardised scheme was adopted, whereby the bomb wing was denoted by a geometric shape, the bomb group by a letter and individual plane by a number. These were painted vertically on the fin as large as space would allow.

Unfortunately, even the B-29's sizeable fin was not big enough and crews reported difficulty in reading the markings. Consequently, after the 73rd and 313th BWs had adopted them, the markings were changed so that the geometric shape took up the entire fin and had

BELOW Before the decision was made to paint the B-29 undersides black, the 28th Bomb Squadron, 19th Bomb Group was selected to test the scheme. Their B-29s received matt-black undersides, the only B-29s to do so. Here the ground crew pose in front of a 28th BS B-29 44-69680 *City of Bakersfield* sporting the matt-black undersides and an impressive tally of mission markings. This B-29 later served with SAC, in overall natural metal (having had the matt-black removed!) before being the first Washington delivered to the RAF. *(Neil Allen)*

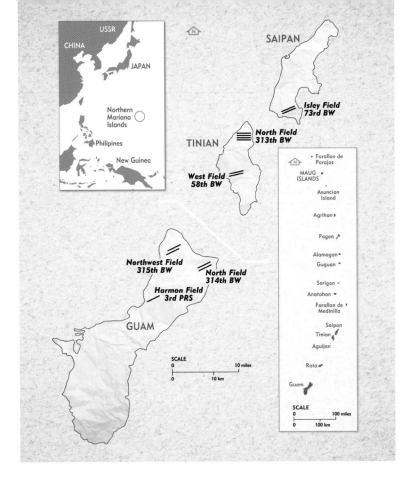

the letter within it. The individual plane number was moved to the rear fuselage. Lead planes were further identified with black or black and yellow bands on the fin or rear fuselage.

The other form of markings was nose art. Again, early aeroplanes had no restrictions with crews decorating the noses of their planes as they wished. Often these were fairly raunchy and apparently resulted in complaints reaching the head of the USAAF after some influential women saw, and were shocked by, the art on returning war-weary B-29s. Reportedly, this did not sit well with the USAAF hierarchy's aspirations to become separate from the Army, and bomb wings were then required to replace raunchy nose art with standardised symbols, an order that was complied with only very sporadically. Just the 313th and 314th BWs fully embraced standardised art; the 73rd sported a yellow spear and black ball – unkindly referred to as a 'chicken on a stick' by the crews – and 314th BW planes carried a stylised globe centred on the USA, with a flag pole positioned at a city and the flag displaying 'City of —'. Other standardised art was limited to bomb groups, the 6th BG adopting an image of the pirate Jean Lafitte.

The order was highly unpopular, as expressed by a mechanic tasked with removing the image of a gorgeous blonde in rather sketchy attire from 'his' plane: 'I won't see this old gal here coming home anymore. Why not? Because some moralist back home, I guess, wrote a letter of complaint. They can see real gals back there. But what do we have to look at?'

HEADQUARTERS, 505TH BOMBARDMENT GROUP
APO #247, % POSTMASTER
San Francisco, California

2 April 1945

MEMORANDUM TO: All Concerned.

1. The following extract from letter, Headquarters, 313th Bombardment Wing, subject: Aircraft Markings dated 31 March 1945 is published.

*   *   *   *

"h. Group Commanders will see that all pictures of women are removed from aircraft of their Group."

*   *   *   *

2. It is with deep regret that I receive and must of course, carry out the above order. I realize what it means to those concerned to remove the "women" from their airplanes; they have somehow become a part of the missions that have been flown. Some of you have spent hard earned "cash" for these "women". All this I realize, but they must go.

3. General Arnold and commanders on down the chain of command somehow feel that the B-29 is a cut above the ordinary airplane and being such is not to be placed in the common class by pictures of nude women.

4. Insignia of sponsors, "Sea Bee" or otherwise may be retained, however, they are to go only on the right side of the nose section in the nose of the comet.

Robert A. Ping

ROBERT A. PING,
Colonel, Air Corps,
Commanding.

DISTRIBUTION:

2 - Ea Sq.
6 - Eng
1 - Ea APC

20th Air Force Tail Markings

XX Bomber Command
58th Bomb Wing – China Burma India Theatre (March 1944 – March 1945)

40th BG
Tail stripe colour denotes squadron:
25th BS – red
44th BS – yellow
45th BS – blue
395th BS – black. Disbanded Oct 1944.

Letter denotes individual aircraft.

444th BG
No squadron identification until October 1944 when a fuselage band was added in the squadron colour:
676th BS – green
677th BS – yellow
678th BS – red
679th BS – none. Disbanded Oct 1944.

Individual aircraft number in diamond.

462nd BG
Before October 1944 the rudder was painted in the squadron colour. After October 1944 all rudders were painted red and a number used to denote the squadron:
768th BS – red then 1
769th BS – yellow then 2
770th BS – green then 3
771st BS – blue. Disbanded Oct 1944.

Letter denotes individual aircraft.

468th BG
Centre of rudder stripe denotes squadron
792nd BS – white
793rd BS – dark blue
794th BS – red until Oct 1944 then yellow
795th BS – yellow. Disbanded Oct 1944

Last three numbers of serial denote individual aircraft.

XXI Bomber Command

XXI BC used a standardized set of unit markings. A geometric shape denoted the Wing while a Letter denoted the Group. Squadrons were each allocated 20 individual plane numbers in squadron numerical order so the lowest numbered squadron in a group received numbers 1 – 20, the next lowest 21 – 40 and the highest numbers 41 – 60. These individual plane numbers were not related to the plane's serial number and were reused should a plane be lost or irreparably damaged. Early XXI BC markings were found to be ineffective and were revised in March 1945 to make the markings more visible. At this time, some units also had their identifying letters changed to avoid confusion with other similarly shaped letters.

58th Bomb Wing – West Field Tinian (April 1945 To VJ Day)

40th BG
Tail tip colour denotes squadron:
25th BS – red
44th BS – yellow
45th BS – blue

444th BG
676th BS
677th BS
678th BS

462nd BG
Red rudder on all planes.
768th BS
769th BS
770th BS

468th BG
Some planes retained the tail stripes from their CBI markings, although others, and replacements, did not.
792nd BS – white
793rd BS – dark blue
794th BS – yellow

73rd Bomb Wing – Isley Field, Saipan. (Prior to April 1945)

497th BG
869th BS
870th BS
871st BS

498th BG
873rd BS
874th BS
875th BS

499th BG
877th BS
878th BS
879th BS

500th BG
881st BS
882nd BS
883rd BS

73rd Bomb Wing – Isley Field, Saipan. (April 1945 to VJ Day)

497th BG
869th BS
870th BS
871st BS

498th BG
873rd BS
874th BS
875th BS

499th BG
877th BS
878th BS
879th BS

500th BG
881st BS
882nd BS
883rd BS

313th Bomb Wing – North Field, Tinian. (Prior to April 1945)

6th BG
24th BS
39th BS
40th BS

9th BG
1st BS
5th BS
99th BS

504th BG
398th BS
421st BS
680th BS

505th BG
482nd BS
483rd BS
484th BS

313th Bomb Wing – North Field, Tinian. (April 1945 to VJ Day)

6th BG
Red group colour painted on fin tips and
engine cowlings.
24th BS
39th BS
40th BS

9th BG
White group colour painted on fin tips and
engine cowlings.
1st BS
5th BS
99th BS

504th BG
Yellow group colour painted on fin tips.
398th BS
421st BS
680th BS

505th BG
Red fin tips.
482nd BS
483rd BS
484th BS

Individual plane number 74 lay outside the initial
allocation of 1 – 60 per group. Towards the end of
WWII planes with higher numbers began to
appear in several groups.

Lead Planes

To improve the effectiveness of bombing, General LeMay introduced lead crews. These were
experienced crews who also received extra training so that they could lead daylight formations
and act as pathfinders for night missions. To allow crews to identify the lead planes while
forming up, they initially carried a black bar on the forward fin (see 444th BG tail). However, this
soon gave way to more dramatic black and yellow bands allowing the planes to be identified
more easily – see 9th, 505th and 330th BG tails. All groups except those in the 315th BW used
similar schemes. The 315th BW flew exclusively by night where lead plane markings had no use.

509th CG
Forward pointing arrow only applied after the end
of WWII. Prior to this the 509th CG planes carried
spurious markings of other groups (see page 61).
The individual plane numbers for the 509th CG
were higher than the standard groups being in the
range 71 – 95.

393rd BS

314th Bomb Wing – North Field, Guam.

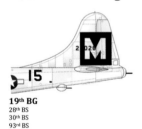

19th BG
28th BS
30th BS
93rd BS

29th BG
6th BS
43rd BS
52nd BS

39th BG
60th BS
61st BS
62nd BS

330th BG
457th BS
458th BS
459th BS

315th Bomb Wing – North West Field, Guam.

16th BG
15th BS
16th BS
17th BS

331st BG
355th BS
356th BS
357th BS

After the cease fire groups began painting
the last four digits of the serials on the fin.

501st BG
21st BS
41st BS
485th BS

502nd BG
402nd BS
411th BS
430th BS

3rd Photo Reconnaissance Squadron

3rd PRS

The 3rd PRS operated F-13A photo planes. Attached to the XXI BC Headquarters for pre and post mission intelligence the F-13s arrived on 31 October 1944 and initially flew from Isley Field, Saipan but after General LeMay took over he moved them to Harmon Field, Guam to be closer to XXI BC Headquarters. The move to Harmon Field took place in January 1945.

Nose Art

Initially nose art was left to the discretion of the airplane crew and highly individual and often raunchy images proliferated. In April 1945 apparently prompted by outrage voiced by influential women in the US after they saw, and were shocked by, the artwork on returning war weary B-29s. The 20th AF hierarchy felt that this could diminish the effectiveness of the B-29 as the medium for the USAAF to gain its independence from the Army and individual nose art was outlawed and standardized nose art was brought in. This order was not well adhered to with only the 73rd and 314th BWs and the 6th BG (within the 313th BW) adopting it.

The 73rd BW adopted a yellow spear bisecting a winged black ball. Individual aircraft names were allowed and painted on the yellow spear. Z-15 was named 'Fire Bug' but is shown during her return to the USA as part of Operation Sunset and flown by a 19th BG crew. This crew named their B-29s after the daughter, Pat Chandler, of their A/C, Vern Chandler, and Fire Bug received the name Princess Pat IV on the right hand side (retaining Fire Bug on the left) as well as some very non-standard white walls for her nose tyres for her flight home.

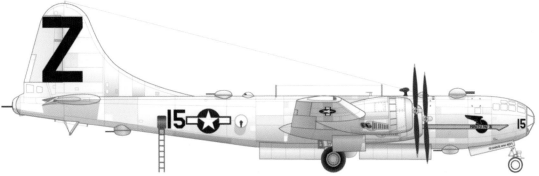

The 314th BW adopted a stylized globe centered on the USA with a giant flagpole inserted on a given city. The city's name being written on the flag as 'City of ....'. It was thought that naming planes after a city would help the War Bond Drive with cities being able to adopt and follow 'their' B-29. Crews were normally left to choose what city the plane was named after.

Below is M-2 City of Bakersfield showing some late war marking in addition to the City of ... nose art. Notable late war markings are the black undersides introduced to help defeat enemy searchlights; yellow filled M denoting M-2 as a lead ship and the 'P.W.SUPPLIES' written under the wings denoting a plane taking part in the PoW camp supply drops after the armistice.

The 6th BW adopted the image of the pirate Jean Lafitte with this displayed on both sides of the nose. The airplane's individual name was written in a flame trailing from the image. Individual crews were allowed to choose the name.

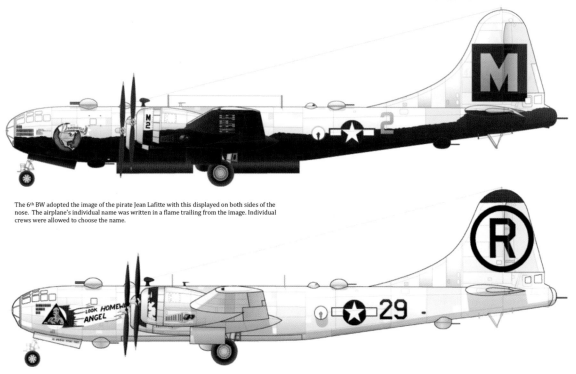

Appendix 3

SAC markings and colours

BELOW B-29 storage facilities and SAC B-29 bases in the USA. (mark@chidgeyacres. demon.co.uk)

SAC units operated B-29s in a mixture of overall natural metal and with black undersides depending on what the plane had applied during the Second World War. The only other painting regime occurred in Korea when once more black undersides, this time extending well up the fuselage sides and on the fin, were ordered to help defeat enemy searchlights.

Initially SAC did not use unit markings. However, in 1948 SAC authorised tail markings, also called tactical aircraft markings, for its bomb wings. These followed the same pattern as the Second World War markings, with large geometric shapes occupying most of the fin, sometimes with a letter within it. However, they did not conform to any standardised pattern and in October 1949 SAC issued a revised set of markings that followed a standardised layout with the geometric shape denoting the air force and the letter within it indicating the bomb wing. Those units that had applied the 1948 tail markings now changed them to the new standardised set. Finally, in April 1950 SAC reorganised the bomb wings and air forces so each air force was based on a geographic area. This also resulted in many of the bomb wings, although often retaining the letter, having to alter the geometric shape following a transfer to a different air force.

When all these amendments are combined with the relocation (and hence re-marking) of bomb wings, tracking the markings used by SAC units is a complex problem, with B-29s within bomb wings sometimes carrying three different types of markings as they transitioned through various policy changes. Also, unlike during the Second World War, individual planes regularly changed their assigned BW, resulting in new markings and, for a while at least, BWs possessing planes with markings from BWs other than their own!

In 1953 SAC dispensed with the tail markings altogether, probably much to the delight of the maintainers.

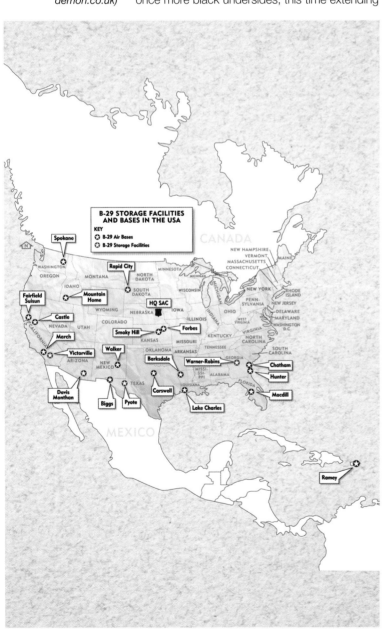

OPPOSITE AND FOLLOWING FOUR PAGES
Tail markings used by post-Second World War B-29 units. (mark@chidgeyacres.demon.co.uk)

From when SAC was created on 21 March 1946 until mid 1947, apart from the 509th CG and some special operations, its aircraft carried no specific tail markings. The 509th CG continued to use the forward pointing arrow in a circle from WWII and aircraft participating in Operation Crossroads carried markings applied for this. From mid 1947 SAC authorized tail markings and these continued to be used until 1953 when tail markings were abandoned. Only B-29 units are covered below, SAC had many more BWs and also fighter wings.

Operation Crossroads Task Group 1.5 B-29 Markings: 1946

T.G. 1.5
Kwajalein, 1946
B – Bomber
F – Photo
W – Weather

Last three digits of serial placed on rear fuselage. Weather B-29 128 had a replacement rudder and hence only a partial W.

Initial SAC Markings for B-29 units: 1947 – October 1949

2nd BG – 8th AF
Davis-Monthan, 1948 / Chatham 1949
20th BS – Yellow
49th BS – Blue
96th BS – Red
2nd ARS – none (KB-29M)

The Buzz numbers on the rear fuselage were a short lived marking on B-29s existing between June 1946 and July 1948. It consisted of a two-letter code separated from the last three digits of the serial by a dash. For B-29s the code was B (Bomber) and F (B-29).

7th BG – 8th AF
Carswell, 1947 - 1948
9th BS – Red
436th BS – Yellow
492nd BS – Blue

22nd BG – 15th AF
Smoky Hill, 1948 - 1949
2nd BS – red
19th BS – blue
33rd BS – yellow

28th BG – 8th AF
Rapid City, 1948 - 1949
77th BS – blue
717th BS – yellow
718th BS – red

43rd BG – 8th AF
Davis-Monthan, 1947 - 1950
63rd BS – yellow and black
64th BS – green
65th BS – red
43rd ARS – blue and white

92nd BG – 15th AF
Spokane, 1948 - 1949
325th BS – red
326th BS – blue
327th BS – yellow

93rd BG – 15th AF
Castle, 1948 - 1949
328th BS – blue
329th BS – red
330th BS – yellow
(Converted to B-50D 1949/1950)

98th BG – 8th AF
Spokane, 1948 - 1949
343rd BS – red
344th BS – green
345th BS – white with black stripes

301st BG – 15th AF
Smoky Hill, 1948 - 1949
32nd BS – yellow
352nd BS – red
353rd BS – blue

307th BG – 15th AF
MacDill, 1948 - 1949
370th BS – red
371st BS – green
372nd BS – blue

509th BG – 8th AF
Walker, 1947 - 1949
393rd BS – yellow
715th BS – green
830th BS – red

Standardized SAC Markings for B-29 units: October 1949 – April 1950

In October 1949 SAC issued its new tactical aircraft markings. These followed a standardized pattern with a geometric shape denoting the numbered Air Force with a letter denoting the unit. A square denoted the 2nd AF, a triangle the 8th and a circle the 15th. The Air Forces were organized by role with 2nd AF operated Strategic Reconnaissance Units, 8th AF operated medium and heavy Bombardment Units and the 15th AF Medium Bombardment Units.

2nd BW
Chatham 1949 - 1950
20th BS – Yellow (B-50A)
49th BS – Blue (B-50A)
96th BS – Red (B-50A)
2nd ARS – none (KB-29M)

5th SRW
Fairfield-Suisun, 1949
23rd SRS – blue
31st SRS – Green
72nd SRS – red
(31st SRS did not carry the Square P as it was assigned to FEAF at Kadena until November 1950.)

9th BW
Fairfield-Suisun, 1949 - 1950
1st BS – none (B-36 after December 1949)
5th BS – none
99th BS – none

22nd BW
March, 1949 - 1950
2nd BS – red
19th BS – blue
33rd BS – yellow
(Circle E assigned in October 1949 but not implemented until spring 1950 as the 22nd BG was on TDY to the UK. 22nd BG retained the earlier Triangle I during this time.)

28th BW
Rapid City, 1949 - 1950
77th BS – blue
717th BS – yellow
718th BS – red

92nd BW
Spokane, 1949
325th BS – red
326th BS – blue
327th BS – yellow

98th BW
Spokane, 1949 – 1950
343rd BS – red
344th BS – green
345th BS – white with black stripes

301st BW
Smoky Hill, 1950
32nd BS – yellow
352nd BS – red
353rd BS – blue

307th BW
MacDill, 1949
370th BS – red
371st BS – green
372nd BS – blue

509th BW
Walker, 1949 - 1951
393rd BS – yellow
715th BS – green
830th BS – red

SAC Markings for B-29 units: April 1950 – April 1953

In April 1950 SAC reorganized the units within each of its numbered Air Forces making the Air Forces geographically based rather than by role. The 2nd AF controlled units in the eastern part of the USA, the 8th AF controlled units in the central part and the 15th AF controlled those units in the western part. This resulted in several units changing their parent AF which require a change to the tail marking. Often this was just a change to the geometric shape with the letter remaining the same.

2nd BW
Hunter, 1951 - 1953
20th BS – Yellow (B-50D)
49th BS – Blue (B-50D)
96th BS – Red (B-50D)
2nd ARS – Green (received KB-29Ps in spring 1951)

5th SRW
Fairfield-Suisun, 1950 - 1952
23rd SRS – blue
31st SRS – yellow
72nd SRS – red
Converted to RB-36 in 1951/52

6th BW
Walker, 1951 - 1953
24th BS – yellow and red
39th BS – red and blue
40th BS – blue and green
307th ARS – (August 1951 – June 1952)
(6th BW formed January 1951. Initial tail marking was an empty triangle. Triangle R (assigned in January 1952.)

9th BW
Fairfield-Suisun, 1950 - 1952
1st SRS – red (B-36 until May 1950)
5th SRS – green
99th SRS – yellow
(The 1950 reorganization saw the 9th SRW re-designated as the 9th BW and losing its B-36s.)

22nd BW
March, 1950 - 1953
2nd BS – red
19th BS – blue
33rd BS – yellow
(22nd BW deployed to Okinawa for combat operations in the Korean War July – October 1950).

43rd BW
Davis-Monthan, 1950 - 1953
63rd BS – black (B-50A)
64th BS – green (B-50A)
65th BS – red (B-50A)
43rd ARS – blue and white (KB-29M)
(A shortage of B-50s resulted in several B-29s joining the unit as a temporary measure.)

44th BW
March, 1951. Lake Charles 1951 - 1953
66th BS – blue
67th BS – yellow
68th BS – red
(Between January and July 1951 while in the 15th AF at March the 44th BW used Circle T as its tail marking. Between July 1951 and September 1952 it was stationed at Lake Charles as an OUT and carried no markings then took on the Square K until April 1953 when all tail codes were removed.).

55th SRW
Ramey, 1950 - 1952. Forbes 1952 - 1953
38th SRS – green and yellow (B-50Ds)
338th SRS – blue and yellow (RB-29s until 1951 then RB-50s)
343rd SRS – red and white (RB-29s until 1951 then RB-50s)
55th ARS – blue and white (KB-29Ms)
(Between November 1950 and October 1952 the 55th SRW was based at Ramey and used the Square V. In October 1952 the unit moved to Forbes and the 15th AF resulting in a change to the tail marking to Circle V.)

68th BW
Lake Charles 1951 - 1953
24th SRS – yellow
51st SRS – green
52nd SRS – red
(68th formed as an SRW and until May 1952 trained using planes borrowed from the 44th BW. After May 1952 the 68th was re-designated a BW and received its first planes. Markings only worn after May 1952.)

90th SRW
Forbes 1952 - 1953
319th SRS – red with white stripes.
320th SRS – blue with white stripes.
321st SRS – yellow with black stripes.
(The 90th BW formed in early 1951 as an Operational Training Unit and carried no tail markings. In September 1952 the 90th BW was re-designated as the 90th SRW and began using the Circle Z tail marking.)

91st SRW
Barksdale 1950 - 1953
322nd SRS – yellow (B-45A)
323rd SRS – red (RB-45C)
324th SRS – blue (RB-45C)
91st ARS – blue and white (KB-29P)

93rd BW
Castle 1950 - 1953
328th BS – blue (B-50D)
329th BS – red (B-50D)
330th BS – yellow (B-50D)
91st ARS – green (KB-29P)
The 93rd BW also placed large plane identification numbers on the rear fuselage comprising the final two digits of the serial and a letter for the squadron: 328th – A, 329th – B and 330th – C. The 93rd ARS had D.

97th BW
Biggs 1950 - 1953
340th BS – red (B-50D)
341st BS – blue (B-50D)
342nd BS – yellow (B-50D)
97th ARS – green (KB-29P)

106th BW / 320th BW
March 1951 - 1953
102nd BS – red
114th BS – yellow
135thBS – blue
106th ARS / 320th ARS – green (KC-97)
The 106th BG was an Air National Guard (ANG) unit inducted into SAC on 1 April 1951. On 1 December 1952 the 320th BW was activated and took over control of all personnel and equipment of the 106th BW that then reverted to the ANG. Markings and sub units remained apart from the 106th ARS being renamed the 320th ARS.

111th SRW
Spokane 1951 - 1953
103rd BS – black and white
129th BS – red and white
130thBS – black and yellow
The 111th BW light was an Air National Guard (ANG) unit inducted into SAC on 1 April 1951 and re-designated as an SRW. The 111th SRW began receiving RB-36s in late 1952. On 1 January 1953 the 99th SRW, Heavy, was activated and took control of all personnel and equipment of the 111th SRW but under new squadron identifications. The 111th SRW reverted to an ANG unit.

301st BW
Barksdale 1950 - 1953
32nd BS – orange
352nd BS – green
353rd BS – blue
301st ARS – red and white (KB-29M)

303rd BW
Davis-Monthan 1951 - 1953
358th BS – black
359th BS – blue
360th BS – red
9th ARS – green (KB-29M)
The image shows the plane in the process of having the 15th AF badge applied to the fin.

305th BW
MacDill 1951 - 1953
364th BS – orange
365th BS – red
366th BS – blue
305th ARS – green (KC-97)
The 305th BW began converting to B-47s in October 1952

306th BW
MacDill 1950 - 1951
367th BS – yellow
368th BS – blue
369th BS – red
The image shows a 306th BW plane having had a replacement rudder – quite a common occurrence. In 1951 the 306th BW began to convert to the B-47 and all B-29s had gone by April 1951.

308th BW
Hunter 1952 - 1953
373rd BS – blue
374thBS – red
375th BS – yellow

310th BW
Smoky Hill 1952 - 1953
379th BS – red
380thBS – blue
381st BS – yellow
310th ARS – green (KC-97)
40th ARS – unknown (KC-97)

376th BW
Barksdale 1951 - 1953
512th BS – blue
513thBS – yellow
514th BS – red

509th BW
Walker 1951 - 1953
393rd BS – yellow (B-50D)
715thBS – blue (B-50D)
830th BS – red (B-50D)
509th ARS – green (KB-29P)

Korean War Markings for B-29 units: 1950 – 1953

22nd BG
Kadena, Okinawa, July – October 1950
2nd BS – red
19th BS – blue
33rd BS – yellow

The October 1949 standardization of tail codes required the 22nd to adopt the Circle E. However the application of this was delayed due to the 22nd BG moving to the UK on a 90 day TDY. When the 22nd BG returned to the US in the spring of 1950 the tail codes began to be changed but the process was not complete when it deployed to Kadena for combat operations in Korea. Consequently the 22nd BG planes went to war with a mixture of Triangle I and Circle E. Eventually all the 22nd BG planes acquired the correct circle E tail marking.

98th BG
Yokota, Japan, August 1950 – 1954
343rd BS – reddish-orange
344th BS – green with white stripes
345th BS – white with black stripes

The April 1950 SAC reorganization saw the 98th BG assigned to the 15th AF with a Circle H marking, However, the 98th was due to permanently transfer to Ramey AFB and the 2nd AF in mid 1950 so, to be more efficient, they actually applied Square H tail markings in anticipation of this move. When the Korean War broke out the transfer of the 98th BG to the 2nd AF was cancelled leaving it in the 15th AF. Hence, when the 98th BG deployed to Yokota in August 1950 it carried the square H tail markings despite being assigned to the 15th AF. In 1951 the 98th BG began changing its tail markings to the correct circle H. In 1951 the 98th also began placing large plane identification numbers on the rear fuselage comprising the final three digits of the serial and a letter for the squadron: 343rd – A, 344th – B and 345th – C.

19th BG
Kadena, Okinawa, June 1950 – 1954
28th BS – green
30th BS – blue
93rd BS –red

92nd BG
Yokota, Japan, July – October 1950
325th BS – red
326th BS – blue
327th BS – yellow

91st SRS
Kadena, Okinawa, July – October 1950
91st SRS - green

307th BG
Kadena, Okinawa, August 1950 – July 1953
370th BS – red
371st BS – yellow
372nd BS – blue

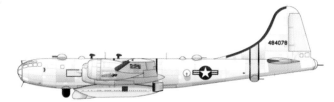

Air Rescue Service
Yokota AB, Japan, 1950 – 1951 / Komaki AB, Japan, 1951 - 1953
One of four SB-29s operated by Flight B, 3rd Air Rescue Squadron (later 37th Air Rescue Squadron, 3rd Air Rescue Group)
Four SB-29s were also operated by Flight D, 2nd ARS, (later 34th ARS, 2nd ARG)

43rd ARS
Operating as Detachment 4 with the 98th BG
Kadena, Okinawa, August 1950 – July 1953
Drogue and probe equipped KB-29Ms to refuel F-80s and F-84s.

Sources

USAAF/USAF Manuals

AN 01-20EJA-1	*Flight Handbook, USAF, Series B-29, B-29A, B-29B and B-29 Receiver* (USAF, Aircraft 15 March 1950)
AN 01-20EJAB-1	*Handbook Flight Operating Instructions, USAF, Series KB-29P Aircraft* (USAF, Revised 1 August 1951)
AN 01-20EJAE-1	*Flight Handbook, USAF, Series SB-29 Aircraft* (USAF, 13 February 1953)
AN 01-20EJ-2	*Erection and Maintenance Instructions for Army Model B-29 and B-29A Airplane* (USAAF, Revised 6 July 1945)
AAF Manual No. 50-9	*The B-29 Airplane Commander Training Manual* (USAAF, Reprinted 1 March 1945)
T.O. 1B-29(T)-1	*Partial Flight Handbook, USAF, Series TB-29 Aircraft* (USAF, 15 March 1956)
T.O. 1B-29W-1	*Flight Handbook WB-29 and WB-29A Aircraft* (USAF, Revised 31 August 1953)
T.O. No. 01-20EJ-3	*Structural Repair Instructions for Army Model B-29 Airplane* (USAAF, November 10, 1943)
T.O. 1B-29-5	*Handbook Basic Weight Check List USAF Model B-29 Aircraft* (USAF, Revised 1 May 1956)

Radar Observer's Bombardment Information File (USAAF, 16 May 1945)

Bombardier's Information File (USAAF, 23 November 1944)

B-29 Mechanic's Field Service Data Book (USAAF, Revised January 1945)

2nd Air Force Manual 65-36 *B-29 Mechanic's Handbook* (USAAF, Revised 1 April 1945)

Books

Birdsall, Steve, *Superfortress The Boeing B-29* (Squadron/Signal Publications, 1980)

Dorr, Robert F., *B-29 Superfortress Units of World War 2* (Osprey Publishing Ltd, 2002)

Farrell, Bud, *No Sweat: The Story of a B-29 Gunner with the 93rd BS, 19th BG, 20th AF during the Korean War 1952–53* (AuthorHouse, 2004)

Freeman, R. A., *Camouflage and Markings No. 19: Boeing B-29 Superfortress: USAAF 1942–1945* (Ducimus Books Limited, 1971)

Hunter, Paul W., *The War Years: The Experiences of a B-29 Flight Engineer in World War II* (self-published, 1999)

Keenan, Richard M., *The 20th Air Force Album* (20th Air Force Association, 1982)

Mann, Robert A., *The B-29 Superfortress A Comprehensive Registry of the Planes and Their Missions* (McFarland & Company, Inc, 2004)

Pimlott, John, *B-29 Superfortress* (Arms and Armour Press, 1980)

Polmar, Norman, *The Enola Gay: The B-29 That Dropped the Atomic Bomb on Hiroshima* (Smithsonian Institution, 2004)

Radar System Engineering (McGraw-Hill Book Company Inc. 1947)

Rodrigues, Rick, *Aircraft Markings of the Strategic Air Command, 1946–1953* (McFarland & Company, Inc, 2006)

Thompson, Warren, *B-29 Superfortress in Korea* (Wings of Fame Volume 16, Aerospace Publishing Ltd, 1999)

Werrell, Kenneth P., *Blankets of Fire: U.S. Bombers over Japan during World War II* (Smithsonian History of Aviation Series, 1996)

Wolf, William, *Boeing B-29 Superfortress – The Ultimate Look: From Drawing Board to VJ–Day* (Schiffer Military History, 2005)

Web

http://www.warbirdsandairshows.com/Aircraft%20manufacturing/usaircraftmanufacturewwii.htm

http://b-29.org

Index